Advance Praise for

WHEN WORDS A

by Valerie Davis Raskin, M.D.

"Once again, Dr. Raskin spans disciplines and provides a wealth of information for women in need and the professionals who care for them. The appendixes alone are worth the purchase. Organized around the questions most on a woman's mind, it reads like the author is sitting beside you. As an obstetrician-gynecologist, I think it will be a valuable resource and I recommend it to anyone who wishes to provide complete care to women."
Kenneth R. Kellner, M.D., Ph.D.
Professor, Department of Obstetrics and Gynecology, College of Medicine, University of Florida

"This book is full of important information and practical suggestions for the millions of women suffering from anxiety and depression."
Nada L. Stotland, M.D.
Chair, Department of Psychiatry, Illinois Masonic Medical Center

"At last, direct answers to complex questions, written with the warmth a woman needs to hear."
Jane Honikman
President, Postpartum Support International

"*When Words Are Not Enough* combines an unusually compassionate approach to women's experiences of depression and anxiety with expert interpretation of the wide array of treatments that can help. Dr. Raskin lets women know that their concerns are valid, shared by many others, and deserving of careful consideration and discussion. As a clinical psychologist, I have great respect for Dr. Raskin's command of the psychiatric research and her ability to integrate it with her significant clinical experience. As a writer, I admire her ability to communicate so much information in such a well-organized and engaging way. But most important, as a depression sufferer, I am grateful to her for a book that I will turn to time after time for my *own* enlightenment and reassurance."
Martha M. Manning, Ph.D.
Clinical Psychologist and Author, *Undercurrents: A Life Beneath the Surface* and *Chasing Grace: Reflections of a Catholic Girl Grown Up*

Also by Valerie Davis Raskin, M.D.

This Isn't What I Expected: Overcoming Postpartum Depression
(coauthored with Karen R. Kleiman, M.S.W.)

WHEN WORDS ARE NOT ENOUGH

The Women's Prescription for Depression and Anxiety

To Jan
Best,
Valerie Davis
Raskin

VALERIE DAVIS RASKIN, M.D.

Broadway Books   New York

BROADWAY

Broadway Books titles may be purchased for business or promotional
use or for special sales. For information, please write to: Special
Markets Department, Bantam Doubleday Dell Publishing Group,
Inc., 1540 Broadway, New York, NY 10036.

BROADWAY BOOKS and its logo, a letter B bisected on the
diagonal, are trademarks of Broadway Books, a division of Bantam
Doubleday Dell Publishing Group, Inc.

Library of Congress Cataloging-in-Publication Data
Raskin, Valerie D.
    When words are not enough : the women's prescription for
depression and anxiety / Valerie Davis Raskin.
        p.   cm.
    Includes bibliographical references and index.
    ISBN 0-553-06713-3 (pbk.)
    1. Women—Mental health.   2. Depression, Mental—Popular
works.   3. Anxiety—Popular works.   4. Antidepressants—Side
effects.   5. Tranquilizing drugs—Side effects.
6. Psychopharmacology.—Sex differences.   I. Title.
RC451.4.W6R37 1997
616.85'27'0082—dc21   96-38081
                                     CIP

FIRST EDITION

Designed by Debbie Glasserman

97 98 99 00 01 10 9 8 7 6 5 4 3 2 1

For permission to reprint, grateful acknowledgment is given to the
following:
Alfred A. Knopf for the excerpt from The Unquiet Mind by Kay
Redfield Jamison. Copyright © 1995 by Kay Redfield Jamison. Used
by permission of Alfred A. Knopf, Inc.

For one who imagines,
one who conducts,
and one who dances

Acknowledgments

I gratefully acknowledge the invaluable guidance, relentless encouragement, artful wisdom, and thoughtful advice of Anne Edelstein, my agent, and Janet Goldstein and Betsy Thorpe, my editors.

I thank those friends and colleagues who read and critiqued parts of this book as it developed: Jill Baskin, D.D.S., Anita Clayton, M.D., Nehama Dresner, M.D., Leslie Hartley Gise, M.D., Karen Kleiman, M.S.W., Laura Miller, M.D., Debbie Pirus, and Katherine Wisner, M.D. Your insight and good judgment I receive with pleasure; your incredibly generous gift of time is especially appreciated. A special thank you to Tracy Schneider, who always kept me from surrendering to chaos.

Contents

Acknowledgments   *vii*

Introduction: When Words Are Not Enough   *xiii*

PART ONE: PROBLEMS AND THEIR SOLUTIONS: Understanding
Mood and Anxiety Disorders and the Choices for Recovery

  1. Do I or Don't I Take Pills? *The Medication
     Dilemma*   3

  2. Why Can't I Shake This? *Clinical Depression*   20

  3. Why Am I So Explosive?
     Premenstrual Depression   54

  4. Why Can't I Just Relax? *Anxiety Disorders*   79

  5. Why Can't I Stop Worrying? *Obsessive Compulsive
     Disorder*   104

  6. Why Can't I Get a Good Night's Rest?
     Sleep Disturbances   121

PART TWO: SOLUTIONS AND THEIR PROBLEMS: Understanding
How Medical Treatment for Depression and Anxiety Affects
Women's Bodies

  7. What Happened to My Sex Life? *Sexual Side
     Effects of Medication for Depression
     and Anxiety*   141

  8. Will Prozac Make Me Fat or Ugly?
     *Medication Side Effects That Might
     Affect Your Physical Appearance*   162

  9. Is This Hormonal? *How Reproductive Hormones
     and Menstruation Affect Prescriptions for
     Depression and Anxiety*   179

10. Oops! What Do I Do Now? *Accidental Pregnancy While Taking Medication for Depression and Anxiety*   193

11. I Want to Have a Baby. *Guidelines for Medication Use During Pregnancy*   204

12. How Can I Take Care of the Baby When I Feel This Bad? *Guidelines for Medication Use After Childbirth*   223

Appendix A: The Biological Basis of Depression and Anxiety   247

Appendix B: Medications for Depression and Anxiety   263

B.1 Brand and Generic Names of Psychopharmacotherapeutic Medications   264

B.2 Classification of Psychotherapeutic Medications   266

Antidepressants   267

B.3 A Comparison of Antidepressants   267

B.4 Antidepressants That Increase Serotonin   268

B.5 Usual Dose Ranges of the SSRIs   269

B.6 Unique Properties of Prozac   270

B.7 Advantages and Disadvantages of Short-Acting Serotonin-Enhancing Antidepressants   271

B.8 How to Adjust the Prozac Dose Downward   272

B.9 Common Side Effects of SSRIs   272

B.10 Usual Dose Ranges of Heterocyclic/Tricyclic Antidepressants   274

B.11 Common Side Effects of Tricyclics   276

B.12 Comparison of Tricyclic Antidepressants   278

B.13 Unique Aspects of Wellbutrin Compared to SSRIs and Tricyclic Antidepressants   279

B.14 Alternatives for Treatment-Resistant Depression   280

Mood Stabilizers   282

B.15 Mood Stabilizers   282

B.16 Available Preparations of Mood Stabilizers   283

B.17 Alternatives to Mood Stabilizers   284

Antianxiety Medications 285

B.18 A Comparison of Preventive Treatments for Panic Disorder
With or Without Agoraphobia 285

B.19 Antianxiety Medications: Comparison of Buspar (Buspirone)
and Tranquilizers (Benzodiazepines) 286

B.20 Comparison of Benzodiazepines 287

General Information 288

B.21 Common Medication Interactions 288

B.22 Cost-Saving Measures for Medications for
Depression and Anxiety 291

B.23 Pregnancy Ratings 292

B.24 The American Academy of Pediatrics Classification of
Medications by Breast-Feeding Women 294

Resources 295

For Further Reading 297

Glossary 305

Index 309

Introduction

WHEN WORDS ARE NOT ENOUGH

When I became a psychiatrist, I learned to heal with words.

I love words. They have helped me through many dark moments.

Perhaps, like me, you spent your girlhood sprawled across a comfortable chair, pretending that you were that carefree princess or that you were the one living in that idyllic little house on the prairie.

Perhaps, like me, you spent your adolescence lost in the lyrics of a song that spoke so clearly to you. How soothing it was to know that you were not the only one, that Joni Mitchell knew exactly how blue felt.

Perhaps, like me, you have been blessed by the words of another: Your sister, your friend, your therapist, your minister, your neighbor has helped you cross a river you couldn't get over by yourself. You may have found sanctuary in a recovery book, a poem, a novel, a prayer, a comforting phrase from a twelve-step program.

You may have found that words which you yourself spoke brought peace: Nurturing another through your words, you filled a little space of your own too. Perhaps, reading aloud to your children at bedtime, you felt released from a malignant childhood, heard yourself say words that prove that you were not destined to inflict the same wounds that you suffered.

If so, you may understand why a young woman who went to medical school intending to specialize in obstetrics and gynecology instead chose to specialize in healing words. I leaped at the opportunity to learn to listen, really, really listen, and to apprentice myself to those doctors who mended through hearing and speaking and the sharing of verbal space.

In my psychiatry residency, I learned to be quiet when it was helpful to let my patient talk and to speak when it was healing to do so. As much as I learned what to say, I learned even more about what *not* to say.

I learned traditional and nontraditional talking therapies. Like almost every psychiatrist trained until very recently, I learned how to listen and how to speak like a Freudian, how to conduct psychoanalytic psychotherapy. Like many psychotherapists of late, I saw with great clarity that psychoanalytic words were a little like spinal manipulation: wonderful for some conditions, worthless for others.

In the last several years, healing words have undergone a huge transformation. During my residency (and after), I also learned radically different ways of using words to help families, couples, individuals find their ways out of dark places, new talk therapies such as cognitive therapy and family systems therapy.

One of the last lessons I learned in my residency training was that not everything my teachers told me about words was true. Many simply had ignored gender; a few even tried to teach me that gender doesn't influence therapeutic communication. But my patients taught me that it was okay, really okay, to listen and speak with a woman's ear and voice. To ignore gender is about as ridiculous as not noticing that one or one's patient is a person of color, a person of another faith or ethnicity, that the life experiences that any two people bring to a healing encounter don't deeply affect the transaction.

Just as I grew comfortable with being a female healer, I learned that women speak about emotional illnesses, symptoms, hope, and relationships with female voices. I heard my female patients talk about their fears that their depression might hurt their children, how they felt ashamed when they couldn't drive carpool because of an anxiety attack, how they couldn't talk with their partners about making love for fear the words would be misunderstood. I heard my female patients talk about family obligations, what others would think of them, how comfortable it felt to sacrifice their own needs on behalf of others. I learned how damaging culture can be to women's souls, how it makes us hate our bodies and believe that if we just tried a little harder, we too could juggle one more ball.

But the most important lesson I learned as a student of words is this: Sometimes words are not enough.

Like every physician before me, I learned the painful reality that the doctor's tools are limited. Whether one has a scalpel or a guide to Jungian dream analysis in one's hand, simple solutions rarely suffice. Human suffering is not simple, and the healing of suffering cannot be simplified.

For many years, psychiatrists simplistically preached that words *were* enough. If words didn't heal, then the words were wrong, they needed to be repeated and repeated or spoken by a different healer, or the patient was resisting the words. Medications were rarely spoken of; they were dispensed by the black sheep of the profession, those too bookish or too blundering to use the best healing tools, words. They were reserved for the most seriously ill, used only when words had failed to cure psychosis, mania, paranoia, or suicidal inclinations. Virtually all early specialists in psychiatric medications were men; to this day, female psychiatrists remain underrepresented in the group of psychiatric practitioners who specialize in the treatment of emotional illnesses by medication.

Prozac changed everything. I was the chief resident of my psychiatry training program the year Prozac came on the market, now almost ten years ago. Until Prozac, medications for depression and anxiety were not only viewed as inferior treatments, they were all too often worse than the disease.* Powerfully sedative, potentially addictive, dangerous in overdose, many of the pre-Prozac antidepressants and antianxiety medications were not effective or not tolerated by the sufferer.

Prozac changed how practitioners of psychotherapy and the public alike viewed mental illness. For the first time, an effective, well-tolerated medication significantly eased, sometimes completely eliminated, the suffering caused by clinical depression, anxiety and panic disorders, and obsessive compulsive disorder. Now psychiatrists and nonmedical psychotherapists could suggest alternatives for the countless people whose symptoms had been untouched or only partly touched by words.

Prozac touched off public, private, and professional debate about how to treat depression and anxiety. The pendulum swings widely: At times, new antidepressants are described as a cure-all, the mental

---

*Since Prozac (fluoxetine), many similar antidepressants, including Zoloft (sertraline) and Paxil (paroxetine), have been introduced. Specifying "Prozac" is not meant to endorse this antidepressant relative to any other medication. In the text, I will give the brand name and generic name at the first mention, then use the brand name thereafter. Both names are listed on pages 264–65.

health fixer-upper we have sought since the beginning of time. At times, these medicines are seen as harmful, agents of political oppression, obstacles to personal and social change. And at other times, these medications are spoken of as life-sustaining medications, evidence of God's grace or the wonders of science.

The controversy about Prozac tells us that we are in the middle of a cultural transformation, as we struggle together to sort out new information about the nature of suffering. Is suffering due to a chemical imbalance? Is a little suffering good, a healthy response to an unhealthy marriage, for example, or to the inevitable disappointments of ordinary life? Is suffering normal, a human response to grief and loss? Is it a hallmark of social failure, poverty and oppression and other obstacles to human fulfillment? Does medication remove the necessary emotional pain along with the excessive pain, rob people of the need to explore critical life issues?

I will not propose to tackle all of these important philosophical questions: The answers vary much from individual to individual. Doctors often know how to fix things without really understanding why the cure works and what the fixing says about the complex nature of the underlying illness. Clearly we are in the midst of a paradigm shift about how we understand depression and anxiety.

But I am certain that one thing will remain true for women struggling with depression and anxiety in the coming years: Sometimes words will not be enough.

Sometimes loving, kind, supportive, insightful, incisive, pragmatic, spiritual, therapeutic words do not help, or not enough. Sometimes depression or anxiety is so severe, you can't even listen in the first place. Sometimes you need medication to feel like yourself again. Sometimes you need medication to enable words to help you make necessary changes. Sometimes you need medication because brain chemistry is more powerful than any words you know how to say or hear. Sometimes you need medication because life is too much: You have too much grief, too much adversity, too much loss to recover without it. Sometimes you need medication because biology is too much: Genes, neurotransmitter imbalances in the brain, physiology, hormone fluctuations, medical illness, or chronic sleep deprivation are too powerful.

My first book was about recovering from postpartum depression. People generally agree that postpartum depression is a bad thing and writing a book to help women with it is a good thing. I got used to being encouraged by friends and strangers alike. This topic is different. It's a woman's guide to medicines for depression and anxiety. "You're warning women about the dangers of medication, right?" "Are you telling them not to let doctors give them pills?" "Is it one of those just-relax-and-take-a-pill-honey books?" "You think it should be added to the drinking water, right?" Everyone has an opinion on what he or she wants me to write!

I believe in the middle ground, and this book will not be about how every woman should be on antidepressants. Although I do not believe that the solution to women's suffering will be found solely in a prescription bottle, I do think that antidepressants are wonderful, and I have seen them bring an end to needless pain and disappointment time and again. But this book will not be about how, in the era of brain chemistry, talk therapies are antiquated. This book will not be about how taking antidepressants or antianxiety medications isn't really different from a relaxing weekend at a spa.

These are serious, powerful medications. But depression and anxiety are serious, powerful, and very real illnesses. They affect women twice as often as they do men, and they affect women's self-esteem, professional selves, family life, spirituality, friendships. Depression and anxiety interfere with a woman's ability to live life to the fullest, to savor the ordinary moments of peace and joy. They also interfere with a woman's ability to struggle when it is appropriate to struggle.

I am incredibly grateful that I have these new tools to relieve suffering. Daily I witness amazing transformations, see ordinary women with extraordinary problems and illnesses make extraordinary gains. A woman who is leaving her job four days a month in tears because of premenstrual depression becomes her everyday competent self again as she responds to a new serotonin re-uptake inhibitor (such as Prozac). A mother who couldn't take her child to the park because of crippling anxiety skips into my office when the antianxiety medication has restored her to her customary competent mothering. A grandmother suffering from both cancer and depression, when the old-fashioned tricyclic antidepressant kicks in, is able to, at last, talk about her fear, her rage, her fatigue. I see medications perform a miracle: They make women feel like themselves again.

In my practice as a specialist in women's psychopharmacology (the treatment of mental illnesses using medication), I sometimes see ordinary women with simple, straightforward concerns about medication. More commonly, I see ordinary women with complex issues and concerns. My patients are women who want to know what to do about the fact that their otherwise perfect antidepressant is robbing them of sexual pleasure, who desperately want to get pregnant but fear damaging their babies if they remain on medication, who have stopped taking medication because they would rather be miserable than weigh twenty pounds more as a side effect. I see women struggling to sort out how long to take the medication. I see women struggling with fallout: Do I tell my new boyfriend about the medication? What will my mother-in-law think? Does this make me an addict? Am I constitutionally weak?

One of the wonderful results of the women's movement, something we now take for granted, is that women no longer take pills prescribed to us like good girls used to. We aren't submissive "honeys" anymore. But sometimes even when we are prepared to be active consumers, we encounter obstacles that prevent us from becoming fully knowledgeable advocates for our own well-being.

These obstacles might be medical: insufficient scientific knowledge, neglect of woman-specific research, HMO nightmares, geographic isolation, miscommunication, or inexperience on the doctor's part. Or they might be on the patient's part: shame, avoidance of conflict, wanting to be a nice person, lack of knowledge about what to tell the doctor.

This is a book of words about pills. Nowhere is communication between the doctor and patient more critical than in mental health treatment. Diagnoses are based on words, what the doctor asks you and what you tell him. The doctor prescribes psychotherapeutic medication based on what you tell her, and you decide whether to take the medication based on what she tells you. You negotiate side effects through words, and you must know what is essential to talk about. I hope these words help you find your voice again, help you regain the ability to feel and express comfort and joy, and help you speak about your concerns and listen to your doctor with a loud and strong voice and critical ear.

Part One

PROBLEMS AND THEIR SOLUTIONS

Understanding Mood and Anxiety Disorders and the Choices for Recovery

Chapter 1

DO I OR DON'T I TAKE PILLS?

The Medication Dilemma

MY PATIENTS

My patients come to me in various ways. Some are sent by medical doctors for general emotional problems: "PMS," depression, anxiety attacks. They come without any set notion about the medication vs. words dilemma, perhaps not even sure what the difference between a psychiatrist and a counselor is.

Others are referred by a therapist who feels that words are not enough, that the therapy is at an impasse. These women have already processed the medication dilemma—do I or don't I take medication?—before they even meet me. Sometimes they are so eager to try medication that they are disappointed if they leave without a prescription.

A few are sent for a specific consultation, such as whether it is advisable to stop breast-feeding in order to take medication, what the impact of a hoped-for pregnancy might be on their illness, or how to get their sex drive back while taking medication that interferes with libido. These women have moved through the medication dilemma already: Their question to me is how to refine the prescription, how to treat their depression or anxiety disorder more gently, more safely.

I confess to a special affinity for those patients who come to me through what I think of as the underground railroad of women suffering from anxiety and depression. This is a semisecret network of women who have overcome emotional illnesses, who now eagerly guide the passage of others entering that painful journey. The routes are convoluted: A new patient will tell me that she got my name from her sister, who works with someone whose neighbor I care for.

The semisecrecy of the underground network exists because we are in a period of changing our cultural perspective on mental illness. It's hard to know whom to ask for help for emotional ill-nesses—it's not at all like asking your neighbor to recommend a gy-necologist—but more and more women are holding their heads up with pride, comfortable with acknowledging that they have struggled with emotional illnesses. Most of my patients confess to having at least a little bit of shame and self-criticism for being sick. But they are raising consciousness too, little by little. No one is more eager to spread the word about the miracle of modern psychiatric treatment than a woman who has been to hell and back.

These underground railroad workers don't necessarily wear "Ask me about Prozac" buttons. They do speak up quietly, telling their stories bit by bit at a barbecue, over the schoolyard fence, at the of-fice coffee break, at a prayer group. They tell their own stories to fight stereotypes and provide reassurance that help is out there. Over and over, my patients tell me that the little bit they reveal about their own experiences with depression or anxiety make them mag-nets for women in crisis. "I'm a one-woman mental health resource guide in my subdivision," one says. Another tells me, "I'm like the Employee Assistance Program for anyone at work looking for a shrink." Some women have banded together to form self-help net-works, since they know that the issue isn't just getting help, it's get-ting the right help.

Julie's Story

Julie approached the medication decision kicking and screaming.

From the very beginning, it was clear that Julie was not the whatever-you-say-is-best-doctor type. Her nurse-midwife was sending her to me to try to treat her severe premenstrual mood swings, but before she would schedule an appointment, she had some questions. I met her first criterion: Yes, I do consider myself a feminist. And, no, I do not automatically put every woman who walks through my door on med-ication. "You're an individual; we'll take it from there."

Her questions were so detailed that I thought she must be a nurse or a doctor. As it turned out, she had read a lot of women's health books, and she needed to know that I would take her seriously. In-deed, her questions were far from trivial. She had a therapist whom she adored—would I try to interfere in that relationship, or did I see the antidepressant medication as compatible with her therapy? Was I comfortable with her use of alternative healing? Would I be available to talk with her partner? Did I think that I might be able to help her, or would she just have to learn to live with it?

I suggested that Julie look at what I had written about psychiatric medications in my first book, even though she did not suffer from postpartum depression. Substitute "PMS" for "postpartum depression," I said, and you'll get a feel for how I approach psychopharmacotherapy (the treatment of emotional syndromes using medications). Sure enough, she came in to her first appointment with yellow Post-its flagging page after page. Some of the Post-its were "Ah-ha" notations: Ah-ha, that sounds just like me. Others were questions: What if I get that side effect? How do you do it differently for women who haven't just had a baby?

Julie is like many of my patients who can't seem to get enough information to help them grapple with the medication dilemma. Tell me more, they say, give me something to read about it. I practice in two very different communities in the Chicago area, and Julie lives in the activist community whose city council voted it a nuclear-free zone. It's a multicultural town that sells more health food and books than shoes, and the neighbors cheer when an electrician moves in because none of the therapists on the block can change a light bulb. The women I treat from this community tend to see me as a medical consultant and ask to call me Valerie. They may choose to accept my advice about whether medication may be helpful, but I'm just one of multiple sources of guidance and information.

Liz's Story

I also practice in a rather traditional suburb, where my patients are far more likely to view me as an authority just because I'm a doctor. Liz, like many women, defers to the advice I give her based on her intuitive sense that I'm trustworthy.

Liz said she came to me for help with anxiety because her neighbor said I was nice and not nearly as strange as most psychiatrists are said to be. You ask about things that matter, she said. You understand what a disaster it is when I can't drive carpool because I'm having a panic attack, or how ashamed I am that I have to ask my mother-in-law to do my grocery shopping.

When I review treatment options with Liz, she tells me: Whatever you think is best, Dr. Raskin. If I push a little, she admits that she is terrified of taking medication regularly, that she wants to try some other things first. She tells me that she wants to keep taking the Ativan (lorazepam) her internist prescribed when things get really out of hand, but she doesn't want to "jump on the Prozac bandwagon" until she is convinced that there is no other way.

Unfortunately, words were not enough to stop Liz's anxiety attacks. After a while, Liz told me that besides being afraid of becoming addicted to medication, she hesitated to take anything because her husband was against the very idea. She brought him to an appointment, and we discussed his fears. He worried that she would become a zombie, too drugged to function normally. He was reassured by my certainty that this would not happen, and he was open to the idea that proper treatment for her anxiety disorder would almost certainly help her function like her old self again.

Once she started antidepressant medication, I had to encourage her repeatedly to tell me about her concerns. Call me if you get side effects, I told Liz, or if the medication isn't working after a few weeks.

The different roles in which my patients place me are challenging in different ways. For Julie, I must be able to explain neurotransmitters at a medical school textbook level. She knows the scientific names for important brain chemicals: serotonin and norepinephrine. She also keeps me from slipping into the paternalistic mode every doctor is vulnerable to. I don't mean that I'm going to stumble and call her "dear." But "trust me" will never be enough—I will always need to explain my recommendation.

Liz, however, demands the opposite: She should be a poster child for the benefits of assertiveness training. She needs me to help her become more comfortable in speaking up for herself, in our work together and in other relationships. Since she isn't used to speaking her mind with doctors, she makes me listen very, very carefully, so I can sense whether she is about to stop the medicine because she worries it might be making her hair fall out, or if she's trying to telegraph to me that she can't have an orgasm due to the medication but is too embarrassed to come right out and say it.

Pathways to Power

I wrote this book with readers like Julie and Liz in mind. Julie needs it because she knows that when it comes to women's health care, knowledge is power. Regardless of her emotional pain, Julie is a smart consumer first and a patient second. She cannot even consider taking psychiatric medication unless she is fully aware of her options, the likelihood of clinical response, and the potential pitfalls.

Liz needs it because she suffers from toxic niceness: She judges her treatment by how nice her doctor is, and she's afraid to ask questions for fear her doctor won't think she's nice. She's convinced that nice girls don't talk about constipation, diarrhea, or heaven forbid, sex, even when asked by a doctor about whether these possible side effects of antidepressants such as Effexor (venlafaxine) and Pamelor (nortriptyline) are bothering her.

Shame

Both Julie and Liz have one thing in common: Deep down inside, both feel embarrassed about taking psychiatric medication.

> Julie had tried everything else under the sun: yoga, therapy, primrose oil, B vitamins, melatonin, herbs, acupuncture, a shaman, and exercise. Some of these had helped a little, but some hadn't done anything. Therapy helped most of all, but she still dreads the week before her period, when "the creature returns, and I become this raging person I don't even know."
>
> I respect her wish to find a natural alternative, but I also see the denial and shame in her quest for anything but medication. Would you have spent five years looking for a natural cure for menstrual cramps, or high blood pressure, or even hay fever? I ask. For Julie, coming to see me feels partly like an opportunity to get better but also, alas, partly like a personal failure.

Her detailed questions about the relationship between serotonin and premenstrual depression are not just her way of establishing equal footing with me. They also help her quiet her inner sense of inadequacy, the nagging self-criticism that she wouldn't need psychiatric medication if only she were stronger, wiser, more mature, less self-indulgent, prettier, wealthier, smarter, or any number of personal qualities she believes would confer mental health.

Liz shares Julie's sense of humiliation. "I feel guilty that I'm not 'normal,' she says. "It's not fair that my kids have to have this neurotic mess of a mom." She sacrificed a lot to be a stay-at-home mother, but sometimes she thinks her kids would be better off without her around so much.

I told both women the same thing when they first came to see me: I understand that you aren't completely convinced that there's a biological abnormality here, but you will believe it when you see the medication work. Having tried deep breathing, progressive relaxation, complete abstinence from caffeine and sugar, and two years of psychotherapy, Liz will believe that her illness is biological only when, two weeks after starting 25 milligrams of Tofranil (imipramine), she stops having panic attacks and decides that "this must be how everyone else feels."

I encouraged Julie to browse through a book I thought she would carry at her bookstore, Susan Sontag's *Illness as Metaphor.* Sontag describes the history of viewing tuberculosis and cancer as conditions caused by personal weakness, "diseases of passion." Until medical scientists isolated the tuberculum bacteria and found specific antibiotics to cure TB, Sontag notes that "TB was understood, like insanity, to be a kind of one-sidedness: a failure of will or an overintensity." Fifteen years after she wrote those words, our culture continues to view depression and anxiety metaphorically, as the inability to pull oneself together (depression) or self-indulgent excessive worrying (anxiety).*

I tell my patients that they are like the consumptive patient of the 1800s, a woman blamed for experiencing an illness that later gener-

---

* I use the term "depression and anxiety" to group together the disorders that tend to respond to the medications I'll be describing in the book. These disorders include obsessive compulsive disorder, clinical depression (including major depression, bipolar depression, and dysthymic disorder), generalized anxiety disorder, panic disorder, agoraphobia, and premenstrual depression. This book is not intended as a complete information resource guide for women with psychosis, such as schizophrenia, affective psychosis, and postpartum psychosis, or for women who have significant concerns about potential self-injury, self-mutilation, or suicide. I also discuss medications for depression and anxiety as coexistent illnesses for women with eating disorders, posttraumatic stress disorder (rape trauma syndrome and domestic violence), breast and gynecologic cancer, and hormone-induced mood disorders.

ations would view as biological. Your granddaughters, I say, will laugh at our quaint notions that depression, obsessive compulsive disorder, and anxiety were primarily disorders of deficient character, faulty toilet-training, or moral inferiority. But I also doubt that simple biochemical models will replace simple moralistic explanatory models. Women suffer from chemical imbalances, but we also suffer from heartache, trauma, grief, and loss.

ARE WE THE "WEAKER SEX"?

The decision to take medication implies at least partial faith in the idea that emotional illnesses have a biochemical basis and are not personal weakness. Mental health consumers and professionals alike have recently banded together to fight the unfair stigma of mental illness, and it's a pleasure to see the word spread. But believing that depression has a physical basis is a far cry from being comfortable taking a prescription yourself. Believing that your body really is different from that of others who do not have panic attacks is a far cry from being comfortable taking a prescription. When a patient is struggling with the medication dilemma, she often asks me to convince her that the illness is "real," that taking medication isn't a sign of weakness. I address the biochemical basis of depression and anxiety in Appendix A, but I want to make a few general comments here.

The cultural notion that experiencing an emotional disorder—and taking medication to recover—is a sign of personal weakness is embedded in our pull-yourself-up-by-your-bootstraps culture. It's embedded in machismo, in real-men-don't-eat-quiche. If we have learned anything at all about women's psychology in the last twenty years, it's that women's lives are relational, that women live in a place of connectedness to others. Rugged individualism is a male archetype that both genders can use less of!

Women's vulnerability to and recovery from emotional illnesses naturally rests in a place of connection to others. Social factors that prevent women from experiencing the pleasure of being connected—violence, divorce, discrimination, loss—make us preferentially vulnerable to emotional disorders. Things that interrupt the buffering experiences of connectedness may matter more to women, may be the unique gender-based factor that allows biological, hormonal, genetic, and physiologic vulnerability to emerge. Our bodies are different, our minds are different, and our minds and bodies are interdependent.

I am often asked why I specialize in women: Don't I know that men suffer anxiety and depression too? Of course they do, but these illnesses are not gender-blind. Women experience twice the incidence of depression as men, across the life cycle and across ethnic and national lines. Women have over twice the incidence of panic disorder and two and one-half times the rate of agoraphobia. Obsessive compulsive disorder is one of the few illnesses that strikes men and women equally, but often it strikes women at a particularly vulnerable time: during pregnancy or just after childbirth.

Historically, women's ailments have been attributed to psychological causes, to some vague sense that we are the weaker sex. Until very recently, we haven't had the technology to investigate the biochemical basis of emotional illness, and words were our only treatments. The stigma of women's illnesses intersected with the stigma of poorly understood mental illnesses. The medical profession is notorious for labeling illnesses as psychosomatic until the cure comes along. As an example, when I started medical school, menstrual cramps were commonly attributed to personality flaws, most notably neurotic conflict about femininity, sexuality, and childbearing. When psychoanalysis failed to cure dysmenorrhea (painful menstruation), the patient was labeled "resistant." Fifteen years later, the remarkable and widespread success of nonsteroidal anti-inflammatory agents (such as Advil and Aleve) has proven beyond a doubt that menstrual cramps respond to biochemical treatment approaches. Our poor mothers!

Recognizing the highly significant role that neurotransmitters (the chemical messengers of the brain) such as serotonin, norepinephrine, GABA, and dopamine play in depression and anxiety by no means proves that psychology, sociology, and family dynamics play no role in panic attacks or in depression. There is ample evidence to the contrary. Women are vulnerable to depression and anxiety for reasons that clearly are not only biological or hormonal. For example, women who are battered by their partners are at much greater risk of developing clinical depression. Women who have survived a rape are far more likely to have anxiety attacks and insomnia. Widows are at increased risk of clinical depression in the year after they lose their husbands. The list goes on and on.

But a mountain of evidence attests that women are not more vulnerable to depression and anxiety than men simply because of our role in society. Women's suffering cannot be reduced to social oppression any more than it can be reduced to neurotransmitter abnormalities or to hormonal swings. We all want simple explanations for emotional illnesses, but sometimes gray is gray. It's natural to feel more comfortable taking medication for a condition that is primarily biological. But many illnesses that we all agree are primarily biological are affected by stress and life circumstances as much as illnesses with emotional symptoms.

Take the common cold, for example. I spend most winters sniffling and sneezing, as I pick up every virus that ever floated past one of my kids' airspace. I know that a cold is a biologically caused illness. I am at higher risk for this illness due to my social role as a mother. I also know that I can absolutely, positively count on being sick the week that the garbage disposal breaks down, the car battery is dead because I left the lights on all night, and my child care arrangements fall through. Therefore, it is important and healthy for me to reduce stress. However, I don't feel better until I take Sudafed. The medicine works even though stress helped bring the illness on.

WHAT CAN WE DO ABOUT DEPRESSION AND ANXIETY?

Anxiety and depression are far more troublesome than a mere cold, but the medications for emotional illnesses are a little like nasal decongestants and antihistamines. They relieve symptoms but do not cure the virus. Medical interventions for emotional illnesses relieve suffering—induce a remission of the illness—but do not cure depression and anxiety. There is no psychiatric equivalent of a vaccine or an antibiotic that eliminates a person's biological vulnerability. For most women, though, medications for depression and anxiety are tremendously helpful in relieving serious emotional pain.

Must We Choose Between Pills and Words?

Unlike medication, psychotherapy can heal deep-seated emotional vulnerabilities for many people—that is, it can be beneficial even after treatment is completed. Successful psychotherapy can be somewhat of a vaccine, boosting immunity to stressful circumstances. Some people think of emotional recovery with an all-or-none mentality. Either you take psychotherapeutic medication or you go into therapy for a "pure" talking cure. It just isn't so. In fact, oftentimes the medication is necessary in order for psychotherapy to proceed. Other times the treatments complement each other. It's like taking muscle relaxants and undergoing physical therapy for back strain: The two treatments work together to get you back on your feet.

WHY PROZAC STARTED A REVOLUTION

If you or someone you love is suffering from clinical depression, obsessive compulsive disorder, premenstrual depression, anxiety attacks, or other emotional symptoms, you couldn't be alive at a better time in history. Antidepressants have been around since the 1960s; for a few generations before that, medical options were limited to addicting or powerful sedatives or to electroshock therapy. The cure was often worse than the disease, and treatments were far from effective. For thousands of years before that, there was simply no medical treatment. Anxiety disorders and moderate depression were, presumably, kept secret, as they still may be today. Severely depressed individuals (like Great-Aunt Mildred, whose nervous breakdown was kept secret for generations) were cut off by society, hidden by families, subject to incarceration or institutionalization, or victims of suicide.

Since antidepressants have been around for forty years, many people wonder why Prozac (fluoxetine) set off a national fury and landed on the cover of *Newsweek* in 1994. A few years ago, people I met in casual conversation shied away from me upon learning that I was a psychiatrist, fearful that I would make some disparaging remarks about their unconscious impulses. Nowadays, people flock to me at cocktail parties, eager to ask me about Zoloft (sertraline), Xanax (alprazolam), or Serzone (nefazodone), sometimes perfectly content to discuss their antidepressants with strangers. Truly, we are witnessing a long-overdue revolution in how our culture conceptualizes mental syndromes.

Prozac and the new psychiatric medications released after it—Zoloft, Paxil (paroxetine), Effexor, Serzone, Wellbutrin (buproprion), and Luvox (fluvoxamine)—created a virtual feeding frenzy for good reason. They work, and they are well tolerated. The older antidepressants, termed "tricyclics" or "heterocyclics" because of their chemical structure, remain highly effective medications still widely used by psychiatrists. However, the side effects are so significant that many women are unable to tolerate them. Since the new antidepressants have unique biochemical effects on neurotransmitters, the 20 to 40 percent of individuals who didn't respond to the old antidepressants suddenly had an alternative.

But, most important, Prozac took the nation by storm because it was the first of several antidepressants that the average American physician (i.e., nonpsychiatrist) can prescribe safely and easily. The tricyclics and the other pre-Prozac antidepressants (called monoamine oxidase inhibitors, or MAOIs, now rarely used) were potentially lethal if taken in overdoses of as little as a week's supply or, in the case of MAOIs, if certain foods or medications were taken in conjunction, even accidentally. After Prozac, nonpsychiatrists were able to offer a new treatment to their patients, without the expertise of the psychiatrist.

Furthermore, the side effects of the early antidepressants necessitate slow dose adjustment upward; lengthy delays in reaching a therapeutic dose were quite common. Because the newest antidepressants are so safe, and because they have fewer side effects and therefore can be prescribed in initial doses that are likely to be effective, today's doctor can put her patient on a beginning dose of Zoloft, see her in three weeks, and expect about a 50–50 chance that the patient's condition will have improved. It's no wonder that Prozac is now the second most prescribed medication (not antidepressant, mind you, *medication*) in the United States, with Zoloft rapidly gaining ground.

The Changing Doctor-Patient Relationship

These scientific breakthroughs are great news for women. Unfortunately, alongside the revolution in understanding chemical imbalances in the brain is another revolution, the revolution in the doctor-patient relationship caused by economic forces. Fewer and fewer Americans have unrestricted choice of doctors, and fewer and fewer doctors can withstand the pressure to move patients through the pipeline as quickly as possible. Because the medication dilemma is so complex, many women feel that they are rushed to make a decision or to get their questions done with.

Unfortunately, rushing mental health care often causes significant problems. For starters, medications may be pushed relative to psychotherapy, which may be viewed as frivolous or may be doled out too sparingly by cost-conscious insurers or HMOs. A patient who needs specialty information, such as what to do if she is taking a psychotropic drug and wants to get pregnant, may have to pay out of pocket to see a doctor who is not in the HMO or list of covered doctors.

The importance of good rapport between doctor and patient is nowhere as critical as in psychiatry. Developing trust and mutual respect is especially important when it comes to mastering the do-I-or-don't-I take medication dilemma. But rapport is important at every step of the way. Sometimes the first medication works right away with few or no side effects. Many times the road to recovery is rocky, with unwanted effects on women's bodies or minds, or incomplete medication response. Judging, during your first appointment, how receptive a doctor is to how you feel about taking medication will give you a good sense of the long-term potential for good communication.

An even greater change in how mental health care is delivered is the much greater role assumed by primary care practitioners. Many, many women receive antidepressant or antianxiety prescriptions from their obstetrician gynecologist, family physician, internist, nurse practitioner, or physician's assistant. Many women taking medication for depression and anxiety have never been so much as in the same room as a psychiatrist. However, general practitioners are far less likely than psychiatrists to have expertise in talk therapy, and it is important to consider whether, just as words are not enough, pills are not enough either.

PUTTING YOURSELF IN CONTROL: A PRESCRIPTION

I cannot put an expert in women's psychotherapeutic medication in every HMO or geographic area, or force policy makers to recognize the importance of equal insurance coverage for mental health treatment. It isn't necessary for every woman with depression or anxiety to be treated by a woman's mental health specialist. However, it is important for every woman to get the most out of her treatment that she can. As a patient, it is important for you to know the crucial questions to ask, to know what to worry about and what not to worry about, to gauge whether your doctor is prescribing according to typical practices, and to know what you must be sure to tell your doctor.

This book is about psychopharmacology for women. I want to say up front that I have a very strong bias in favor of combining prescriptions with psychotherapy, but not just any psychotherapy. Just as Prozac is not the answer to every psychiatric condition under the sun, no one form of psychotherapy is the answer to all human suffering. I will tell you what I know about when words are better than pills, when pills are better than words, and when words and pills are the best choice. Almost always, the best treatment for a serious emotional syndrome such as obsessive compulsive disorder, depression, or anxiety is a combination of psychotherapeutic medication and psychotherapy and/or self-help, spiritual work, lifestyle changes, and other methods of promoting emotional resilience and sustaining healthy relationships.

Getting Good Help

Only medical professionals can prescribe medication. In most communities, that means a medical doctor such as a family physician or a psychiatrist. In some areas, nurse practitioners or physician's assistants also prescribe antidepressants under medical supervision (although you may never actually see the doctor).

Psychotherapists come in many forms. Most but not all psychiatrists also practice psychotherapy, but some do not because they specialize in medications only, or because the insurer or health plan wants less expensive practitioners to serve that role. Psychiatrists charge the most for psychotherapy; psychologists are usually next; and social workers generally charge the least amount. No one has ever proven that cost translates into quality. There are extremely gifted social workers who charge $70 a session and extremely incompetent psychiatrists who charge $140. I do feel that in some cases, seeing a psychiatrist for therapy and medication—one-stop shopping—is the most efficient and productive treatment for those who are not already in mental health treatment. But many women start with a therapist and see a doctor only after they want to explore medication, often while continuing with the original therapist. It is perfectly acceptable to see a therapist for words and a doctor for medications, and personally I often practice this way.

I encourage you to seek mental health treatment only from certified and licensed practitioners. All states regulate psychotherapists, and licensing makes sure that the therapist or doctor has met certain minimum standards of education and credentialing. Whom you turn to will have some impact on what type of treatment is offered. However, one sign of competent professionals is whether they know their limits and whether they are open to considering alternatives. Good social workers know when a medical consultation is needed. Good internists know when to refer you to a psychologist for marital counseling. Good psychiatrists know when to refer you to a geriatric specialist or a family therapist. Mental health treatment is complex, and few professionals are so smart that they don't ever need help. A good clinician should talk over your options with you. A nonmedical therapist who ridicules or automatically dismisses medication is suspect. A doctor who ridicules or automatically dismisses therapy is equally suspect. Thoughtful, nondefensive, nonjudgmental consideration is a hallmark of competence.

I won't be emphasizing psychological and interpersonal treatments in this book, in part because there are so many terrific books out there already. (See p. 297.)

In This Book

In Part One of the book, I'll tell you about the different kinds of anxiety and depressive disorders that affect women, including common symptoms. At this time, the diagnosis of emotional illness is basically made through words. Medical tests may eliminate identifiable organic causes of mood or anxiety symptoms, but right now, there exist no clinically useful ways of diagnosing psychiatric conditions except by identifying and labeling symptom clusters. There is no equivalent electrocardiogram or X ray for depressive or anxiety disorders.

The American Psychiatric Association has compiled what practitioners call *DSM-IV*, the fourth consensus manual about diagnosis based on reported symptoms. The full title is *Diagnostic and Statistical Manual of Mental Disorders, Fourth Edition.* You may well have seen this book in your doctor's or therapist's office; most psychiatrists own and use this regularly, including for insurance billing. When I discuss emotional syndromes such as clinical depression and panic disorder, I will describe the diagnostic criteria found in this so-called bible.

I'll talk about women's issues for each disorder, including biological information about etiology and treatment. I'll also give you the basics to help you make educated choices about your medication and nonmedication treatment options. These chapters will help you decide whether you should consider taking a medication for your emotional symptoms.

While some readers may not have made the medication decision yet, many will be undergoing medical treatment for depression or anxiety. In Part Two, I assume that you are taking or have taken psychotropic medication. Here I address issues that are specific to women: pregnancy, breast-feeding, childbirth, menstruation, sexuality, body image and weight, hormones, and contraception, including abortion. I consider it likely that the readers of this book soon will know more than some doctors do about how medications for anxiety and depression affect women's bodies. For this reason, I also include professional references for you to share with your doctor. (See p. 299.)

Some readers will be wondering whether they are overmedicated by doctors used to dosing for men or whether their doctors appreciate the unique issues of certain side effects for women, such as being too sedated to wake up at night when a baby cries. They may feel intimidated, dismissed, misunderstood, hurried, or misinformed by their doctors. They may suspect that their doctors just don't know or don't understand. This book will help these readers know when to ask, what to ask, and how to get answers.

The two appendixes elaborate on the biological basis of mood and anxiety disorders and describe the various medications in detail. You can check here for a quick overview of usual dosages, side effects, and interactions with other medications.

Certain themes are repeated throughout this book. One is the importance of tailoring the treatment to the individual. This book is intended as a supplemental source of information. It cannot and must not serve to replace individual medical attention. You should never make medical decisions based on this information without consulting your doctor. Your doctor may have very specific reasons for treating you differently than I describe, and it is important to receive individual medical advice from your physician. I do not know each reader's personal medical history and can discuss the issues only in a general way. Use this information to clarify, challenge, explore, discuss, and negotiate your treatment.

Another repeated theme is that the cure should never be worse than the disease. Psychopharmacology for depression and anxiety should not leave you feeling like a zombie, cause you not to care when your one-year-old heads for the electric outlet with fork in hand, or make you feel as horribly buzzed as that time in college when you took your friend's speed in order to finish a term paper. It is reasonable to expect that side effects will be mild and bearable.

Taking Care of Yourself

You will also see me encouraging you over and over again to feel comfortable with receiving treatment for an emotional condition, just because it makes you feel better. Women are often other-oriented, putting their own needs at the bottom of the list. In my practice, I've noticed that many women make the decision to take medication for depression or anxiety only in the context of what it will do for someone else.

Annabelle tells me she wants to try medication because she can't stand yelling at her kids when her period is coming. Esther doesn't want to be such a burden to her adult daughter, who has to drive her own children all over town as well as take Esther to the grocery store because she's too anxious and agoraphobic to drive by herself. Janetta is worried that her boyfriend will dump her if she doesn't get her act together. Wendy feels guilty because she never asks anyone over to her house anymore and worries that it will hurt her husband at work if his colleagues find out she's clinically depressed. Lynn wishes she could help out her siblings more with caring for their ailing mother, but she can't even manage to cook dinner for her own family, let alone take care of anything extra.

Like all of these women, you have a right to feel better, period, even if no one but you notices the difference. You have a right to benefit from new discoveries about the relationship between neuro-transmitters and emotional syndromes. You have a right to competent medical treatment and to expect that your doctor knows or is pre-pared to learn about the specific issues that women care about.

When I was working on this book, one of my patients left me a message telling me that the Zoloft I had prescribed was working. As most women do long before coming to the doctor, Mindy had tried many different remedies to shake off her chronic low-grade depres-sion. We thought we had solved the problem when a blood test re-vealed hypothyroidism, but correcting her underactive thyroid gland provided only partial relief. Within a few weeks of starting Zoloft, she felt like her old self. "It's a miracle in a pill," she said, "a miracle I thought I'd never personally experience. My husband is thrilled."

I'm delighted that her husband is thrilled with her response to Zoloft, which increases the brain chemical serotonin. But mostly I'm thrilled for Mindy. She deserves to feel good every day—or, to put it another way, to feel *appropriately* sad when things are sad and not to feel sad when things are not sad. She deserves to know about her al-ternatives and to have her doctor listen to her concerns. She deserves to know as much as she wants to about her medications and to expect that her doctor can answer the unique questions that concern her as a woman.

So do you.

Chapter 2

WHY CAN'T I SHAKE THIS?

Clinical Depression

KEY POINTS

• One in five women will suffer from clinical depression at some point in her life. Women are twice as likely as men to experience clinical depression.

• Serious depression is associated with chemical imbalances in the brain that may not respond to talk therapy alone.

• Depression is a highly treatable illness that has a strong biological and genetic basis.

• If you respond to antidepressants, you should remain on the dose that got you well for at least four to nine months after you recover.

By far, depression is the most common emotional illness from which women suffer. Stephanie is one of the 7 million women in America who is battling depression right now.

Stephanie's divorce lawyer sat her down one day and recommended that she talk to her doctor about depression. "I see this a lot in my business," the attorney said. "All your hopes and dreams go down the tubes, your mother says thanks to you she'll never have grandkids, and you have to see this asshole in court every time you turn around. Who wouldn't be depressed?" Stephanie had to admit it: In the last two months, she woke up at 4 A.M. every night, cried at the drop of a hat, and was so fatigued that she hadn't even gotten around to packing a single box.

Her doctor did an exam and a blood test and told her that everything was okay physically. He asked Stephanie about other common symptoms of depression: inability to relax and have fun, irritability, and a sense of futility. Her physician joked that the divorce lawyer was an excellent diagnostician, and he handed her a prescription.

YOU ARE NOT THE ONLY ONE

Stephanie is not alone. The numbers are simply astonishing. Currently one out of sixteen American women is suffering from clinical depression. Women see psychiatrists 2 million times each year for depression, and the number of women receiving antidepressant medication who have never seen a psychiatrist is skyrocketing. Each of us has a one in five chance that this disease will hit us at some point in our lives, and once you've suffered an episode of clinical depression, you have a 50–50 chance of getting it again.

That depression is so very common means that one of the members of your aerobics class, one of the women standing in line at the grocery store, one of the mothers of every kindergarten class in America, one of the graduates of your childbirth preparation class, one of your grandmother's former sorority sisters, one member of an all female volleyball game, or two or more women in the average law school class has the illness called clinical depression.

When I'm asked to help doctors try to predict which of their patients are vulnerable to depression, I say: all of them. With the odds at 20 percent, no woman is immune. That's higher than the risk of breast cancer, infertility, miscarriage, or abnormal Pap smears, and we know that these conditions can happen to anyone. Everyone knows a woman who has suffered from clinical depression; you just may not know that you do.

WHY CAN'T I JUST SNAP OUT OF IT?

Although it is so common, depression is seriously undertreated. Most depressed women receive no professional help whatsoever, medication or otherwise. Most are aware that something is wrong and will have tried to fix things on their own. Long before they come to my office for help, my patients have tried to "snap out of it." Often, someone, perhaps with the best of intentions, will have instructed them simply to get it together, try harder, stop being so self-indulgent. Some will have watched *Oprah* religiously, hoping for the flash of insight that will release them. Some will have tried retail therapy: shopping and shopping, looking for the purchase that will ease the pain. Some will have found temporary relief in Häagen-Dazs, others in compulsive exercising. Many will have been to the health food store, running through melatonin, multivitamins, herbal teas, or other promises of natural relief.

But serious suffering is unlikely to respond to a weekend away, a deep massage, a good manicure. Serious suffering is unlikely to respond to willpower. Many of the things women do to lift a low mood work when things are just a little bad. Mostly, however, chocolate doesn't fix significant depression. Indeed, most women with depression struggle along, going through the motions. If you believe what the movies say, everyone in America has seen a therapist and been on Prozac (fluoxetine). It just isn't so. No other disease is so highly treatable yet so woefully undertreated. Seventy percent of women with clinical depression never get any treatment whatsoever. Unfortunately, even fewer get appropriate treatment.

Obstacles to proper treatment may be pragmatic, such as how to squeeze in an appointment between shuttling kids to Little League and piano lessons; financial; or clinical: Your obstetrician may know everything about reproductive hormones but just the rudiments of Prozac and only Prozac, while your psychiatrist may know all the ins and outs of multiple antidepressants but nothing about women's bodies, or even birth control pills. Many women will need to make treatment decisions in the context of pregnancy, breast-feeding, contraception, and/or menstruation, yet the information about these gender-specific factors are either very poorly researched or not widely known by practitioners.

But the very nature of depression creates obstacles to proper treatment. Depression causes low self-esteem, pessimism, and fatigue. Low self-esteem may make you feel so personally inadequate that you believe that you are defective, not sick. Pessimism may make you feel that your condition is futile: Nothing will help anyway. Exhaustion and fatigue may make you feel so overwhelmed that you can't muster up the energy to take the first step toward recovery.

You do not have to suffer like this. You can feel like yourself again, but you will need to take active steps to overcome depression. Why suffer for one day longer than necessary? Many women avoid treatment because they think getting help feels like too much effort. The reality is that overcoming depression reduces the effort that even simple tasks take now. Getting help makes everything easier, from looking for a new job to nursing a baby in the middle of the night. Getting help makes sense; it is, in fact, highly efficient. It isn't one more ball to juggle: It is a way to manage the balls that are already there much more effectively.

I can't think of a single patient I've treated who felt that she had a lot of time to dabble. Women generally do not enter treatment looking for lengthy solutions; the days of a six-month rest cure in the country are gone. The intensity of competing demands for time means that many women will give professional treatment a try, but they won't stick around long waiting for relief. Getting professional help for depression is terribly important, but getting appropriate, accessible, effective treatment is crucial.

How can you get such treatment? It's easier to get good treatment if you know what's wrong. You're a better consumer if you know which questions to ask and you usually get well more quickly if you know where to go for help. This chapter is designed to make you an efficient consumer. First, I'll go over the diagnosis of depression. Using *DSM-IV* as a guide, I'll review the subtypes of clinical depression. I'll talk about some of the special circumstances that raise the risk of depression for women. Then I'll review what is known about the cause of depression (although I reserve a detailed discussion of brain chemistry for Appendix A). I'll give you guidelines about which kind of treatment is best for which kind of depression, and review what's known about effective treatments, comparing different types of therapy with different medication approaches.

DEPRESSION: THE DIAGNOSIS

Mental health professionals diagnose depression solely with words. There is no blood test, X ray, hormone analysis, or other biological test to diagnose depression. A doctor may order some laboratory tests to eliminate known physical causes of depression, such as an underactive thyroid. You may be asked to take a standardized questionnaire that rates symptoms of depression. But mostly, you will simply be asked about particular symptoms of clinical depression.

Fortunately, often it is rather easy to diagnose depression, especially the most serious types. In the modern medical era, many people are skeptical of the diagnosis, believing that the lack of a laboratory test means that it is not a real illness. Although the diagnosis of depression is an imperfect science, it isn't mumbo-jumbo either. Just as an old-fashioned, experienced doctor was darn good at picking up anemia without a blood test, experience and judgment enhance psychiatric diagnostic accuracy, and good clinicians make reliable diagnoses. In truth, there is so much useful information available that many women go to the doctor with a pretty good idea of what their diagnosis is. It is more usual for someone to request an appointment with me for depression than because she just doesn't feel like herself.

While I encourage you to tell your doctor or therapist what you think is wrong with you, be sure that neither of you assume that you are correct without carefully reviewing your symptoms. The list of symptoms on page 28 will help you know what to be sure to tell your doctor about, but it cannot substitute for clinical judgment and experience. Along with evaluating your specific symptoms, the doctor will consider your overall general health, your family history, the severity of symptoms, your global functioning, and other conditions that mimic depression, whether they are physical or emotional. The doctor may order lab tests before diagnosing depression.

Basically, a clinician makes a diagnosis of depression when a certain cluster of symptoms have been present for two or more weeks. That's it. Biological revolution notwithstanding, the diagnosis comes down to a judgment call. But many other diagnoses also are made on the basis of the doctor's clinical judgment about the patient's symptoms: Migraine headaches, dysmenorrhea (menstrual cramps), hay fever, muscle spasm, chronic back pain, and many viral syndromes are diagnosed purely by symptom patterns.

The very term "depression" may be confusing because it is used both for a specific group of illnesses and, everyday, as a synonym for feeling sad. There are different ways to classify depression, and some readers will be interested in the specifics. If you are not, skip ahead. According to the *DSM-IV*, clinical depression is divided into two types: major depressive episode and dysthymic disorder. A major depressive episode, the most common type of depression, is characterized by acute onset and by severe symptoms. Major depressive episodes may be caused by one of two illnesses: unipolar disorder or bipolar disorder. In contrast, dysthymic disorder is an insidious illness, a low-grade but chronic mood disorder that is present for at least two years (see the box below).

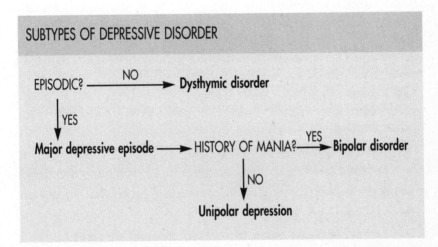

SUBTYPES OF DEPRESSIVE DISORDER

Depressive disorders may be further divided into subtypes, including seasonal pattern ("winter depression") and postpartum-onset. Depressive disorder is also known as mood disorder or affective disorder. Bipolar disorder is also known as manic-depressive disorder and bipolar affective disorder. Unipolar disorder is further divided into single episode and recurrent (more than one). While the *DSM-IV* classifies premenstrual depression as a type of depressive disorder, I discuss it separately in Chapter 3.

Is This Manic-Depressive Illness?

Probably the single most important diagnostic issue is whether you have "pure" depression (i.e., "unipolar") or have manic-depressive illness ("bipolar"). Women are twenty times more likely to have unipolar depression as bipolar disorder. Whenever possible, unipolar depression should be distinguished from bipolar depression. This distinction is important in order to determine appropriate treatment. Women with bipolar disorder run special risks when they take antidepressants. The 1 percent of the population that suffers from bipolar disorder illness usually gets the kind of depression that fails to respond to talk therapy alone. If you have ever experienced a manic or near-manic spell for a few days or weeks in the past, you are far more likely to require medication. The next box presents the symptoms of mania or near mania.

SYMPTOMS OF MANIA OR NEAR MANIA ("HYPOMANIA")

Several days or more of elevated or irritable mood, with uncharacteristic thoughts and actions, including:
- Racing thoughts that jump from topic to topic
- Decreased need for sleep, often accompanied by excessive energy and activity such as painting walls, cleaning, making phone calls. These activities may be productive but may become pointless over time
- Extreme talkativeness, often to the point that others can't interrupt you
- Dramatic increase in sex drive, uncharacteristic love affairs, or uncharacteristic sexual experimentation
- Grandiose sense of self, such as believing that you have special creativity, special purpose, or invulnerability
- Recklessness and impulsivity, such as speeding or wild spending

Medication treatment is much more complex for women with bipolar disorder. One of the most important facts that you can tell your doctor before starting to take an antidepressant is whether you have ever experienced a near-manic or manic episode, or if a parent, sibling, or child has bipolar disorder. If you are suffering from bipolar disorder, taking an antidepressant can switch you from depression into mania, which can have extremely serious consequences. Usually I recommend that women with bipolar disorder remain under the care of a psychiatrist rather than a general physician and that they take a mood stabilizer (such as lithium) along with an antidepressant.

If you have a family history of bipolar disorder but haven't ever had any manic symptoms, it's not possible to predict with certainty that you will not experience medication-induced switching or that you may ultimately turn out to have bipolar rather than unipolar disorder. This is partly because most individuals with bipolar disorder have one or more depressive episodes before they experience a manic episode. Many women are not diagnosed as having bipolar disorder until years into the illness. Having relatives with manic-depressive illness does not mean that it is your destiny to suffer the illness as well; having the illness in your gene pool, however, does increase your risk of unipolar depression.

Clinical Depression: Unipolar Type

The next box lists symptoms of a major depressive episode. At least one symptom must be sad or depressed mood ("dysphoria") or loss of pleasure in life ("anhedonia"). In order to be classified as a major depressive episode, the symptoms must not be due to a specific medical condition (such as a medication side effect) and must be severe enough to cause some impairment in your functioning. Not uncommonly, doctors will focus on employment-related functioning, without also recognizing that depression may affect women's social and family functioning. As you review your own symptoms, consider whether poor concentration is affecting your ability to grocery shop, or if irritability is keeping you from being the mother you usually are, or if you've become so needy that your boyfriend doesn't call as often.

Unlike many other emotional conditions in which symptoms fluctuate, the symptoms of a depressive episode are like a fog that never clears. The symptoms are there most of the day, most days. Although the symptoms must be present for two weeks, most women do not seek treatment until the symptoms have existed for months.

It is common for women with depression to have suicidal thoughts. Usually these thoughts are passive, such as fantasies of just not waking up one morning or developing a fatal illness. If things are this bad for you, you should seek professional help. However, those who are experiencing any active suicidal thoughts should immedi-

SYMPTOMS OF CLINICAL DEPRESSION

The presence of five or more of the following symptoms suggests that you are suffering from a major depressive episode:

- Feeling depressed, empty, blue, or sad
- No longer enjoying things that used to bring you pleasure, ranging from loss of enthusiasm for your job, your hobbies, your family, your favorite television show, or almost any once-interesting activity
- Change in your appetite (either loss of appetite or increased appetite), or an unexplained 5 percent increase or decrease in your weight
- Difficulty falling asleep, restless sleep, premature wakening, or excessive daytime sleeping
- Noticeable anxiety, agitation, pacing, restlessness, or, conversely, slowed motor activity as seen in lack of facial expression and decreased spontaneous movement
- Tiredness, low energy, fatigued by minimal activity
- Low self-esteem, including feelings of inferiority, of worthlessness, or of guilt
- Poor concentration or difficulty making decisions
- Wishes for death or a fatal illness or accident, thoughts about killing yourself, or a plan of how to kill yourself

ately seek medical attention. These include having the thought that your family would be better off if you were dead or any plan about how you would kill yourself if you had the energy or nerve to do it. **If you have any actual suicidal activity, such as stockpiling pills, purchasing a gun, mentally composing a suicide note, or thinking about times when you could be sure that your children would not be home to find your body, go to the nearest emergency room right now and tell them how you feel.**

Dysthymic Disorder

In one sense, dysthymic disorder is a "low-grade" form of depression. Symptoms are less severe, and this form is not usually associated with suicidal tendencies or profound loss of ability to function. However, dysthymic disorder can be very disabling due to its persistent, chronic nature. The very fact that it is so gradual in onset may keep women (or their families or doctors) from recognizing that it is a treatable illness rather than a gloomy personality. Some researchers feel that dysthymic disorder actually may represent a partially resolved major depressive episode and/or may be a warning of one. When a major depressive episode is superimposed on dysthymic disorder, it is called double depression. Dysthymia is a synonym for dysthymic disorder. The next box lists symptoms of dysthymic disorder.

SYMPTOMS OF DYSTHYMIC DISORDER

The presence of a depressed mood for most days over a two-year period, along with at least two of the following symptoms, suggests that you may be suffering from dysthymic disorder:

- Appetite changes (chronic overeating or low appetite)
- Sleep changes (chronic oversleeping or insomnia)
- Chronic feelings of fatigue
- Low sense of self-worth
- Difficulty concentrating or chronic indecisiveness
- Chronic pessimism or lack of hopeful feelings

Some researchers note that dysthymic disorder has other symptoms, including persistent guilt, irritability, withdrawal from friends and family, and low productivity. Dysthymic disorder may worsen regularly premenstrually, and some women attribute the mood disorder to "PMS." This is discussed more in the next chapter.

DEPRESSION: IS THERE MORE THAN ONE KIND?

In addition to breaking down depressive disorders into the categories of unipolar, bipolar, and dysthymic disorder, *DSM-IV* also differentiates postpartum onset and seasonal subtype.

Postpartum Depression

For the first time, the current *DSM* includes the specific diagnosis of postpartum depression. According to *DSM-IV*, postpartum depression is diagnosed if the syndrome occurs within four weeks of childbirth. Many postpartum specialists, myself included, feel that this period is too short. We believe that depression that occurs within the first year after childbirth is postpartum depression. The symptoms are generally similar to "ordinary" depression, but women with postpartum depression are especially likely to be plagued by guilt feelings, feelings of maternal inadequacy, and anxiety attacks. Also, the sleep disturbance is somewhat distinctive in postpartum depression. Women with postpartum depression are usually exhausted but unable to fall asleep even when the baby is sleeping. Two groups of women are especially susceptible to postpartum depression: those with a past episode of postpartum depression and those with bipolar disorder. To read more about postpartum depression, I refer you to my first book, *This Isn't What I Expected*, and Chapter 12.

Seasonal Affective Disorder

DSM-IV also describes the seasonal affective disorder subtype of depression, which sometimes is called winter depression or seasonal pattern depression. As many as 90 percent of individuals with this form of depression are women, and seasonal depression is more common in northern climates where winter days are short and cold. The symptoms may be somewhat distinctive, more characteristic of typical female depressive symptoms: Excessive sleeping, sugar craving, compulsive eating, and weight gain are common.

Seasonal depression generally begins in fall or winter and resolves with the return of spring and sunlight. However, a minority of women with seasonal depression have summer depressions instead. The key feature is at least two seasonal episodes with full recovery when the season passes, without nonseasonal episodes in between.

Light therapy is an option for women with seasonal affective disorder. Also called therapeutic lighting or phototherapy, this type of treatment is not likely to be helpful for "ordinary" clinical depression. Used in place of medication, light therapy works best for the milder type of winter blues. Women with more severe seasonal depression may do best combining light therapy with standard antidepressants, and some, particularly women with a history of mania or hypomania, may require a mood stabilizer such as lithium also. Phototherapy requires daily exposure to a light box (or a portable light visor), preferably in the morning, for the entire at-risk season. Fortunately, the therapeutic trend is to expose people to shorter periods of more intense light, so women don't have to put their lives on hold for a few hours a day.

Patients usually tolerate light therapy well, but, while a "natural" treatment, it can have side effects. It can be so stimulating that it causes irritability, and it may even precipitate a manic or near-manic episode, just like antidepressant medication. Milder side effects can include headache and insomnia. The now-standard ultraviolet (UV) shielded light (as opposed to "full-spectrum" light) minimizes the long-term risks of skin or eye damage.

Occasionally medical insurers cover the cost of light boxes, but usually they do not. Since patients will most likely have to pay out of pocket, I recommend starting with a rental or choosing a company with a thirty-day money-back policy. Light therapy takes effect quickly when it works; if you don't respond, you can send the unit back. While light boxes can be obtained without prescription, I highly recommend that they be used under medical supervision.

"Of Course She's Depressed"

The fact that the diagnosis is made largely by symptom expression (rather than by causation) means that the *DSM-IV* doesn't address many common situations in which women are especially vulnerable to depression. Stress of all sorts increases the risk of clinical depression in men and women alike. However, women are especially prone to depression in particular gender-linked life circumstances. These include bereavement, breast and gynecologic cancer, sexual assault, and domestic violence.

When the specifically treatable condition of clinical depression coincides with one of these circumstances, it may be dismissed or overlooked. My friend Nehama Dresner, M.D., director of outpatient psychiatry at Northwestern Memorial Hospital, calls this the of-course-she's-depressed syndrome. Everyone from family members to doctors to therapists may see the depression as being expectable, only natural. The problem is that even if it is "sensible" to be depressed when you have breast cancer or when you just lost a baby, you still have a condition that can be treated. Dr. Dresner likens this to saying of course her leg is broken, she was hit by a truck. You still apply a cast, even if you think it is reasonable to have a broken leg under such circumstances. Indeed, treatment for coexisting depression may facilitate a person's ability to cope with the underlying stress.

Bereavement

It is a biological fact of life that women are more likely to be widowed than men are to lose their spouses. Also, miscarriage or stillbirth is more likely to lead to depression in women than in their partners. While grief is not an emotional illness, it is one of the most common precursors to depression.

In fact, bereavement often feels just like depression. After the death of a loved one, it is normal to feel sad, to cry, to have trouble concentrating, to sleep fitfully, to forget to eat, to lose the ability to enjoy life in the same way, and to find it difficult to go through the motions of everyday life, whether work or family life. When grief does turn into depression, an antidepressant may help the depression as well as the grief. Clinical depression overwhelms your ability to move through the pain of the loss, and proper treatment will help you put the pieces back together.

Because culture shapes how people mourn a loved one, it isn't always possible to draw sharp lines demarcating grief from depression. You may find it helpful to consult someone from within your own culture. Ask: Is this more than usual, atypical? A religious leader, a doctor or a nurse, or a counselor from within your community may be a very helpful sounding board.

Depression often is distinguished from grief by how long the acute pain lasts: Usually, after two to three months, "normal" grief begins to subside (although you shouldn't expect to recover fully by two months and likely you will never feel entirely free of pain when you lose someone who really matters). Aside from duration, certain very pronounced symptoms are common when depression complicates the mourning process. These symptoms are suicidal thoughts (including wishes that you had died too, even if you don't have plans or impulses to harm yourself), inability to go through the motions at all (not caring for children, not being able to get out of bed to go to work), extreme guilt (obsessing about something you should have done for the deceased person or some way you should have prevented the death), or a deep sense of being unworthy, useless, or inconsequential.

Cancer

Depression complicates cancer every day. Between one-third and one-half of women who are undergoing treatment for a malignancy will experience a bout of clinical depression. Cancer is a massive emotional trauma. It is normal to be terrified, or to feel exhausted and depleted by radiation or chemotherapy. It is normal to feel irritable, distracted, withdrawn, worried, and to feel outraged when others are blatantly insensitive, when they say "just be glad you're alive," or "at least your kids are in high school." It isn't normal to lose hope, to lose the will to fight, to lose the ability to experience joyful moments.

Being diagnosed with breast or gynecologic cancer may be uniquely traumatic because the treatment may be disfiguring and may injure a woman's sense of herself as feminine or sexual or youthful. However, a pervasive sense of being physically defective, utterly deformed, may be a hallmark of depression. Absolute inability to feel attractive or sexual, profound loss of self-esteem and self-worth are not expectable reactions to having breast or gynecologic malignancies.

Aside from culturally mediated body image issues, certain cancer treatments certain (including chemotherapy for breast cancer or surgical removal of the ovaries) precipitate actual or physiologic menopause. While natural—gradual—menopause is not associated with an increased risk of depression after the first year, abrupt menopause is an entirely different matter. Surgery or chemotherapy for cancer that suddenly removes the ovary's supply of the natural female hormone estrogen can precipitate depression. The effect may be a direct physiological one (estrogen's effects on brain chemistry is discussed in Appendix A), or it may be a secondary effect from hot flashes, sexual discomfort, and the like.

Some doctors feel that treatment of depression may have direct medical benefits for women with cancer. You may have seen reports that emotional health improves a person's medical outcome from cancer, especially breast cancer, or even that emotional imbalance was the cause of someone's cancer in the first place. This makes me see red. First of all, we just do not have the scientific evidence to make such a claim. It may be that depression itself is more likely to affect women with more advanced illness who have to undergo more aggressive treatment. Second, results of studies are in conflict; some research shows that depression and anxiety actually help survival rates. Mark Twain said there are lies, damn lies, and statistics. If you have cancer, be skeptical, and resist internalizing any message that if you tried harder, were more emotionally competent, you wouldn't have this cancer or you would have a better outcome. New Age insistence that the mind-body are always intertwined are just beliefs, not God's truth. I am outraged when I see anything that smacks of blaming the victim.

Furthermore, you don't need to justify treatment of depression as a way to improve your cancer prognosis. It is enough to treat depression in order to feel better. Much of what women with cancer go through is not avoidable. However, clinical depression is not a necessary part of cancer treatment. It isn't like hair loss, an unavoidable side effect of chemotherapy. When you are fighting cancer, you have enough on your plate without adding depression. If you talk to your doctor or oncology nurse about depression, you should expect to be taken very seriously. Neglect of a treatable illness just because you are doubly burdened by cancer is nothing short of appalling. Overcoming clinical depression will help you tap into your natural strength in enduring adversity.

Sexual Assault

According to statistics, approximately 25 percent of women will be raped in their lifetime. Rape is unspeakably horrible, one of the worst traumas that human beings can experience. The most common emotional reaction to sexual assault, called rape trauma syndrome (or posttraumatic stress disorder in *DSM-IV*), is characterized by anxiety, repeated mental reliving of the rape through nightmares and flashbacks, hyperactive alertness and easy startle reflexes, and aversion or suppression of reminders or memories of the attack. Transient sleep and appetite changes are common. Most rape victims experience serious emotional symptoms, but by no means do all experience an emotional illness. As with any psychiatric condition, symptoms are considered an illness if they are persistent, severe, and interfere with day-to-day living.

Medication should not be the main treatment used for rape trauma syndrome. Most cities have rape crisis centers staffed largely by volunteers who can be very helpful in the immediate aftermath of a rape. Also, professional treatment with a counselor who specializes in trauma recovery can help many rape survivors. Much of the research on antidepressant medications for posttraumatic stress disorder is conducted on war veterans, performed at Veterans Administration hospitals, and it isn't clear how applicable these findings are for female survivors of sexual trauma. However, at this time, healing words seem to aid trauma recovery much better than medication.

However, clinical depression is the single most common disorder found in conjunction with posttraumatic stress disorder. If posttraumatic stress disorder develops after a woman is raped, she is likely also to develop clinical depression. As is true for other conditions, treatment for depression facilitates recovery from posttraumatic stress disorder. It is very difficult for victims of sexual assault who also are depressed to learn to trust again, to venture out in the world, to get a good night's sleep, to reconnect with people. Aggressive treatment for depression also will make it easier for women to be involved in the legal system, should they be pursuing criminal charges.

Domestic Violence

Battered women are at very high risk for clinical depression. Helplessness is a clear precursor of depression, and abused women typically feel trapped. Unfortunately, many physicians overlook the importance of treating clinical depression in abused women, believing that it is only natural for a woman to feel depressed when her husband is beating her. Doctors aren't always terribly good about helping battered women, but even when they attend to the issues, they focus on ending the violence, on helping a woman find a safe and violence-free environment. If they refer a battered woman to a shelter and she doesn't go there, many caregivers are frustrated and quit trying.

However, treatment of depression may allow a battered woman to hope again. Depression itself feeds the sense of futility and helplessness that accompany domestic violence. Leaving an abusive relationship is incredibly challenging and overwhelming, and it doesn't take much for a woman to believe that she can't escape, can't make it alone, can't feed her children or find a place of her own or hide herself successfully. Appropriate treatment for depression will bring strength to many battered women. It may make all the difference in their ability to get help, to imagine a different way of living, to take the necessary steps.

WHAT CAUSES DEPRESSION?

Why Is It Always Us?

Women are twice as likely as men to suffer from depression, for reasons that are only partly known. Women's social roles and responsibilities are part but not all of the cause. The single highest known situational risk factor for depression is being a homemaker caring for small children, a condition that increases a woman's vulnerability to depression by two and one-half times. That's not too surprising, since caring for children is a high-stakes job with many competing and conflicting demands, little predictability, no breaks, no pay, isolation from adult company, and no genuine societal appreciation of its importance.

Reproductive Links

However, homemakers are also at higher risk for biological conditions that increase vulnerability to depression: pregnancy and recent childbirth. An individual woman's vulnerability to experiencing a mood disorder is highest in the first three months after childbirth, a time of enormous physical stress including hormonal transitions and chronic sleep deprivation and fatigue. In fact, if the social factors known to increase women's risk of depression—lower socioeconomic status, caregiving responsibilities, and the like—are eliminated, women still have an unexplained (presumably biological) 40 percent increased risk for depression.

Rates of depression begin to increase following menarche (onset of menstruation) and peak at the ages of twenty to forty-five, the years during which many women are bearing or raising children. Despite the stereotype that menopausal women are unhappy, hormone-depleted empty nesters, the reality is that women are less vulnerable to depression after menopause. Instead, depression afflicts women at a time in their lives when they typically have little opportunity to take care of themselves. The average age of onset is twenty-seven.

Is It My Situation?

The evidence that biological factors predispose individuals to clinical depression is overwhelming. But simplistic biological explanations do not suffice; multiple factors combine to cause depression. Stressful life events, how a woman was raised to feel about herself, the quality of her marriage, the safety of her neighborhood, the availability of nurturing people to buffer disappointments, and her individual opportunity to accomplish things that make her feel good all contribute to her likelihood of experiencing depression.

But situational factors are not the only cause. The fact is, almost everybody—male or female, rich or poor, brown or pink, born-again Christian or third-generation atheist, doctor or hospital cleaning woman—*almost everybody* has suffered pain and loss. It comes with being human. But clinical depression doesn't inevitably follow human tragedy, and, conversely, many of my patients tell me that they've gotten through much harder times than whatever seemed to precipitate the current episode of depression that brought them to see me now.

In fact, that was true for Stephanie, whom you read about previously.

Stephanie told me that she couldn't believe the depression was hitting her now, because she wanted this divorce as much as her ex-husband did. She had lost her best friend in high school to leukemia and suffered date rape in college without developing depression, so why now? But her family history was loaded: Several relatives were depressed, including a cousin who hadn't started having problems until she too was in her thirties. Their shared grandmother was a chronic complainer who had a long history of unexplained aches and pains, and Stephanie felt that her mother struggled with demons she couldn't or wouldn't share with anyone. Realizing that she had a good track record of overcoming adversity helped Stephanie feel more optimistic about her future, since she was terrified that she would never feel good again. Like her mother and grandmother, Stephanie had the potential for severe depression. Unlike them, she was determined to get well again, whatever it took.

Stephanie was puzzled by why the divorce triggered her depression, but she saw clearly that one followed the other. Sometimes it is easy to pinpoint what sets off depression. Extreme stress alone can do it, as it did for my postpartum patient Monica, who had a cesarean section delivery following forty-eight hours of hard labor, struggled with a milk-allergic, extremely colicky baby who literally screamed for hours on end, and had to return to work at four weeks postpartum because her husband got laid off and they needed the money. On the other hand, my postpartum patient Cindy had sailed through a previous baby without any problems, but she developed a very severe depression when her thyroid replacement medication was lowered abruptly in error, an obviously biological trigger.

Predisposed to Depression

If it isn't just heartache and misery, what then seems to account for why individuals suffer from depression? In my view, situational and emotional stress may lead to depression for people with the biological or genetic predisposition. In general, I believe that the greater the biological predisposition, the more susceptible a person is to emotional stress; however, even women with no biological predisposition may experience clinical depression, given enough stress, fatigue, or loss.

Conversely, women with a strong biological tendency may experience clinical depression in the absence of any stress. A biological tendency to depression may show up in several ways: close blood relatives with depression, recurrent bouts (especially three or more) of depression, a tendency toward very severe symptoms and/or strong physical depressive symptoms, and past response to antidepressant medication. In fact, while stress (especially loss) is often a precipitant to the first or second depressive episode in women with multiple episodes of depression, eventually the depression has a life of its own.

One explanation of this tendency is called kindling; it's as if once a person has had depression, the embers remain quietly lit, ready to burst into flame at an ever lower threshold. In other words, once the final common pathway of brain chemical imbalance has been reached, the individual is prone to subsequent imbalance. Some researchers feel that women are especially vulnerable to hormonally sensitive kindling. (See p. 260).

Genes

Depression is partly genetic. A person's risks of suffering from depression triples if she has a biological parent, sibling, or child with depression. Some families keep mental illnesses well hidden. Mary Karr, in her memoir *The Liars Club*, describes how the fact that "Mother's family was inherently Nervous" was secret. Many of my patients say, "Trust me, no one would talk about being depressed even if they were."

Bipolar disorder is even more genetic than unipolar depression — that is, it is more likely to cluster in families, and the genetic patterns are slightly different. Having relatives with unipolar depression increases a person's risk of unipolar depression only, whereas relatives of individuals with bipolar disorder have higher rates of both unipolar and bipolar depression.

The genetic predisposition appears to play itself out in various neurotransmitter dysfunctions, called by many chemical imbalances. Briefly, neurotransmitters are the chemicals that brain cells use to communicate information. These neurotransmitters function according to their location in the brain: At one site, a neurotransmitter may communicate the command "run" whereas in another part of the brain, the chemical message may be "feel peaceful." Neurotransmitters are involved sensory experiences, emotional states, involuntary automatic functions such as breathing, voluntary muscle activity, appetite, and sleep. Many people have heard of the neurotransmitter serotonin. Others include dopamine, norepinephrine, GABA, and acetylcholine.

Appendix A presents evidence that clinical depression is caused by physiologic, genetic, and biochemical imbalances in the brain. Some readers are very interested in the chemical aspects of depression; others' eyes glaze over at the mention of the word "neurotransmitter." Some of my patients want highly technical explanations; others are happy to take my word for it.

Neurotransmitters: Chemical Messengers in the Brain

Here's the short version: In clinical depression, neurotransmitters are not functioning properly. Antidepressants normalize neurotransmitters.

When I talk about neurotransmitters with my patients, I shrug and frown a lot and look puzzled. I tell them how much is unknown, undiscovered. At a lecture I attended recently, a very prominent researcher said, "When you are depressed, your brain juices are all out of whack"—dispelling my notion that psychiatrists more clever than I could explain neurotransmitters in a concise but sophisticated manner. Medical psychiatry is in its infancy: We know brain juices are out of whack, we know how to help, but that's about it. The bottom-line reason why clinical depression isn't a symptom of weakness or something you should be able to pull yourself out of is because your brain juices are out of whack.

While it looks as if many factors, ranging from stress, grief, injuries to self-esteem, medical illness, hormones, medications, genetics, and addictions, can lead to depression, in the most serious cases of depression, neurotransmitter dysfunction appears to be the final common pathway. Brain juices can go out of whack on their own, or they can be pushed by recent and remote emotional experiences. Some women have a strong physiologic or genetic tendency to have these chemical imbalances, and they may struggle with depression on and off for their entire lives, even under the best of circumstances. Some women have strong physiologic or genetic tendencies yet appear to have some sort of unusual immunity to depression, protective life experiences or circumstances that counteract the biological tendency. Other women, such as incest survivors, may have been robbed of the necessary emotional vitamins that protect against depression in later life.

Apparently the psychosocial and neurotransmitter dysfunctions feed off one another in the mood center of the brain. For example, habitual negative thinking or stressful life events may lead to the chemical imbalances in the brain. However, the chemical imbalances also cause distortions of thought and perception, so that the person's self-esteem lowers, she is unable to find pleasure in usual outlets, and the spiral goes ever more downward. This is why combined biochemical and psychological treatment usually works best.

Other biological abnormalities in clinical depression are well documented. Aside from neurotransmitter imbalances and dysregulation, depressed individuals have physical differences in sleep electroencephalograms (EEGs), subtle hormone abnormalities in the pituitary and adrenal glands, and abnormal biological clock functions. The brain regulates sleep, controls the functioning of the pituitary and adrenal glands at a site called the hypothalamus, and sets the circadian rhythms (the twenty-four-hour cycle). The abnormalities that have been verified are more evidence that clinical depression isn't just in the mind, it's in the brain too.

Life Circumstances

As more research is done, we will have a much clearer understanding of what the specific, unique causes of depression are. Right now, things are murky, but I believe that ultimately we will find out that both nature (brain chemistry) and nurture (life experience) contribute to depression. Briefly, here are some of the "life experience" models of what cause depression.

Sigmund Freud predicted that eventually a biological basis of mental illness would be discovered. In the meantime, he suggested that childhood psychosexual developmental fixation leads to adult vulnerability to major depression. While mental health professionals have largely dismissed this theory, Freud left a legacy that cannot be denied: the belief that we bring our childhood experiences with us wherever we go, as long as we live. Freud taught us that early losses have emotional impact throughout our adulthood. We all filter the present through experiences of the past, even when we are not aware of doing so.

Another psychological theory about the cause of depression is called learned helplessness, a theory modeled after animal studies in which dogs unable to avoid painful physical stimuli eventually quit trying and sink into a passivity that looks like despair. Applied to humans, this model supposes that the individual's experience of uncontrollable events cause her to feel unable to exert influence over any/all future events, to feel helpless in general. This model best explains why depression is so common in abuse and trauma victims. After enough externally imposed pain, it's natural to feel depressed and hopeless about your ability to control what happens to you. A fascinating study showed that the dogs who were made to act helpless stopped doing so when given antidepressants; this provides indirect evidence that situational depression may improve with medical treatment.

Another widely accepted psychological theory of what causes depression is the cognitive-behavioral model proposed by Aaron Beck and popularized by Dr. David Burns. In this model, negative patterns of thought and action (essentially, always seeing the cup as half empty rather than half full, and acting like it's empty) lead to the syndrome of clinical depression.

Comorbidity

Depression often is seen as a secondary diagnosis with other conditions, called comorbidity (coexistent illness). Women with panic disorder, obsessive compulsive disorder, posttraumatic stress disorder, eating disorders, addiction, and personality disorders are at higher risk of comorbid clinical depression.

WHAT ARE THE TREATMENTS FOR DEPRESSION?

Talk Therapy

The more severe the symptoms, the more likely a person is to need medication, since talk therapy alone is usually effective only for mild to moderate forms of clinical depression. At the milder end of the spectrum, it is perfectly appropriate to use nonmedical approaches to recovery. It is not appropriate to rush to medication in mild to moderate depression. Proven treatments for mild depression include exercise, stress reduction, lifestyle changes, relationship changes, and short-term psychotherapy. **If these methods are not effective, or if symptoms get worse despite these interventions, medication should be considered.**

Short-term therapy usually lasts for six to twenty sessions. Most people who are going to respond to therapy feel some improvement within the first month of treatment, even within the first session. If you do not have faith and trust in your therapist, or just don't feel that the two of you hit it off, chances are that the therapy will not work. It's simply not true that you need to feel worse before you feel better. True, talking about your emotional pain will feel bad. For therapy to work, however, you must feel that the therapist is in your corner, that he or she is there to support you through this. Two specific types of short-term therapy that have proven efficacy for depression are: cognitive therapy and interpersonal therapy. Supportive and psychodynamic therapy can also be adapted for short-term treatment, when the goal is also that of providing quick symptom relief and restoring previous functioning. Most psychiatrists do not feel that psychoanalysis or extended psychoanalytic therapy is sufficient or usually appropriate for acute clinical depression.

Unlike longer term psychodynamic therapy or psychoanalysis, which lasts one or a few years, brief therapy will not change your underlying personality and therefore will not help you build your psychological immunity to depression down the road. Unfortunately, recently one of the major shifts in mental health coverage is toward symptom relief and restabilization, with very few companies or HMOs willing to pay for long-term therapy. If you decide that you would like to undergo extensive psychotherapy, chances are that you will have to foot the bill. Less expensive alternatives include choosing a nonmedical therapist and group therapy. If private therapy is too expensive, check into training programs at a university graduate or medical school. Many have clinics in which residents and graduate-level therapists are available on a sliding fee scale. If you are seeing a therapist in training, be sure that he or she is supervised by an experienced faculty member. In large cities, fully trained mental health professionals who are undergoing advanced training in psychoanalysis often can be seen at reduced cost at psychoanalytic institutes.

Sally's Story

Most of us know someone like Sally: She can't see the blue sky because of a single cloud, she can't accept a compliment gracefully, and sometimes you feel like you'll scream if she predicts one more disaster that never materializes. But the depression that hit Sally after a breakup with her boyfriend was much more than her usual pessimism. Her predictions of gloom and doom got much worse, and she began to feel that she would never go on a date again, let alone get married. She ignored the fact that everyone told her that her ex always broke it off whenever he started to get close to a woman and felt certain that her personal flaws were the problem. In cognitive therapy, Sally learned to recognize her tendency to catastrophize and saw that she consistently negated the positive while amplifying the negative. She learned specific ways to interrupt her automatic negative thoughts and began to replace the automatic self-criticisms with more realistic appraisals.

A therapist who focused on interpersonal relationships might have tackled Sally's problems from the point of view of enhancing her relationships rather than targeting her negative thinking. In this type of therapy, Sally would have been encouraged to communicate more effectively, including learning how to "read" others better. Her therapist would have pointed out that Sally gets in a needy-clingy-suffocating mode and helped her to recognize that expecting any one person to meet all of her emotional needs is not possible or healthy. At the end of treatment, Sally would have replaced her obsession with finding a husband with a wish to have many strong, satisfying, healthy relationships. A few therapists (most of whom are in New York City) have been trained in a standardized form of relationship therapy called interpersonal psychotherapy (IPT).

In brief dynamic therapy, Sally would have explored the childhood roots of her susceptibility to rejection in a highly focused way. Dynamic (also called psychodynamic) therapy centers on transference, the exploration of how past ways of relating continue to color present relationships. Unlike psychoanalysis, in dynamic therapy Sally's therapist would give her lots of feedback while looking at how her parents' divorce left a deep imprint that continues to cause her pain years later. Sally would come to see that she was drawn to unstable creative types who almost always had problems committing to relationships. The therapist would suggest that Sally was trying to undo the abandonment that she experienced when her father, a poet, left her mother for a girl barely old enough to baby-sit the then nine-year-old Sally. Unintentionally, Sally pursued men who might fix the hurt but kept finding time and again that she couldn't change the tiger's stripes. As therapy ended, Sally would have felt much more in control as she vowed to open her eyes to the world of men who were looking for a nice, boring, till-death-do-us part relationship.

Sally might also have responded to nonspecific supportive therapy, in which she would ventilate her feelings and learn new coping skills. She might have chosen pastoral counseling, which integrates faith and spirituality as part of the healing process. However, if Sally was moderately depressed, her therapist might have pointed out that the current U.S. Public Health Service Guidelines state that appropriate treatment includes an antidepressant, especially if the counseling didn't pull her out of it. If Sally was severely depressed, she would have found it impossible to focus at all in therapy, at least until the medication began to work. If people can't sleep, can't eat, and can't concentrate, they can't work psychologically until they have some symptom relief.

When Words Are Not Enough: Medical Therapy for Depression

It might be helpful to consider the model of cardiac disease in thinking about when medication is appropriate. In mild cases, exercise and diet changes may be all that are needed to relieve the disease. In severe cases, the patient could die if suitably aggressive treatment is withheld. Mild to moderate depression affect the quality of life, and each individual needs to make the decision about whether medication will help them live life to the fullest. Given the many nonmedical alternatives, it may be inappropriate to turn to antidepressants too soon if one has never tried therapy or self-help. However, severe depression is a life-threatening illness that must be treated aggressively.

Symptoms that suggest that medication is necessary include: suicidal thoughts, complete loss of pleasure in response to pleasant events (i.e., you would feel down even if you won the lottery), waking several hours earlier than usual every morning, consistently feeling worse first thing in the morning, weight loss, and agitation. Panic attacks, trouble falling asleep, obsessive worrying, and excessive guilt also predict response to medication. If you previously had an episode in which you needed to take medication, chances are very high that you will need to again. Also, if a close blood relative responded to an antidepressant, your chances of responding to medication are also good. In mild cases, you should consider medication if you do not improve after two to four months of therapy. Any loss of contact with reality, including hallucinations (hearing voices or sounds), bizarre beliefs, or paranoia will not improve unless medication is started (usually both an antidepressant and an antipsychotic medication and sometimes lithium). Women with bipolar disorder generally do not respond to words alone.

Stephanie's Recovery

It is well documented that combined medication and psychotherapy is the most appropriate treatment for moderate to severe cases of depression. Stephanie responded to this combination:

> Stephanie's family doctor handed her a prescription for Prozac. At first, she was scared because a few years back, she had heard that Prozac caused people to become wild and aggressive. Her doctor reassured her and said he liked the medication because it caused so few side effects.
>
> For the first few days, Stephanie felt queasy about an hour after she took the Prozac. This quickly passed, and by her appointment a month later, she was much better. Because it was taking her two hours to fall asleep every night, her doctor gave her a second prescription for a tiny dose of Desyrel (trazodone), a very sedating antidepressant. Tiny or not, it did the trick.
>
> The doctor told Stephanie that he wanted her to take the medication for at least six months. He also recommended that she see a social worker to talk over the divorce. Stephanie met with the therapist weekly for three months, and the support was just what she needed. During this time, she talked about how painful it was that her own mother wasn't there for her when things got rough. She saw the pattern: just like when her first true love dumped her in college, just like when she couldn't find a job for five months after graduation, just like when her pet kitten got run over by a car when Stephanie was in eighth grade, her mother's response was always: What did you do to bring this on yourself?
>
> Her therapist helped her to realize that along with losing a husband, she was also losing a wish left over from childhood, the wish that her mommy would hug her and kiss her and tell her everything would be okay. "She would if she could, I'm sure," Stephanie's therapist said. "You and I don't know what keeps her from being able to be

more supportive. We just know that it's time to stop banging your head against this particular wall."

Stephanie felt great when she finished therapy, but she decided to follow her doctor's advice and continue the medication for another few months. Six months later she stopped the Prozac. Two weeks later she stopped the Desyrel and found that she could once again fall asleep easily. At a checkup a year later, she was pleased to report that even though she had gone through some hard moments, the depression stayed away.

HOW MEDICATIONS WORK

Doctors choose a particular medication based on their formal training as well as a host of informal sources of information. By far, psychiatrists have the most formal training in prescribing antidepressants. Most family physicians have some formal psychiatry training as part of their postgraduate residencies, but many older family physicians and general practitioners (GPs) and most gynecologists and internists did not get this training during their residencies. However, good doctors in any specialty undergo continuing medical education, attending seminars and lectures to learn about innovations in clinical practice.

Generally you can assume that a psychiatrist has had training and experience in using antidepressants (although many psychoanalysts do not; you should check if your doctor calls himself an analyst). Nonmedical therapists such as clinical psychologists and social workers cannot prescribe medications, but they can refer you to a doctor. You should feel free to ask your primary care doctor if he or she commonly prescribes antidepressants, since it isn't a good idea to be your doctor's first anything. If your doctor is offended by your questions, find a new doctor. All doctors should know and be comfortable with their limitations: Defensiveness and omnipotence in a doctor are bad news.

We physicians are highly influenced by how a medication affected a previous patient. Seeing good effects from one medication often causes a doctor to stick with that particular antidepressant. Similarly, a single case of severe side effects may make us stay away from that medication, even if it's not really logical to do so. Since antidepressants are generally comparable in effectiveness, knowing which medication to use for which patient is as much an art as it is a science. If I feel that several different antidepressants are clinically appropriate, I discuss the pros and cons of the alternative drugs, to let my patients tell me which risks they feel most willing to tolerate.

Antidepressants all influence one or more neurotransmitter in the brain, usually by slowing down the re-uptake of the neurotransmitter. (See p. 253.) Exactly how this happens is still somewhat of a mystery. Doctors use various metaphors to express what is known about how antidepressants work: They reset the thermostat, repair chemical imbalances, fix brain juices that are out of whack. My personal favorite is that antidepressants are the equivalent of kicking a broken vending machine. We can speculate that the kick loosens springs, lines up mechanical components, or shakes the Diet Pepsi can free. The indisputable, observable fact is that the kick makes the vending machine function properly. Antidepressants are indisputably, observably helpful in treating clinical depression.

Antidepressants do not work as quickly as kicking the vending machine, however. Although a minority of women notice partial symptom relief within days of starting an antidepressant, most women don't begin to feel like themselves again for at least two to three weeks. This suggests that the antidepressants—all of which are known to increase neurotransmitter activity after a single dose—trigger a chain reaction in the brain that takes time. This fact is absolutely critical to appreciate, because it is often tempting to stop the medication after a few days. If it isn't working yet, keep in mind that it isn't supposed to. Since side effects are almost always worst in the first few weeks, I encourage my patients to stick with the medication for at least a few weeks, a month if they can, because two miraculous things happen: They start to feel good again, and the side effects diminish.

After people have taken an antidepressant for months on end, the faulty mechanism is somehow fixed. But this crude "repair" needs a chance to settle in. To use the earlier analogy, if you kick the vending machine long enough, it suddenly starts functioning on its own again, and it remains fixed. If you stay on antidepressants long enough, your chemical imbalance is much less likely to come right back. That's why most doctors recommend a period of maintenance medication, even when you are feeling yourself again.

How Long Do I Need Medication?

Often the first question a patient asks me is "How long do I have to take this stuff?" The answer always must be individualized, based on the patient's unique situation. However, most women with a single episode of depression should stay on antidepressants for four to nine months after the symptoms resolve. Many women are tempted to stop the medication as soon as they feel well. It's hard to take a pill for an invisible condition. **However, stopping too soon greatly increases the risk of relapse.**

For patients who have had two episodes, I encourage a full year's maintenance and sometimes as much as two years. If patients have suffered three bouts of clinical depression, I recommend they stay on medication indefinitely, since the chances of recurrence are high. About half of women with a single depressive episode will remain well after an adequate maintenance period. Even those who eventually do relapse may not do so for many years. However, if my patient relapses soon after stopping maintenance medication, I recommend a longer period of maintenance (such as one or two more years) and then try to taper the medication again. I also usually recommend two years' maintenance therapy for women with dysthymic disorder and often recommend indefinite medication if the dysthmic disorder recurs after the medication is stopped.

Maintenance medication is different for women with bipolar disorder. Usually psychiatrists recommend a shorter period of antidepressant therapy for them, followed by indefinite maintenance therapy with a mood stabilizer (most commonly, lithium, Tegretol [carbamazepine], or Depakote [valproic acid]). This course of treatment is taken because mood stabilizers often are effective at preventing relapse and antidepressants may have a paradoxical worsening effect by precipitating bouts of mania. Some psychiatrists prefer Wellbutrin (buproprion) as a first choice for women with bipolar disorder, because it may be the least likely to induce manic episodes.

Doctors are also likely to recommend longer periods of maintenance antidepressant therapy for especially bad cases, such as when suicide was attempted, or in the rare instance in which shock therapy (electroconvulsive therapy [ECT]) was necessary to recover because medication was ineffective.

Types of Antidepressants

The first antidepressants were discovered in the late 1950s, when by chance certain drugs were noted to improve depression rather than the original conditions they were being tested on (tuberculosis and schizophrenia). Virtually all the new-generation antidepressants have been engineered in the laboratory, based on how they influence neurotransmitters. Because of chemical refinement, medications concocted in the lab are less likely than those found by chance to have unwanted and unnecessary side effects, including less risk of death due to overdose. Doctors generally prescribe one of the new antidepressants because of their safety, unless there is a specific reason to prescribe an older drug.

The new group of antidepressants include Prozac, Luvox (fluvoxamine), Paxil (paroxetine), Serzone (nefazodone), and Zoloft (sertraline). These medications increase serotonin activity and are also called selective serotonin re-uptake inhibitors (SSRIs). Effexor (velafaxine) and Remeron* (mirtazapine) inhibit re-uptake of serotonin and norepinephrine. Wellbutrin (buproprion) inhibits dopamine re-uptake. These new generation antidepressants may also be referred to as "atypical" or "novel" antidepressants.

The heterocyclics, also called tricyclic antidepressants, were the mainstay of treatment for clinical depression up until the mid-1980s. These include Elavil (amitriptyline), Norpramin (desipramine), Tofranil (imipramine), Pamelor (nortriptyline), and many others. Heterocyclics usually cause more severe side effects than the new antidepressants, but not always. Some women feel jittery and buzzed by the new antidepressants, and would much rather have the dry mouth and constipation that is common with heterocyclics. Most primary care doctors do not prescribe heterocyclics, while psychiatrists often do. When primary care doctors do prescribe heterocyclics, often the dose is too low.

Circumstances in which I prescribe a heterocyclic as my first choice include pregnancy and breast-feeding, since the longer a drug is on the market, the better opportunity we have to assess the poten-

---

* Remeron has just come on the market. Usually the medical community needs at least a year to learn more about a new medication, and doctors typically do not prescribe brand-new drugs except for individuals who haven't responded to previously available drugs. Remeron looks to be very sedating, which would limit its use.

tial for delayed-onset side effects in fetuses and babies exposed to it. Otherwise, like many other doctors, I use heterocyclics as a second choice if someone did not tolerate or did not respond to a newer antidepressant. (Many of my colleagues try two different serotonin-enhancing antidepressants before switching to a tricyclic.) Because heterocyclics are more sedating, many doctors prescribe them for women with marked sleep disturbance. Finally, since heterocyclics are available as generics, they are much less expensive than new generation antidepressants.

The most problematic side effect for women taking serotonin-enhancing antidepressants is that they may interfere with sexual pleasure or functioning. (See Chapter 7.) The most problematic side effect for women taking heterocyclics is that they often increase appetite and may cause weight gain. (See Chapter 8.) Wellbutrin, which is in a class by itself, causes neither weight gain nor sexual dysfunction. However, it must be taken two or three times a day (as opposed to once for most others), and it is dangerous in women with bulimia or anorexia nervosa, substance abuse, or epilepsy.

In deciding on a course of treatment, to some extent, you and your doctor have to pick your poison. However, as none of these side effects is certain to happen, it may make sense to take a wait-and-see approach before deciding that you cannot tolerate a particular drug. Your doctor should warn you of common side effects, and you should be involved in the medication choice based on your own sense of which side effects would be most troublesome. Fortunately, far more women have mild side effects or none rather than the alternative many women fear: turning into zombies.

When Should I See a Specialist?

A subgroup of women have treatment-resistant depression, which is defined as depression that fails to respond to two trials of adequate doses of medication taken for an appropriate length of time. Medication issues are very complex for these individuals, many of whom need to take more than one medication, or take a special kind of antidepressant called a monoamine oxidase inhibitor (MAOI). Table B.14, on page 280, lists some alternatives.

Women with treatment-resistant depression should be cared for by a psychiatrist with expertise in prescribing medication. If you got your prescription from a primary care doctor, I encourage you to see a psychiatrist if you have not responded to a first-line antidepressant, just as you would see a specialist for any illness that didn't respond to the efforts made by your primary care physician.

CONCLUSION

Antidepressants are often called quick-fix solutions, as if solving a problem rapidly is a terrible thing. Here are a few other medical quick fixes: penicillin, tubal ligations, insulin, and open heart surgery. These scientific breakthroughs improve the quality of life. But I believe that antidepressants usually are best thought of as merely one aspect of fixing the problem. My patient Natalie had a quick-fix response to Zoloft, a serotonin-enhancing antidepressant. Her symptoms of profound sadness, irritability, and insomnia got better within weeks, and her boss noticed that she was doing her job like her old self. She then threw herself into therapy, which hadn't been helpful until she started the medication. One of the first things she noticed after the Zoloft kicked in was that she began to cry in therapy, but this time the tears made sense. Instead of a diffuse sadness, she could work with her therapist on those things that were, in reality, sad and painful. For Natalie, the antidepressant gave her the strength to do some very deep and very necessary psychological work.

Other women respond so well to antidepressants that they no longer feel the need for therapy. Sometimes when a therapist refers a patient to me, I start her on antidepressants, and she recovers and then asks if it's okay not to see the therapist who made the referral. While this situation may be professionally embarrassing, remember, you're not responsible for making your therapist or psychiatrist feel needed and wanted or employed, so you should trust your instincts about what feels right. When I'm asked this question, I usually respond that the woman should ask her therapist's opinion, since he or she may recommend treatment to get at underlying vulnerabilities, which is certainly valid. However, if your therapist can't state treatment goals for you, or if you've accomplished the goals that feel right to you, it's okay to move on.

Viewing antidepressants as an either/or treatment is unrealistic. Some women will respond fully to psychotherapy. Some women will respond fully to an antidepressant. Individual women have different values and beliefs about what kind of treatment is best or feel strongly that they wish to try one approach and not another. There's an old joke about how many psychiatrists it takes to change a light bulb: one, but the light bulb has to want to change. The light bulb also has to want to take Prozac. If you are opposed to medication, it's okay to try other avenues of treatment. Do consider setting a time frame in your mind—for example, tell yourself you'll try therapy for two months, then reconsider medication if you don't notice significant improvement. Also consider getting another professional opinion. Finally, try to hear what people who love you are saying. If your mother, partner, brother, therapist, best friend, and doctor are all advising that you take an antidepressant, give it some real thought.

Chapter 3

WHY AM I SO EXPLOSIVE?

Premenstrual Depression

KEY POINTS

- Premenstrual syndrome ("PMS") is a fuzzy term that refers to a wide variety of physical or emotional symptoms that fluctuate across the menstrual cycle.
- Premenstrual depression (PMD) is a depressive disorder that may cause irritability and a sad mood for a week or more before your period and resolves with menstrual flow.
- Many other disorders may fluctuate symptomatically prior to menses. It is very important to avoid mistakenly attributing all emotional symptoms to "PMS." The most common illness that masquerades as "PMS" is premenstrual exacerbation of a major mood disorder.
- Natural remedies may not be enough for PMD.
- While serotonin-enhancing antidepressants are effective medical treatment for premenstrual mood disorders, there are a number of alternative medications.

Nowadays, when a woman calls me for an appointment and asks for help with depression, nine times out of ten she is indeed suffering from clinical depression. However, when I am asked to help someone with "PMS," anything goes. This is so because in our culture, we use the term "PMS" to describe everything from breast tenderness to rage attacks. Unfortunately, the term also is used to belittle and mock women, all too often being a synonym for "bitchy." When you talk about "PMS" with your doctor or therapist, carefully review each and every symptom. Never assume that you are on the same wavelength.

Clarity about the exact symptoms is crucial because while many women with depression note the effect of their menstrual cycles on mood, just 3 to 5 percent of women actually has the illness called premenstrual depression (PMD). Questions about "PMS" are very common, and it is natural to wonder whether hormones might be influencing your mood. The first thing I try to do is sort out whether the main problem is primarily physical (bloating, food cravings, cramps) or primarily emotional (irritability, crying jags, feeling overwhelmed and hopeless). When emotional symptoms are the main problem, my patient and I next try to figure out whether things are bad throughout the cycle but really, really bad premenstrually ("premenstrual magnification") or whether things are *only* really, really bad premenstrually. Charting your symptoms throughout your menstrual cycle—either on your own or using a chart provided by your doctor—is useful as a diagnostic tool and for monitoring treatment progress. A sample chart is found at the end of this chapter.

Marti is a forty-two-year-old divorced mother of two teenagers who made an appointment to see if I could help her with "PMS." The first thing I did was ask Marti to begin charting her symptoms, even before our appointment.

Make a list of five or more things that bother you, I said, and make a quick note each day of how severe the symptoms were. I asked her to rate the symptoms as absent, mild, moderate, severe on a daily basis.

Marti easily picked the most bothersome symptom. Absolutely, positively, she said, it's anger. Every little thing ticks me off, she says, stuff that doesn't get to me most of the time. Each month, during the week before her period, she is "constantly at war" with her teenagers. She tells me that raising teens is no piece of cake, but during the week before her period she cannot ignore the fact that they never come down for breakfast until one second before they have to go to school, and then it seems that they stand in front of the refrigerator for hours pondering the merits of orange juice vs. milk. "I hate the way their stupid baggy jeans look, their music drives me bonkers, and I cannot stand to tell them one more time to put their own dishes in the dishwasher. I go from annoyed to screaming in an instant. Then I get my period, it feels like the alien force leaves my body, and I look back and realize that I've been way overreacting for the past week."

If Marti's kids or her boyfriend try to tell her she's acting "PMSy" she gets even more irritated, convinced that they're trying to brush her off. Her tendency to explode isn't only with her kids. For a week every month, she's pounding on her horn at the slightest traffic nuisance, and her secretary seems to do no right. Sometimes Marti's so frustrated and overwhelmed that she cries at anything at all, and she feels down and draggy all the time.

When Marti brings her menstrual cycle symptom chart in, a quick glance confirms her self-assessment. She has a twenty-six-day cycle, menstruating from day 1 to day 5. She believes that she ovulates on day 12 (she experiences low back pain and has a thick, clear discharge around that time) and feels good for several days after this. Beginning on day 17, she starts noting slight irritability and oversensitivity. By the next day, she has moderate symptoms, and on days 19 through 26 she has severe irritability, oversensitivity, feelings of being overwhelmed, and mood swings. She also has moderate sugar cravings, anxiety, and tearfulness. Once her period starts again, she has a so-so day for the first day but is completely back to herself on day 2.

I tell Marti that I use the term "premenstrual depressive disorder" for her condition. I do that partly because that's what the *DSM-IV* calls it and partly, as mentioned previously, I'd remove the term "PMS" from the language if I could.

PREMENSTRUAL DEPRESSION: THE DIAGNOSIS

The ease with which Marti pinpoints her most bothersome symptoms is classic for PMD. I have found that the single most troublesome PMD symptom—the one that weighs most heavily in the medication decision—is irritability. In this situation, your fuse is extremely short, and you feel unable to let things just roll off your back. Little things loom large, and daily hassles feel enormously overwhelming.

Irritability affects other people—not just the woman suffers! But it's perfectly okay to take medication for PMD because *you* feel miserable, not just because you're making your family miserable too. Don't overlook symptoms that are purely subjective, such as cyclic depression and self-criticism. The box below presents the symptoms of premenstrual dysphoric disorder.

SYMPTOMS OF PREMENSTRUAL DYSPHORIC DISORDER

You may have PMD if you have five of the following symptoms present during the premenstrual week *and* the symptoms resolve within the first few days of your menstrual flow. The symptoms should be documented by daily charting over two consecutive periods.

- Irritability, anger, arguments with others
- Sad, gloomy feelings, including feeling worthless or useless
- Abrupt mood swings, with sudden tears, anger, or personal oversensitivity
- Feelings of anxiety, edginess, and tension
- Diminished ability to concentrate
- Low energy, getting tired too easily
- Loss of interest in the things that you usually enjoy
- Sugar, salt, or junk food cravings, or other changes in your usual eating habits or appetite
- Feeling easily overwhelmed or unable to manage things you usually can handle
- Changes in your sleep habits: either oversleeping, napping, or insomnia
- Physical changes including breast soreness or engorgement, headaches, and bloating

The American Psychiatric Association compiled a work group of advisors to tackle the complex issue of diagnostic criteria for PMD. There are almost 100 different definitions of PMD, some of which are mostly physical ("PMS") and some of which are mostly emotional. The *DSM-IV* took a compromise position, including the list of "research" criteria for PMD cited in the box, while postponing full endorsement as an official psychiatric diagnosis.

Even these criteria are not without controversy. Personally, to give just one example, I don't believe that premenstrual headaches belong in this list, since premenstrual migraines are a legitimate independent diagnosis. I'm not terribly bothered by this, however, since most women who meet these strict diagnostic criteria for PMD will do so on the basis of emotional symptoms alone.

A BRIEF HISTORY OF THE PREMENSTRUAL CONTROVERSY

Part of the controversy about the diagnostic criteria is clinical while part is purely political. Nowadays, any expression of anger, displeasure, conflict, or even sometimes authority by a woman is subject to being called "PMS." In fact, this societal tendency to ridicule women's anger and attribute pathology to women's normal reproductive and hormonal changes has caused considerable confusion and dissension among clinicians and researchers investigating PMD.

Some feminists within the women's health movement are completely opposed to having the American Psychiatric Association include PMD as a bona fide disorder in the *Diagnostic and Statistical Manual.* They feel that doing so will essentially backfire against women, increasing the likelihood that we will be seen as disabled due to the fact that we menstruate. They note that many, many women experience mild emotional changes across the menstrual cycle that should not be labeled psychiatrically or treated professionally.

Other doctors, nurses, and therapists with equally passionate commitment to women's health feel that it is important to validate the individual woman's experience, believing that failing to acknowledge those women with severe PMD ignores politically problematic reality. It also hampers desperately needed research, since lack of uniform diagnostic criteria means that scientific findings are not reproducible from one research protocol to the next (since the researchers may not be treating the same illness).

PREMENSTRUAL DEPRESSION: IS THERE MORE THAN ONE KIND?

Before describing treatment options for PMD, I want to spend some time talking about what PMD is *not*. The self-diagnosis of PMD is often mistaken. In fact, the numbers are astonishing: As many as 80 percent of women who volunteer to be subjects in PMD study protocols will not show premenstrual emotional changes when they actually chart their cycles. This means that many women are attributing the wrong thing to PMD, which can prevent them from getting appropriate and effective treatments. It also means that patients must be clear with their nurse-practitioner or doctor about symptoms: They should describe specific emotional or physical changes and avoid the catch-all term "PMS."

Premenstrual Physical Symptoms: Not PMD

One of the things that PMD is *not* is a syndrome characterized mostly by physical symptoms, either premenstrual or menstrual. If your major symptoms are physical symptoms of headache, water retention, painful breasts, back pain, and stomach upset, you do not have premenstrual depressive disorder. You may be emotionally bothered by these symptoms, just as you would be by any other physical ailment. But unless you have emotional symptoms that are very distressing to you or that affect how you live your life, you do not have PMD. You may have endometriosis, migraine headaches, underactive thyroid, or simply annoying but not pathological uncomfortable physical symptoms that might be relieved by dietary changes (especially reducing caffeine), exercise, a mild diuretic (medication that enhances water elimination), or even birth control pills.

Menstrual Physical Symptoms: Not PMD

If your major problem is menstrual cramps that begin when your period starts and go away when it's over, you may have a condition called dysmenorrhea ("painful menstruation"), which almost always can be treated easily with nonsteroidal pain relievers or birth control pills. Nonsteroidal pain relievers available without prescription include Advil (ibuprofen), Aleve (sodium naproxen), and Orutis (ketoprofen). If you haven't done so recently, you should have a physical examination including a pelvic exam to check for any new or progressive physical symptoms. Some other physical conditions, such as headaches or endometriosis, may worsen during the menstrual cycle. Again, it's normal to be cranky when you are in pain; this isn't PMD.

Mild Premenstrual Blues: Not PMD

Another thing PMD is *not* is mild irritability or other changes, lasting a day or two. If your premenstrual changes consist of uncharacteristically yelling at your kids once or twice, or feeling draggy for a day or two, or sneaking two candy bars when no one is looking, or having that once-a-month fight with your lover about which restaurant you're going to, things are not severe enough to warrant either a psychiatric diagnosis or medication. PMD warrants treatment (medical or otherwise) when it impairs how you function, either in personal relationships or at work, or if the emotional distress lasts for a week or more. If you can shake it off, if words are enough, or if it's mildly bothersome but not getting in the way of your life, you should not jump to take a medication or to label normal fluctuations as a disease.

Instead, make an effort to get yourself healthier physically. Pay attention to what you eat, especially reducing salt, caffeine, and alcohol, and try once more to quit smoking. Go back to the aerobics class, and make a plan to nurture yourself during the few troublesome days. Do not schedule your child's birthday party for the day before your period, and ask for more help from your partner if that's an option. These measures are a good idea for anyone with any menstrual cycle problem, so that those days don't just creep up on you and take you by surprise month after month.

Feeling Angry: Not PMD

PMD is *not* the cause of sensible anger. Anger can feel very bad, even if it is totally justified and rational. It's scary to feel powerful anger and to fear losing control. Unless you grew up in unusual circumstances, you have been socialized as a woman to avoid anger, to make nice at all times. In fact, the rampant use of the term "PMS" when equated with "bitch" can be seen in part as a tool our culture uses to warn women to stay nice: Be polite, or we're going to bring up those raging hormones again.

If you are angry because the guys at work put a girlie calendar up over the coffee machine, because your husband didn't tell you for the seven hundredth time in a row that he was working late, because your boss knows how to tell you it's done wrong but doesn't know how to tell you when it's done right, because your ex-husband married someone two years older than your eldest son, or because your neighbor repeatedly asks you to drive her kids home from school once or twice a week because, after all, you don't "work," you are sensibly angry. It's time to stop pinning it on "PMS" and use your anger to make changes. Anger is a natural emotion that comes with being human. It's a way that nice girls feel at times and an important stimulus for growth. My two favorite books to recommend on this subject are Harriet Lerner's *The Dance of Anger* and a funny and wise book called *Getting in Touch with Your Inner Bitch* by Elizabeth Hilts.

Premenstrual Exacerbation: Not PMD

Another thing that PMD is *not* is premenstrual exacerbation of another emotional condition, especially a mood or anxiety disorder. Two situations commonly misattributed to PMD are a primary mood or anxiety disorder present most of the month but that is somewhat or very much worse premenstrually and a noncyclic emotional condition. In the latter case, it seems like you are worse premenstrually, but when you actually monitor your cycle, you have symptoms on and off randomly throughout the month.

PREMENSTRUAL MAGNIFICATION: LUPE'S STORY

Lupe has the most common condition for which PMD is misdiagnosed. Her proper diagnosis is clinical depression, also called a major depressive episode, which is worse just before her period. This condition has been termed premenstrual exacerbation of depression or premenstrual magnification (PMM).

Lupe has PMM, which was clear when she charted her symptoms over the course of her menstrual cycle. She came in for treatment because she couldn't cope any longer with the terrible moodiness she suffered every month, which seemed to start midcycle. She thought she had "PMS," especially because she usually felt better after about four days of her menstrual cycle. She had experienced a month or two of depression in the distant past, once in high school when her grandmother died and once eight years ago after the birth of her only child, when she was twenty-four.

In the past six months, Lupe's job had taken over her life. Corporate cutbacks at the telecommunications firm where she worked had left fewer people to do more work, at the same time that she received a promotion. She knew that people were saying that she got her supervisory job because she was a double–Affirmative Action statistic as a Hispanic woman, which both hurt her and enraged her. At first she knew that these were just sour grapes by envious coworkers, but lately she couldn't muster up her usual self-esteem and wondered if she was indeed up to the job.

She focused on her premenstrual symptoms of crying spells, restless sleep, loss of energy, and the loss of joy in her life. She was easily annoyed, but it seemed that the worst thing was her feeling that she just couldn't go on working twelve-hour days while caring for her son and trying to be a good wife. She never wanted to have sex anymore, and she worried that her husband was losing patience.

When Lupe and I looked at her menstrual cycle symptom chart, we discovered that she wasn't actually feeling so great during the first two weeks of her cycle. Although her symptoms were mild to moderate during that time frame, they were clearly there. It was also clear that she felt worse premenstrually, leading to her self-diagnosis of "PMS." My diagnosis was recurrent unipolar depression with premenstrual magnification (PMM).

Unlike what occurs in classic premenstrual depression, we were able to find a clear precipitant to Lupe's depression: job stress and ethnic prejudice by a few former coworkers who were now her subordinates. Her previous two episodes suggested that she suffers from a biological predisposition to develop clinical depression when under stress, which was clearly the case lately. Understanding the role of job stress helped Lupe turn to the Employee Assistance Program at her company, which in turn linked her up with a group of minority managers that met monthly for lunch and brainstorming.

She also decided to go into therapy, focusing on how her difficulty setting limits and her tendency to avoid any interpersonal unpleasantness contributed to her vulnerability to depression. All too often, she said yes when she wanted to say no, or backed down just to avoid conflict, and she knew she was paying the price. Since she saw this as partly just her, partly a female thing, and partly a Mexican American female thing, she decided to see a Latina therapist in addition to taking an antidepressant I recommended that she continue for at least a year.

Since her episodes of depression have been separated by very long stretches, we don't know for sure whether the talk therapy will help protect her from future depressive relapses; her past episodes make it more likely than not that Lupe will struggle with depression at some point down the road. We do know that she found therapy to be quite helpful; Lupe felt stronger, more in touch with her feelings, and more able to speak up for herself. As is usually the case with premenstrual magnification of depression but not true PMD, Lupe has been off the antidepressant for over a year now with no symptoms of relapse. Even though she had experienced three episodes of clinical depression, Lupe decided not to take an antidepressant indefinitely because they were so far apart. She promised herself that she would get right back into therapy at the earliest warning sign and would probably stay on medicine if she had another serious bout.

Many emotional syndromes besides depressive disorder may have premenstrual exacerbation, but major depression and dysthymic disorder are by far the most likely to worsen premenstrually. Other possibilities include obsessive compulsive disorder, panic disorder, eating disorders, bipolar disorder, and anxiety disorders. After I talk about the treatment of PMD later in this chapter, I'll also discuss strategies for treating premenstrual exacerbation syndromes.

IT MAY NOT BE PREMENSTRUAL ANYTHING

Many women whose menstrual cycles do not indicate a cyclic pattern suffer from a variety of easy-to-treat emotional conditions falsely pinned on "PMS," including all of the most common and most treatable forms of depression and anxiety. This means that you should seek help even if you chart your symptoms and don't find a menstrual cycle pattern. Instead of starting with your gynecologist, however, you should consult a psychiatrist or another mental health professional who can perform a diagnostic assessment.

There are a number of reasons why women tend to overdiagnose "PMS" in themselves. For starters, keep in mind that since ancient times, people have attributed all kinds of things to women's menstrual cycles, including volcanic eruptions, good crops, and whether the king had many sons. Thousands of years of collective unconscious tells us that menstruation is a tremendously powerful force, and it doesn't surprise me that we would associate changes in our psyche with changes in our bodies.

However, I also believe that many women view "PMS" as a more acceptable diagnosis than pure depression or anxiety. "PMS" is typically seen as partly physical rather than purely mental and therefore lower on the hierarchy of stigmatized illnesses. It's more acceptable to tell your coworker that you are having problems related to your period than it is to say that you have depression. You may criticize yourself less for having "PMS" and feel less like it's your own fault. Any and all of these are understandable, but proper diagnosis is the first crucial step to recovery. You must keep an open and objective mind about your diagnosis and work on accepting yourself as you are.

WHAT CAUSES PREMENSTRUAL DEPRESSION

As is true for most other forms of anxiety and depression, the diagnosis of PMD indicates a particular set of symptoms that cluster together in a particular pattern, not an illness with a single known cause. In other words, PMD is more like migraines than it is like strep throat, in that we don't yet know what causes it.

We do know some things that don't cause PMD. No single abnormality of estrogen or progesterone causes PMD, a fact that many people find surprising. Progesterone deficiency is commonly believed to underlie PMD, but study after study disproves this. No ovarian hormone fluctuations across the menstrual cycle have been proven to cause PMD. However, many experts believe that PMD is a premenopausal syndrome, an early warning signal that subclinical ovarian changes due to aging are underway. PMD usually starts in the late thirties and early forties and is rare in teens and young adults. As discussed in Appendix A, reproductive hormones may affect mood in susceptible individuals, and repeated cyclic changes in female hormones may trigger electrochemical imbalances in the brain, called kindling. (See p. 260.) Intuitively, women with PMD often feel that they are going through early menopause and are astonished or frustrated when their hormone tests are normal. The brain may be aware of subtle changes many years before the levels drop sufficiently to show up in the bloodstream.

A fascinating study published in 1991 in the medical profession's most prestigious journal, the *New England Journal of Medicine*, showed that when menstruation was brought on early, in artificially induced periods, the PMD symptoms did not correlate with these periods but instead occurred when the study volunteer would naturally have been premenstrual. In other words, it looks as if the PMD is cyclic but independent of the reproductive hormone changes.

This finding suggests that PMD may be an independent cyclic mood disorder that has been synchronized with the menstrual cycle chronologically, a coincidence in time that is not causative. "Ordinary" clinical depression typically affects many of the brain's inner clocks, ranging from twenty-four-hour-clock disturbances (disrupted sleep-wake cycles and physiological circadian rhythm abnormalities) to annual clock disturbances (winter depression or seasonal affective disorder), and it isn't a big stretch to guess that the monthly time clock is also vulnerable to mood disorders.

One of the known risk factors for PMD is a personal and/or a family history of depression. This genetic vulnerability to PMD supports the idea that it may be best thought of as a variant of other forms of depression rather than as a primary reproductive hormone imbalance. Indeed, PMD may be the aftermath of prior depression, especially postpartum depression.

However, these theories do not explain why PMD disappears at menopause or why the very extreme measure of surgical removal of the ovaries (or the chemical equivalent, which will be discussed later) alleviates it.

The list of hypothesized causes of PMD is lengthy, which is always a sure sign that the medical community has no idea what causes the condition. Speculated causes include vitamin and mineral deficiencies, hypoglycemia or other carbohydrate metabolism abnormalities, subclinical endocrine abnormalities, melatonin disruption, sensitivity to cyclic changes in endorphins, and/or serotonin deficiencies (one study has shown menstrual cycle changes in the metabolic byproducts of serotonin in women with PMD). As a researcher pointed out, part of the difficulty is determining the cause: "When trying to identify possible causes for PMS, the question why not all women suffer from PMS may be as important as why some women do." In other words, since all menstruating women have cyclic hormonal changes, any theory will need to explain why only a few have PMD.

I believe that the brain chemical messenger serotonin is definitely out of balance in PMD, but we just don't know yet how to identify the complex interactions among reproductive hormone fluctuations, brain neurotransmitter functioning, and the brain's monthly inner clock. This is extremely frustrating for women who suffer from PMD, but as in many other partially explained medical conditions, relief is available even though the "why?" question is unanswered.

A doctor does not need to know which specific bacteria is causing a child's middle ear infection in order to treat it successfully with antibiotics. Her personal experience and that of her fellow pediatricians using a particular antibiotic with other kids guides her choice of which medication to use. This approach is called empiric therapy, which means that the prescribed medication is based on clinical observations of response and not on a model of causation. Doctors and patients alike want to know *why* something works, but when it comes to PMD, you will need to be satisfied with an empiric therapy: If it works, it works.

WHAT ARE THE TREATMENTS FOR PMD AND PMM?

Nonmedical Treatments for PMD

Since there is a huge industry of over-the-counter remedies for "PMS," the overwhelming majority of women seeking treatment for PMD will have tried one or more natural alternatives. These include herbal teas, vitamins (especially vitamin B_6), calcium, multivitamin and mineral preparations, and evening primrose oil.

Buyer Beware

Obviously a natural remedy would be better than taking prescription medication, but many women find that these preparations do not work or provide only minimal relief. Many of these preparations are as helpful as Aunt Lydia's Magic Elixir, the 1890s cure-all that promised to relieve everything from cancer to dyspepsia. While I am not opposed to alternative measures, I do feel that you should not receive your primary medical advice for any condition, PMD or otherwise, from a clerk at a health food store.

The following treatments are *not* effective for PMD: progesterone, including synthetic and natural preparations, vaginal suppositories, or the oral micronized form (in fact, progesterone may exacerbate depression, as in birth control pills); diuretics (which are effective for premenstrual water retention but not depression or irritability); nonsteroidal anti-inflammatory agents (which are effective for cramps, backache, and headache); and ordinary one-a-day-vitamins.

Why Did the Vitamins Help at First?

PMD appears to have a high placebo response that does not last longer than a few cycles. This means that although a treatment may seem to be working for a few months, it may not stand the test of time. This nonsustained response has been called the halo response, because it is as if an angel steps in for a bit, but then her halo slips. I'm not sure why there is such a dramatic transient response in PMD, but it is very discouraging to women who get relief only to fall back into the pit. If this happens to you, don't give up. PMD treatment is a long-term commitment, with trial and error, dose adjustments, and medication changes to be expected.

The halo effect confounds studies about effective treatments for PMD. Several widely used natural or nonantidepressant medical remedies have shown mixed clinical results in treatment studies. In such cases, a medication works in one study sample but not in another. This makes it hard to make a firm recommendation for or against a particular remedy. However, since PMD is a chronic condition (it comes back if you stop the medication, until you stop menstruating), it is quite reasonable to try possibly effective natural remedies before jumping to an antidepressant, if you haven't done so already. I also think it's reasonable to go straight to the antidepressant in many cases. The choice depends partly on what fits for you.

Possibly Effective Natural Remedies: Over-the-Counter Pills

The following box lists natural remedies that have shown mixed results for PMD and may be worth trying as a single or combined regimen.

REMEDY	DOSE	COMMENTS
Calcium	500 mg twice daily	Beneficial for preventing bone loss
Evening primrose oil	400–500 mg three times daily	May be necessary to take all month
High potency vitamin and mineral supplement (such as Optivite)	Single pill daily	Confirm total daily B-6 less than 100 mg
Magnesium	360 mg three times daily	Begin day 15 of cycle
St. John's wort	300 mg three times daily	Verify that the preparation is standardized to contain .15 percent hypericin
Vitamin B-6	25–50 mg	Toxic at doses of 100 mg daily or higher

Possibly Effective Natural Remedies: Lifestyle Changes

Exercise and diet changes may be quite helpful, either alone or in combination with other strategies. I recommend a minimum of twenty minutes of aerobic exercise three times per week. Once you move past the initial pain to the point that you miss it when you can't find the time for your usual routine, exercise has a natural antidepressant activity.

Some women respond very dramatically to a modified hypoglycemia diet, so I recommend that all my PMD patients give it a try. In the PMD diet, small but frequent meals are the rule, in order to avoid low blood sugar intervals. You must never go longer than three hours while awake without eating and should eat just after you get up in the morning and just before you go to bed. Equally important, you should replace sweets with complex carbohydrates, which include whole grains, rice, potatoes, beans, pasta, breads, and crackers. Avoid sugar-rich foods, and try to have six carbohydrate snacks per day. Don't gasp: If you don't add sugar or fat to carbohydrates, you can easily have six starches a day and not gain weight. Here's an example:

7:00 A.M.	oatmeal
10:00 A.M.	half a bagel
12:30 P.M.	sandwich
3:30 P.M.	4 pretzels
6:30 P.M.	potato with dinner
9:00 P.M.	rice cake
10:30 P.M.	rice cake

When Words Are Not Enough: Medical Treatments for PMD

If you have anything but mild PMD, likely you will need more aggressive treatment than these natural remedies. These measures include hormonal treatments, antidepressants, and antianxiety medications. While many of my patients would prefer hormonal treatment (in part because taking hormones seems to validate PMD as a "real" illness), I believe that the typical patient with PMD is better off taking a psychotropic medication (medication that causes emotional changes due to effects on brain chemistry) than hormones (perhaps with the exception of birth control pills). Although natural, hormones are powerful medications, too, which should not be taken lightly.

The box on page 70 summarizes my own typical way of treating PMD. Most women seeking psychiatric medication have spent years lingering in the first step, the search for natural methods.

Hormones

Oral contraceptives are widely prescribed for PMD with mixed results. The effect of birth control pills is variable: Some women feel much better on them, some experience no effect, and others find that their PMD actually gets worse. As discussed on page 64, PMD may be a sign that the ovaries are beginning the gradual hormonal decline that culminates in menopause, before blood tests show detectable abnormalities. When the levels for the hormones are normal, it isn't sensible to use powerful hormone replacement therapy as if the patient were menopausal anyway (at menopause, the risk of

HIERARCHY OF PMD APPROACHES

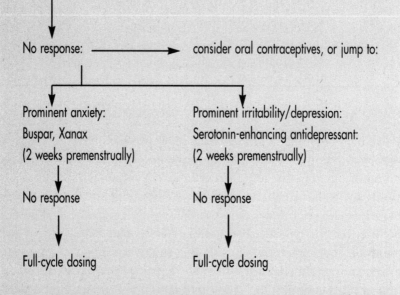

First, try natural methods, including exercise, complex carbohydrate rich diet, megavitamin therapy, primrose oil, moderate vitamin B-6, calcium and/or magnesium

No response: ⟶ consider oral contraceptives, or jump to:

Prominent anxiety: Prominent irritability/depression:
Buspar, Xanax   Serotonin-enhancing antidepressant:
(2 weeks premenstrually)   (2 weeks premenstrually)

No response   No response

Full-cycle dosing   Full-cycle dosing

No response: Consider switching within class (e.g., stop Zoloft, try Serzone, or switch to other class, e.g., no response to Prozac, switch to Buspar). May also switch if unable to tolerate side effects of a particular medication.

bone loss or heart attacks often justifies the use of stronger hormones). Increasingly, physicians prescribe birth control pills as a compromise, in the hopes that a small boost in female hormones will do the trick. Typically, the doctor will prescribe a low dose birth control pill, increasing to a higher dose only as necessary. Birth control pills are contraindicated in women over thirty-five who smoke and in some other medical conditions.

An area that remains unstudied is whether low dose birth control pills might help antidepressants work better for PMD. From time to time, I've had patients in their thirties and forties note an additive effect of birth control pills when taken along with antidepressants or Buspar (buspirone).

I mentioned that progesterone is an ineffective treatment for PMD. A few scattered studies indicate that the form of estrogen worn as a skin patch may be helpful. It's not clear that the oral forms of estrogen (such as Premarin, taken by postmenopausal women) are effective for PMD. As described in Appendix A, the effects of estrogen on the brain may positively influence mood, especially its impact on the neurotransmitter serotonin. However, estrogen may cause uncomfortable side effects such as nausea, headache, and weight gain. But most important, estrogen alone (without progesterone) may increase the risk of breast or uterine cancer and may cause other significant health problems, so its usefulness is limited.

The most dramatic hormonal treatment for PMD is the induction of so-called medical menopause, in which the ovaries are literally shut down hormonally, most typically with "put-back therapy," in which the patient then receives estrogen and progesterone replacement in order to prevent bone loss and heart disease, as in natural menopause. These extremely involved, poorly studied major interventions should be undertaken only in extreme cases as a last resort. The long-term effects are not known. A synthetic steroid called Danocrine (danazol), used to induce menopause, can in and of itself cause marked emotional symptoms as well as masculinization (including increasing the risk of heart disease). The other way of inducing medical menopause is by Lupron (leuprolide) injections. Surgical removal of the ovaries is not appropriate therapy now that so many effective alternatives exist. I believe that these approaches to PMD sometimes fall into the category of treatments that are worse than the disease.

Antianxiety Medications for PMD

Psychotropic medications are far less likely than hormones to cause intolerable or dangerous side effects. Most women with PMD have few side effects from antidepressant or antianxiety medication, and these drugs are highly effective for well-defined PMD.

Two medications usually prescribed for anxiety have been shown to be effective for PMD, even when the main symptoms are sadness or irritability and not anxiety. They are Xanax (alprazolam) and Buspar. Xanax has had mixed results, but more studies than not indicate a beneficial effect on anxiety, irritability, depressed mood, and restless sleep. The doses used in the study were relatively small, in the neighborhood of 0.25 mg three to four times per day, taken between one to two weeks premenstrually until the second day of the period, tapering the medication during menstruation to avoid withdrawal. One clear advantage of this approach compared to daily antidepressants is that you don't have to take medication on days when you feel fine, and you can start the Xanax immediately upon developing PMD symptoms.

The disadvantage is that Xanax can become habit-forming (avoid this drug if you have a personal or strong family history of addiction) and can be too sedating to allow you to function properly or even to drive safely. I recommend that my patients test to be sure Xanax isn't too sedating on a day when they don't have to go to work or drive carpool or engage in anything too demanding. Also, Xanax may "take the edge off" of the irritability (other-directed symptoms) without correcting the underlying sadness (inner-directed symptoms). At least one well-conducted study showed Xanax to have no beneficial effect, so it's not a cure-all.

Buspar is a nonaddictive antianxiety medication that has been found to be helpful in a few small studies of women with PMD. It may be beneficial even when taken only day 15 until menstruation, but some women need to take it the entire month. Doses range from 5 mg to a usual maximum of 20 mg three times per day. At typical doses, the side effects, such as transient stomach upset, are usually mild. Buspar seems especially likely to target the symptom of irritability.

Antidepressants for PMD

My usual approach when the previous measures fail—or as a starting point in severe cases—is to prescribe a serotonin-enhancing antidepressant: Effexor (venlafaxine), Luvox (fluvoxamine), Paxil (paroxetine), Prozac (fluoxetine), Serzone (nefazodone), or Zoloft (sertraline). Anafranil (clomipramine) is also effective. (You can read more about these medications in Appendix B.) One puzzling fact is that serotonin-enhancing antidepressants are more effective for PMD than other antidepressants, which is not the case with ordinary depression.*

Many—not all—women with PMD respond to lower-than-usual doses of these serotonin-enhancing antidepressants. This fact may explain the wide differences in dosages used by gynecologists and psychiatrists when treating PMD. Psychiatrists usually prescribe higher dosages, perhaps because we see more severe cases.

Marti's Recovery

Marti's family doctor had given her a prescription for Xanax when she saw him for PMD. She never even filled it, she told me, because "that stuff is addictive." The daughter of an alcoholic, Marti was far more comfortable taking an antidepressant, which has no potential for abuse.

But she was startled to learn that she may well need to take antidepressant medication for the entire month. She hated the idea of taking something when she felt fine, which led me to recommend Prozac for her. I started her at 10 mg per day for the last two weeks of her cycle. This "took the edge off," but she still didn't feel like her usual self. After three months, I increased her dose to 20 mg per day during those two weeks. She didn't sleep as soundly as usual during the times that she took medication, but she felt that the benefits of the medication far outweighed this side effect.

Since Prozac remains in the system for a much longer time than other antidepressants, I often try to exploit its long half-life and medicate only during the premenstrual phase. I prescribe 10 to 20 mg daily for the two weeks prior to menstruation, which is the equivalent of taking 5 to 10 mg throughout the month. If this dose proves inadequate, I use the other serotonin-enhancing antidepressants interchangeably or recommend daily Prozac. PMD may take a few months to respond fully, so I adjust the dose upward very gradually as needed, to the maximum recommended doses for each.

When daily medication is acceptable, Serzone is often the best

---

* This is highly atypical for antidepressants, since they are usually distinguished by side effects rather than by clinical effectiveness.

medication for PMD. As mentioned in Chapter 7, Serzone is the only selective serotonin re-uptake inhibitor that doesn't interfere with libido or orgasm. However, because its sedative properties take time to get used to, the dose must be adjusted upward very gradually, which can delay response in acute clinical depression. Because women with PMD have two or three weeks without symptoms, and because PMD may respond to lower doses of any particular antidepressant, Serzone may be easier to get used to and better tolerated in the long run.

HOW LONG DO I NEED MEDICATION?

One of the reasons why it is so very important to diagnose PMD accurately is that true PMD is likely to recur if proper treatment is stopped. Unfortunately, PMD actually may worsen the closer you get to menopause and may peak symptomatically if untreated just as your periods begin to get irregular.* Many of my patients are disheartened to hear this: No one ever likes to face years of medication. However, they usually have an inkling that this is only to be expected: It makes sense that as long as you menstruate, you will have PMD. PMD treatment is purely a matter of preventing symptoms or relieving them once they are present. The only cure is menopause.

Since PMD may precede menopause by ten or more years, many sufferers are not willing to commit to indefinite medication. Others are so delighted to find relief that they beg their doctors to promise them a lifetime prescription. Those who are uncomfortable committing to an open-ended period of medication may wish to try to stop the medication, preferably after two years. Then, if the PMD recurs, they may be much more comfortable taking the medication for years.

---

* This progression of PMD in the year or two prior to menopause leaves many women at an impasse with their doctors. When your doctor does hormone tests (usually LSH and FH), they show up normal, and your doctor states that "it isn't menopause." Your intuition is screaming the exact opposite. You *and* your doctor are right. Your doctor is right that you are not medically categorized as menopausal while your reproductive hormones are active. You are right that your brain is sensing the impending change, but modern medicine just doesn't know yet how to capture this diagnostically.

I find that women who developed a gradually escalating PMD syndrome are least likely to stop antidepressants without relapsing. At the other end of the spectrum are women who have PMD following an episode of classic clinical depression, including postpartum. For these women, I recommend a trial off medication after one or two years without PMD symptoms.

TREATMENT OF PREMENSTRUAL MAGNIFICATION

If, like Lupe, you suffer from premenstrual exacerbation of another anxiety or mood disorder, the first step is to treat that disorder appropriately, for as long as necessary based on the underlying illness. In Lupe's case, I recommended that she take the antidepressant Norpramin (desipramine) for a year. Since she doesn't have true PMD, it isn't necessary for her to take medication for years and years.

> It took ten days to stabilize Lupe's dosage, which was lower than the usual maximum since Latina (and Asian) women often respond to lower doses than Caucasian women. She began to notice improvement within a month, but those bad premenstrual days weren't really touched by the medication. I recommended waiting another cycle to see whether the premenstrual depressive symptoms were simply the last to go away or whether they were truly lingering. Fortunately, after two months, Lupe felt good throughout her menstrual cycle.

Had Lupe's premenstrual symptoms lingered, I would have ordered blood tests at different times in her cycle (as described in Chapter 9) or simply increased the dose of the antidepressant for the two weeks premenstrually. This approach may be helpful regardless of the specific antidepressant. If someone is taking 50 mg Zoloft daily, for example, but has breakthrough symptoms premenstrually, I recommend increasing the dose to 75 or 100 mg for the two weeks before menses. If the tricyclic antidepressant didn't work, I might have switched Lupe to a medication that enhances serotonin, such as Paxil. Or I might have recommended that she take Xanax premenstrually.

The menstrual cycle may affect how women with bipolar disorder in particular respond to medication across the cycle, with breakthrough symptoms sometimes incorrectly attributed to "PMS." These issues are discussed in Chapter 9.

CONCLUSION

Premenstrual depression and premenstrual magnification can be very frustrating. If you aren't getting the help you need, try to find the balance between patience and aggressive treatment. With PMD and PMM, it's all too easy to put off help, especially when you're not premenstrual and things seem okay. Stick with it, and shop around until you find someone you trust. PMD can fall between the cracks of primary care, gynecology, and psychiatry, when each clinician knows a little piece but doesn't see the whole picture. The expert you need may be a nurse practitioner, a gynecologist, an internist, a GP, a psychiatrist, or a psychotherapist who can put you in touch with the right medical person. Don't suffer needlessly, and don't settle for "there's nothing that can be done about it."

MENSTUAL CYCLE SYMPTOM CHART

Instructions: Choose five or more symptoms to chart. Write each symptom in the space provided at the top of the columns. At the end of each day, make a note of whether these symptoms were present or absent. If you were bothered by that symptom at all, enter a 0. If the symptom was mild, enter a 1. If the symptom was somewhat bothersome, enter a 2. For severe symptoms, enter a 3.

You may use your own words to describe any particularly bothersome symptom, or you may wish to choose from the following: angry outbursts; irritability; interpersonal conflict; sadness; low self-esteem; oversensitivity; mood swings; anxiety; tension; poor concentration; fatigue; inability to enjoy yourself; food cravings; decreased ability to cope with stress; sleep changes; and physical symptoms, such as breast tenderness, bloating, or headache.

Day 1 is the first day of your menstrual flow. The last day of your cycle is the day prior to the next month's period. Place a checkmark next to each day that you menstruate.

Day Number	EXAMPLE: irritability					Comments
1 ✓	2					
2 ✓	0					
3 ✓	0					
4 ✓	1					
5 ✓	0					
6	0					
7	0					
8	1					
9	0					
10	0					
11	2					
12	0					
13	0					
14	0					
15	0					
16	0					
17	1					
18	1					
19	2					

Day Number	EXAMPLE: irritability					Comments
20	2					
21	1					
22	2					
23	2					
24	3					
25	2					
26	3					
27	3					
28	3					
29 last day						
30						
31						
32						
33						
34						
35						

(enter additional days as needed)

Chapter 4

WHY CAN'T I JUST RELAX?

Anxiety Disorders

KEY POINTS

- Anxiety disorders are common and may cause considerable suffering.
- Anxiety may be generalized or may be limited to discrete panic attacks. Most women with panic attacks worry at some point that they have an undiagnosed medical illness.
- Panic disorder may be associated with agoraphobia, which is a phobia about leaving home or traveling alone.
- Cognitive-behavioral therapies are effective talk therapies for anxiety disorders.
- Antidepressants are effective for anxiety as well as for depression, but often much lower doses are used. Other medications may be very helpful also.

Anxiety is one of the most common reasons women seek mental health treatment. Anxiety disorders typically hit in the early adult years, as they did for Annette.*

Annette came to see me during the semester break of her freshman year of college. She had started college with great anticipation. She had done well in high school and was accepted by her first-choice university. She felt blessed by all the good things in her life: parents who could comfortably afford her tuition, a roommate with whom she

---

* Chapter 5 deals with the form of anxiety disorder called obsessive compulsive disorder.

clicked immediately, and more good professors than bad ones. She had broken off with her high school boyfriend in August, but the decision had been a mutual one.

Unfortunately, instead of feeling on top of the world, Annette had never felt worse. Beginning in October, she began having difficulty falling asleep, even if she had three beers in a row to try to knock herself out. She developed stomach aches and bouts of diarrhea, which the health service called irritable bowel syndrome. She worried that something terrible was wrong physically, but the doctors kept telling her she was fine.

By mid-October, she told me, "I was a basket case." She was walking to class one day when she had a massive anxiety attack. She went straight to the emergency room, certain that she was having a heart attack. Her heart was pounding, skipping beats, and she couldn't catch her breath. Her hands shook, and she thought that she might faint. Suddenly things looked "weird"—completely unreal—and she started to worry that she was having a stroke. Whatever was happening, she was terrified that she was about to die.

By the time she walked across campus to the nearby medical school emergency room, Annette was starting to feel better. Convinced that she had barely escaped death, she told the triage nurse that she thought she might have just had a small heart attack, and she was whisked back to a medical bed immediately. Her electrocardiogram and multiple blood tests were negative, and the doctor's neurological exam showed no signs of damage. He informed her that she might have a condition called hyperthyroidism, but that he would call later in the week when the blood test came back if it was abnormal. Otherwise, he said, the diagnosis is costochondritis: inflammation of the cartilage between the ribs and the breast bone. He suggested that she follow up at student health services the next day.

She felt shaky all day, but the terrible sensations did not return. At her next day's appointment, a doctor that she hadn't met before raised the possibility of an anxiety disorder. She explained that the sensations Annette experienced the day before were classic symptoms of a panic attack and that perhaps the stomach upset and difficulty sleeping were earlier manifestations of the same illness. She explained that it made good sense to rule out an overactive thyroid, since the symptoms can be identical, but that she was guessing that the tests would be normal (which they were).

YOU ARE NOT THE ONLY ONE

Annette has very typical symptoms of panic disorder. She also has a problem that many women battle, one that is twice as common in women as it is in men: anxiety. Although about 3 percent of women will experience panic disorder in their lifetime, as many as one in seven have experienced a single panic attack. Generalized anxiety disorder troubles almost twice as many women as panic disorder, but women are far more likely to seek professional help for panic disorder than for generalized anxiety disorder. About one-third of women with panic disorder will struggle with agoraphobia.

OBSTACLES TO CARE

Unfortunately, women with anxiety disorders face some significant obstacles to getting proper treatment. First, these illnesses mimic physical ailments: pounding heart, upset stomach, breathing problems. It is natural to feel that something is wrong medically: a heart condition, asthma, an undiagnosed stomach ailment, maybe even something deadly. All too often, healthy young women with anxiety disorders spend considerable time, money, and discomfort getting blood tests, X rays, and electrocardiograms (EKGs). By the time everything comes back normal, both the doctor and patient alike are frustrated by the conclusion "there's nothing wrong with you." A wise consumer and a wise physician will consider the diagnosis of anxiety early in the game. There is indeed something wrong, but, fortunately, it's not a heart condition.

Another obstacle to treatment is the tendency to confuse anxiety with personality. Sometimes anxious people are so used to being anxious that it's easy to overlook the fact that anxiety is a symptom, not a character trait. Also, many women don't seek medical help for anxiety because they are too afraid that their doctor will give them medicine that is addicting. However, medical treatment for anxiety disorder does not have to be "addictive."

But the biggest obstacle to treatment is the tendency to underestimate how debilitating anxiety is. Over and over, women with anxiety disorders are advised to "relax," "stop worrying," "pull yourself together," or "snap out of it." People with the best intentions may see anxiety as a weakness to be overcome: Your partner, your mother, the doctor who says "you're fine, forget it"—all may subtly or not so subtly imply that you aren't trying hard enough.

Honor yourself. If you have an anxiety disorder, you know how bad you feel. Don't let others discourage you from getting help.

PANIC DISORDER: THE DIAGNOSIS

Fortunately, sensitivity to the diagnosis of anxiety disorder is increasing. Between watching the *Ricki Lake Show,* reading *Women's Day* magazine, and watching *ER,* many women have heard of panic disorder, and doctors and therapists are more successful at figuring it out. The list in the following box may help you zero in on the proper diagnosis. First, consider whether you have had a panic attack.

The specific diagnosis of panic disorder is made only if you have recurrent panic attacks that leave you terrified of experiencing another one or that cause you to make changes (such as moving back home) in the hopes of avoiding another one. Panic disorder is distinguished from a specific phobia in that you have panic attacks out of the blue; situational attacks such as a burst of anxiety prior to speaking in public don't count.

Panic attacks also may be caused by another anxiety disorder, such as obsessive compulsive disorder (a panic attack about contamination, for example), by a traumatic experience (such as panicking in an elevator because you were raped in one), or by clinical depression. In general, **panic attacks that are due to depression occur with all the other symptoms of depression. (See p. 28.)**

Just as depression can cause panic attacks, anxiety disorders can lead to depression. Feeling sad after having a panic attack does not mean that you are clinically depressed. Indeed, it is common to feel blue when you are having panic attacks, but feeling a complete, all-day, everyday loss of enjoyment of life is not typical of "pure" panic disorder. **Differentiating panic disorder from depression is especially important after childbirth, when doctors may ascribe postpartum depression to any emotional symptoms.**

More confusing still, these diseases are not either/or: You can have two anxiety disorders or panic disorder and clinical depression. This

SYMPTOMS OF A PANIC ATTACK

Sudden, unexpected period of profound apprehension, nervousness, or uneasiness that usually reaches a crescendo within ten minutes and that includes at least four of the following symptoms*:
- Awareness of your heart beating, racing, or skipping beats
- Feelings of suffocating, or difficulty catching or slowing your breath
- Dizziness, feeling that you might faint
- Physical pain or discomfort in your chest
- Stomach upset, including queasiness or diarrhea
- Out-of-body sensations, as if you are watching or outside of yourself, or misperceiving the immediate environment
- Being afraid that you will "lose it," or go crazy, as if you are crawling out of your skin
- Fearing that you might die, or suffer a heart attack or stroke, or sensing an impending catastrophe
- Tingling or numbness, especially around your lips or in your hands and/or feet
- Waves of hot flashes or chills
- Breaking out in a sweat
- Feeling as if you are choking or cannot swallow
- Shaking or trembling hands

* Many women with panic disorder have what they refer to "big ones" and "little ones." A big attack is a full-blown attack as described above. Doctors referred to a little attack as a limited-symptom attack; it may include only one or two symptoms from the list, plus the period of fear and discomfort. Many individuals have both types.

situation is referred to as comorbidity, which means having coexisting illnesses. Rarely do primary care physicians have the clinical expertise to sift through the confusing syndrome of comorbidity. In such situations, I feel assessment and treatment by a psychiatrist is strongly preferable.

But I Swear I'm Having a Heart Attack

In reaching the diagnosis of panic disorder, try to keep the possibility of an undiagnosed medical condition in perspective. Many people believe they are having a heart attack; in fact, one-fifth of those who go to an emergency room for acute chest pain actually have had a panic attack, not a heart attack. A complete physical exam is necessary for patients with panic attacks, and I usually order a blood test to rule out thyroid disease. Although comorbidity is possible, doctors may incorrectly diagnose women with panic disorder as having irritable bowel syndrome, costochondritis (which Annette was diagnosed with), migraine headache, "PMS," smoking, and "stress."

Hypoglycemia, or low blood sugar, is another medical diagnosis often given to many women with panic disorder. This disease is something of a fad, and may be offered by well-meaning but misinformed sources, such as your local health food store clerk. Hypoglycemia is much rarer than is generally believed and should be diagnosed only after a specific set of sequential blood tests following oral glucose dosing. If hypoglycemia is causing your anxiety attacks, you will experience your typical symptoms at the same time that your blood sugar level goes down during the blood testing. I hate to see people feel ashamed that they have panic disorder instead of hypoglycemia. Each problem is equally "real," and neither is a sign of personal weakness, stupidity, self-indulgence, or not trying hard enough.

The most confusing physical disorder associated with panic disorder is mitral valve prolapse. This benign abnormality of one of the heart valves can cause symptoms that overlap with panic attacks: palpitations, chest pains, and difficulty breathing. Individuals who have mitral valve prolapse have higher than average rates of panic disorder, and vice versa. It isn't clear whether this is a coincidence or if the one condition predisposes to the other.

Although I consider medical causes of anxiety attacks with every woman I treat for new-onset panic disorder, I am more likely to be aggressive about trying to identify a medical condition that could mimic it in patients who don't fit the following typical profile of an individual with panic disorder: onset in late teens through their twenties (panic disorder almost never starts after menopause), one or more relatives with an anxiety disorder, and physiological supersensitivity to stimulating substances such as caffeine, nasal decongestants such as Sudafed or Contac, and classical full-blown attacks. Often individuals with panic disorder have a history of transient anxiety during childhood, and frequently they tell me that they smoked marijuana once and quit because they had a severe anxiety attack.

ANXIETY DISORDER: IS THERE MORE THAN ONE KIND?

The most common anxiety disorder that causes abrupt attacks of anxiety is panic disorder. Some women with panic disorder have a subtype, called panic disorder with agoraphobia. Women who have persistent anxiety but who do not have panic disorder most commonly have a condition called generalized anxiety disorder.

Agoraphobia

Sometimes my panic disorder patients want me to keep what I know to myself. Anxious people are anxious, and many patients worry that they will talk themselves into further anxiety if I bring up certain issues. Others find that information is reassuring. As you read this section, bear in mind that if you do not have agoraphobia (fear of leaving home or avoidance of traveling alone), you cannot "talk" yourself into it by reading about it.

Although Annette can't stand to be alone during an attack, she does not suffer from agoraphobia: She doesn't avoid going by herself to places or situations where she couldn't stand to have a panic attack. Over 95 percent of women with agoraphobia also have panic disorder, but the reverse is not true: Only a minority of women with panic disorder develop agoraphobia, and even then, the agoraphobia may be mild. Read that again: Even though you may have panic disorder, you are not inevitably cursed also to have agoraphobia. A few rare individuals have been reported as having agoraphobia without ever having panic disorder.

Kristy has panic disorder with agoraphobia:

The biggest challenge to treating Kristy was getting her to my office. A thirty-nine-year-old homemaker, mother of three, she had not driven even half a block by herself for four years. Her dependence on others was overwhelming: She could not grocery-shop unaccompanied, could not drive her daughter the short distance to preschool unless there was another adult with her in the car, and for years, she hadn't been able to throw the kids in the car and hop over to the beach, or make a run to McDonald's, or get her hair cut on a whim. She hated asking anyone to take her to my office, because she felt that she already asked way too much of those few family members and close friends who knew her secret. Her agoraphobia gradually built up after a series of paralyzing panic attacks, attacks that ironically, rarely bother her anymore. The disability caused by her agoraphobia eclipsed the initial panic attacks. She couldn't drive anywhere alone, and she couldn't drive at all on major roads, even if her husband was with her in the car. Several female relatives had panic disorder, but Kristy believed that she was the only one with agoraphobia. Somehow she mustered up the courage to ask someone to come with her. She had flirted with medication briefly in the past: A low-dose tricyclic antidepressant hadn't worked, and she was afraid of getting addicted to tranquilizers, so she never took the Klonopin (clonazepam) that was prescribed a few years back.

Kristy has many common symptoms of agoraphobia. Even though her anxiety disorder began with panic attacks, she rarely has an attack now. Instead, she struggles most with the limitations of being agoraphobic. She is a wonderful mother, wife, and friend, but this illness has placed many obstacles in her life.

Agoraphobia, which typically begins within months to a year of the first panic attack, can be very disabling. Women are disproportionately afflicted with agoraphobia, perhaps in part due to the fact that dependence on other people and/or becoming somewhat housebound are even less socially acceptable for men. Fortunately, despite the drastic impact it can have on your life, agoraphobia is partly a result of mistaken beliefs—if I don't go outside my home, I won't have a panic attack, and I cannot tolerate any anxiety at all. Remaining at home becomes a deeply ingrained habit, as you tell yourself over and over that you cannot cope outside the cocoon you have developed for yourself. Do absolutely everything in your control to nip agoraphobic tendencies in the bud before they get stronger and stronger. If you have changed your behavior due to the mistaken belief that you must limit your activities, know that cognitive and behavioral psychotherapy and psychotherapeutic medications are highly effective, even in severe cases.

Generalized Anxiety Disorder

As with panic disorder, abnormal body sensations are also characteristic of generalized anxiety disorder (hereafter, GAD). In addition to worry, women with GAD report feeling edgy and irritable, can't concentrate, and often feel that their muscles are constantly tight and tense. It's exhausting to worry all day, but the sense of fatigue that women with GAD report also may be due to the poor sleep that is often part of the syndrome. However, while women with panic disorder (with or without agoraphobia) worry first and foremost about having a panic attack, women with generalized anxiety disorder worry all the time, about everything. Apprehension and a sense of impending catastrophe must be present for at least six months for someone to be diagnosed with GAD, according to the *DSM-IV*. Women who have GAD try very hard to control their anxiety but find that they cannot. Two-thirds of people who suffer from GAD are female.

WHAT CAUSES ANXIETY DISORDERS?

Biological Causes

Much evidence indicates that significant biological and genetic factors predispose women to anxiety disorders. Having a close blood relative with panic disorder raises a person's own risk of panic disorder tenfold. Relatives of individuals with GAD have approximately six times the incidence of the disorder as the general public. This fact probably cannot be entirely pinned on genetics alone, since growing up in a family affected by anxiety could raise the risks that children become similarly anxious. However, in comparisons of identical twins (who have identical genes) and fraternal twins (who share half their genes, like nontwin siblings), the identical twin of a person with panic disorder is five times as likely to have panic disorder as is the fraternal twin who has an affected twin. This finding is very compelling evidence that anxiety disorders are transmitted genetically.

In addition to genetic transmission, the evidence of a physiological abnormality in people with anxiety disorders is overwhelming. The biological aspects of anxiety disorders, including the role of neurotransmitters, are discussed in Appendix A.

The short version is this: Women with anxiety disorders appear to have a biological supersensitivity to very specific chemicals and stressors, ranging from caffeine to laboratory chemicals. This supersensitivity is centered in a specific part of the brain called the locus coeruleus, and it probably involves the brain mistakenly sending and/or receiving distress signals. Humans are physically programmed to experience anxiety—it's part of basic animal survival—but anxiety-prone people are hardwired to experience physical and emotional distress signals even in the absence of danger.

Evolutionary Advantages of Anxiety

Were I designing human beings, I would place such a high value on the survival advantage of perceiving danger that I would err on the side of making some brains more anxiety-prone rather than risking having too little. Many valuable innate human characteristics—beauty, agility, intelligence—fall on a spectrum, with most of us sort of in the middle. With these characteristics, having more than most is generally a blessing. With anxiety, however, having more than most is generally a curse (although there probably are evolutionary advantages to being able to imagine and thereby ward off disaster).

Women who have panic disorder are often very sensitive to environmental changes and physiologic stressors. Sleep deprivation and fatigue are known triggers for panic attacks, which may appear as severe nightmares when they occur during sleep (called nocturnal panic attacks). I believe that, in cases of postpartum panic disorder, sleep deprivation is the single most stressful precipitant in predisposed women.

Again, were I designing mothers, I would make them anxious. As the individuals responsible for the most vulnerable members of the species—babies—they should be able to imagine all the terrible things that could happen. I would want them to wake easily, be vigilant, and not be complacent. I'd make women of reproductive age even more anxious than prepubescent and postmenopausal women, who are not as directly responsible for the survival of the species. Nature apparently agrees: At sexual maturity, girls begin to outpace boys in anxiety disorders, and panic disorder generally abates with middle and older age.

Emotional Causes of Anxiety Disorder

Although I personally believe that anxiety disorders are primarily biologically rooted, competing psychological theories are popular. While today few agree with Sigmund Freud's early theories about childhood psychosexual conflicts resulting in panic attacks, the prevailing psychological explanation of panic attacks relates to separation anxiety, the sense that estrangement from a caregiving person cannot be tolerated. Many women with panic disorder and agoraphobia recall suffering greatly as children when forced to separate from their mothers, often when going to school. Like Annette, women often have their first panic attack shortly after suffering a relationship disruption, either through a broken-off relationship, change in family ties, or the death of a significant person. The central importance of social connections in women's lives may account in part for their vulnerability to anxiety disorders.

The cognitive-behavioral explanation of panic disorder holds that anxiety is a maladaptive learned response that feeds on itself. This model emphasizes the tendency to misinterpret physiologic cues as if they were signs of impending disaster, with a person making the mental leap from awareness of a rapid heartbeat to anxiety about having a heart attack, for example. While I advocate cognitive-behavioral therapy as a treatment, I believe that this model fails to advance our understanding of what actually causes panic disorder.

Can You Think Yourself into Agoraphobia?

Misinterpretation often plays a role in the development of agoraphobia. After a person has a panic attack, she naturally looks for an explanation: It was being out in public, driving in the rain, being in the elevator, and so on. These explanations can be comforting at first: Kristy, for example, thought that she would gain control over her panic attacks by avoiding those situations she misinterpreted as making her vulnerable. Unfortunately, with this line of thinking, soon there is no place to go but home, and, even there, spontaneous panic attacks may occur.

Another cognitive misinterpretation that can lead to agoraphobia is the person's false belief that she will be locked in, unable to escape the disaster that the panic attack seems to herald. We'd all agree that being stuck alone in an elevator while you have a heart attack would be a disaster, but having a panic attack on a bridge or in the grocery store is absolutely no more dangerous than having one at home. Interestingly, many of the situations that women with agoraphobia avoid have evolutionary (biological) value: High places and enclosed spaces *are* more dangerous if you are being attacked by predators, be it on a cliff or a bridge, or in a cave or an elevator.

WHAT ARE THE TREATMENTS FOR ANXIETY DISORDERS?

In the 1990s, many effective alternatives have been developed for people suffering from panic disorder, including agoraphobia. Solid medical and talking treatments are widely available. Modern psychiatric treatment can help most people suffering from an anxiety disorder. Many will become completely symptom-free with treatment. People often ask me if being a psychiatrist isn't horribly depressing. I laugh because witnessing the dramatic recoveries made by women with anxiety disorders is nothing short of exhilarating.

Talk Therapy

Most women try words or "relaxation" before they try medication for anxiety disorder. Many women who are suffering from anxiety disorders will respond well to words, and some will recover fully. Others will feel much better after therapy and take antianxiety medication only sporadically, for a rare panic attack, or before an anxiety-provoking situation, such as flying or public speaking, or for a temporary period of sleeplessness. For the most severe cases, a treatment approach that combines psychotherapy and medication is often best. Not uncommonly, the treatments overlap: Patients start medication for immediate relief, with the plan to taper it off after gains have been made in talk therapy.

Annette, the young woman who developed panic disorder in her first semester of college, got better with talk therapy and an occasional tranquilizer:

The doctor at campus health services informed Annette that anxiety disorders were quite common in young adult women and that starting college was a common precipitant to a panic attack. She gave her a prescription for five Xanax (alprazolam) and suggested that she try one if the symptoms came back. In the meantime, she referred Annette to a clinical psychologist at the health services and suggested that counseling might help.

Counseling did help Annette. Her therapist provided her with information about what was happening to her body, explaining that a panic attack was a manifestation of an ancient physiological reflex called the fight-or-flight response, in which she had all the emotional and physical symptoms of being under attack. Your body is sending you distress signals, she said, but there is no actual danger to you. The therapist noted that one theory explains panic attacks as "false suffocation alarms," caused by electrical misfiring in the brain, which wants you to react as if you are truly suffocating, so that you can do what you need to do in order to save yourself. Annette said that's exactly how she feels during a panic attack: gasping for air. Her therapist told her that while these responses are uncomfortable, to say the least, they could not actually harm her. She taught Annette to let the anxiety run its course and helped her see that the harder she fought the panic, the stronger its grip became. Annette learned to label these sensations as a panic attack and got better at letting the anxiety float through; her sense of control when hit by an attack improved greatly.

If you choose to try words, or if you are frustrated because words haven't helped, be sure that you get the right kind of words. Just as medicines should be tailored to a specific disorder, some types of talk therapies will not touch anxiety disorders. A therapist who has a one-size-fits-all approach is unlikely to be as helpful as one who is knowledgeable about specific forms of therapy for anxiety. Classical, on-the-couch psychoanalysis has proven ineffective for panic disorder and agoraphobia, and psychodynamic psychotherapy may not help either. Education about what is happening to your body during a panic attack should be part of any treatment. There is good evidence that much shorter-term cognitive and behavioral therapies are highly effective.

How Long Should It Take?

Talk therapies for acute anxiety disorders should be helpful in providing partial symptom relief within a month, and you should be feeling much better within three to six months into cognitive or behavioral therapy.

"Insight-oriented" psychotherapy consists of looking back on who you are and how you got there and how that history affects your coping skills and ability to nurture and soothe yourself now. While this form of therapy is unlikely to relieve symptoms quickly (insight-oriented therapy generally lasts six months to two years), it may be very personally enriching in the long run. It also may help you become stronger and ultimately may provide some preventive "rewiring" that helps you be less panic prone, especially if you come from a long line of anxious women who weren't equipped to help you overcome your own tendency to anxiety.

Talk therapy (including a supportive approach that encourages expression of emotions) is a must if you have developed an anxiety disorder in the context of crisis, such as significant relationship changes, bereavement, trauma, or a professional catastrophe. As a rule of thumb, if you don't feel connected with your therapist after four sessions, you should seriously consider switching to another therapist. You may have to pay for therapy on your own, depending on your health insurance. For low cost strategies, see page 43.

The state-of-the-art words for anxiety disorders are spoken in cognitive-behavioral therapy. This relatively new therapy is well described in a recent book, *The Sky Is Falling*, by Rae Dumont. Cognitive-behavioral therapy may include identifying and mentally labeling symptoms, interrupting automatic negative thoughts such as this-must-be-a-catastrophe, developing relaxation and coping skills, learning to use distraction, and progressively exposing yourself to the anxiety-producing situation, sometimes in the company of the therapist.

Every woman who has an anxiety disorder has been told time and again to "just relax," as if that hadn't occurred to her. No one would like to relax more than a person who just had a panic attack. But "relaxation" isn't for everyone. Relaxation therapy is often helpful for generalized anxiety disorder, but it may have a paradoxical effect in panic disorder. During a highly symptomatic time, relaxation actually may provoke a panic attack, perhaps because the brain perceives itself to be in danger, when relaxation is the exact wrong thing to do. I generally advise my patients to consider biofeedback and/or meditation to reduce physiological edginess but to discontinue these techniques if they cause a paradoxical worsening of anxiety.

When Words Are Not Enough: Medical Therapy for Anxiety Disorders

Often words are not enough. They don't work quickly enough, the illness is too severe, or the words help some but not enough. If psychotherapy isn't helping, if you simply are just sick of feeling anxious and panicky all the time, if you are living a life in which you fear the fear, or if you are having frequent or disabling attacks, medical treatment for anxiety disorder is well worth considering.

How Medications Work: Immediate vs. Delayed Relief

If you decide to try medication for an anxiety disorder, you have an alternative that women with depression do not: You may be able to take medication sporadically. Talk with your doctor about the advantages and disadvantages of taking antianxiety medications on and off as compared to everyday. This type of use is called PRN, a medical abbreviation for the Latin term *pro re nata*, "as the situation demands."*

Medications often prescribed on a PRN basis for anxiety—tranquilizers—work by producing an immediate calming of the brain via the specific neurotransmitter GABA. (See p. 254.) Long-term medications—antidepressants—also work for anxiety disorders by restoring the balance of the neurotransmitters norepinephrine and serotonin via a chain reaction that may take weeks.

---

* "PRN" is pronounced by reading each letter individually.

Taking Medication Once in a While

PRN use of antianxiety medication is appropriate only for mild to moderate cases. Since panic disorder by nature waxes and wanes in severity, some women will choose PRN use when their symptoms are mild, moving to regular medication at other times in their lives. Some women would rather have an occasional attack rather than take medication every day. Others would rather take medication every day for the next fifty years if it means not having another attack. This is a judgment call that only the patient can make.

If you opt for PRN medication, your doctor may advise you to take a tranquilizer at the first sign of a panic attack. He should explain that although the first attack is already under way, the goal of the medication is to prevent another attack and to help you feel less jittery after the initial one. Be sure to ask when you can repeat the medication if the first dose doesn't take care of the problem, and be sure you know how many you can take in a twenty-four-hour period. (Often women suffering from anxiety tend to undermedicate themselves.) You might ask your doctor whether you can let the medication dissolve under your tongue (sublingually) for quicker action than would occur if you swallowed it. Both Ativan (lorazepam) and Xanax can be taken sublingually. Some women who take PRN tranquilizers have told me that on the days they have an anxiety attack, they take an extra tranquilizer that night because a good night's sleep seems to help prevent escalation of anxiety the next day.

The only medications that will be helpful if used on a PRN basis are benzodiazepines, which are in the general family of Valium (diazepam)-type medications, also called minor tranquilizers. If you have a personal or very strong family history of addiction, when even occasional use of a potentially abused medication such as Xanax is too risky, you probably shouldn't consider the PRN alternative. Also, PRN use is often sensible for panic disorder (which comes and goes) but not usually optimal for GAD or agoraphobia (which are ever-present).

Xanax, Klonopin, and Ativan are the most widely prescribed medications in this class of drugs (called anxiolytics or benzodiazepines; see p. 266). The other benzodiazepines are nonspecific for panic attacks but effectively reduce the anxiety that follows an attack. Other medications a doctor might prescribe on a PRN basis include Tranxene (clorazepate) or Serax (oxazepam).

While all of these medications work relatively quickly (as opposed to Valium, for example, which enters and leaves the bloodstream slowly), I prefer Xanax, because it takes effect rapidly and is out of the system rapidly. How fast a medication leaves the system is important because while the anxiety attack "revs" a person up, typically counterbalancing the sedative effect of anxiolytic medication, feeling groggy for the rest of the day, unable to work or pay attention to the kids is too high a price for aborting further attacks.

Unfortunately, the benzodiazepines with the quickest onset of action generally have the highest potential for "reinforcement." Reinforcement is the brain's chemical response that makes someone want to take more and more of potentially addictive substances, ranging from alcohol to cocaine. For this reason, many doctors prefer to limit benzodiazepines to PRN use and may prescribe these drugs for daily use only when other alternatives aren't effective.

Taking Medication Every Day

In severe cases of panic disorder, in most cases of agoraphobia, and for GAD, I recommend regular antianxiety medication.* If you have been changing your lifestyle or self-image because of your anxiety disorder, regular use is worth considering. If you are suffering greatly but going through the motions okay, regular medication also is appropriate. One of my patients was having difficulties at work, because she was afraid that she might humiliate herself if she was making a staff presentation and had a panic attack. The fear led her to avoid a critical part of her job. The option of taking a Xanax while everyone was watching her was not acceptable, so she was a good candidate for preventive—daily—treatment.

Annette's doctor at the campus health services gave her Xanax to use on a PRN basis in combination with therapy.

---

* Most of what I'll say about medication is better documented for the treatment of panic disorder with or without agoraphobia than for GAD, simply because more women with panic attacks seek medical help.

Although the therapy helped Annette focus on accepting that her sensations were caused by anxiety and anxiety alone—which kept her from adding her own layers of dread and doom—her panic attacks exhausted her. She hated the ever-present knowledge that another attack was almost certainly lurking in the distance.

Annette was still having a panic attack every week or so. When she arrived home for semester break, her mother witnessed an attack and promptly called me to arrange an appointment for her daughter. After confirming that Annette herself wished to see me, I scheduled her immediately. Annette had taken all of the Xanax that her family physician had given her and then two refills. She carried a Xanax wherever she went and, with half a laugh, told me that discovering she had accidentally left it at home could precipitate an anxiety attack in and of itself.

She described a very typical response to Xanax: Within half an hour, the medication calmed her down and seemed to ease her tendency to get lost in what she called the racing rapids of attack after attack. Of course, she said, by the time the Xanax kicks in, the first panic attack is basically over, but it quieted her sense of being on the verge of losing it forever. She was very worried that she would become addicted to Xanax, yet she said "I can't take this anymore. Fix it." Like just about every woman of her generation, she knew lots of people taking Prozac (fluoxetine) or similar medications, and she wondered whether Prozac would be the miracle in the bottle she was looking for.

Annette has three options for preventive treatment of panic disorder. Two of her choices are classified as antidepressants, because when they entered the market in the 1960s, no one realized that they were also effective antipanic drugs. Regular daily use (between two and four times per day) of Xanax or Klonopin is the third alternative. (These options are compared on p. 285.) The antidepressant Wellbutrin is not effective for anxiety disorders.

Tricyclic Antidepressants for Anxiety Disorder

Of the three choices, I recommended a low-dose tricyclic to Annette. Most anxiety-disorder patients respond to much lower doses of tricyclics than are used for depression (for example, 25 mg of Elavil [amitriptyline], as opposed to 200 mg for clinical depression), which means that the side effects are rarely problematic.

When Annette and I talked about the possible sexual side effects of using Prozac, she decided that she'd rather go with the tricyclic. Annette said, "Imagine, I meet the man of my dreams, we have sex, I can't climax, and when I tell him it's because I'm taking Prozac, he's out the door. No thanks."

I started Annette on 10 mg Tofranil (imipramine) at bedtime. Within a week, she felt more grounded but still "not right." She experienced two little panic attacks during this first week; while she was delighted that they didn't escalate, she was disappointed that she needed to take Xanax twice.* Since she had absolutely no side effects, I upped her dose to 20 mg for another week, then 25 mg taken once at bedtime, and asked her to give the new dose three or four weeks to kick in. She called me from college about a month later and was delighted to report "I'm back! I'm me again!"

Medication-Induced Jitteriness

Annette was fortunate that she did not require higher doses, which might have caused dry mouth, constipation, daytime sleepiness, or an uncomfortable but not dangerous condition called tricyclic jitteriness syndrome. Women with anxiety disorders not uncommonly feel worse before they feel better when they start a tricyclic, because initially, the medication can worsen symptoms of anxiety, causing shakiness, nervousness, and a sense of buzzing all over. (A similar phenomenon is seen with selective serotonin re-uptake inhibitors.)

Of the four most commonly prescribed tricyclics used for anxiety disorders—Adapin (doxepin), Elavil, Norpramin (desipramine), and Tofranil—Norapramin is the most likely to cause this initial jitteriness if the initial dose is too high. It may be preferable in the long run, however, because it is the least likely to cause other problematic side effects, including dry mouth, constipation, and sedation. I usu-

---

* While taking two psychiatric medications is common practice, drug-drug interactions are common. Always check with your doctor about the safety of combining medications. Don't assume any combination is safe or dangerous until you have checked.

ally prescribe an initial dose of 10 mg of a tricyclic for panic disorder patients, even though the final dose often is between 25 and 50 mg. If patients are not jittery on the initial dose, I may increase the dose within a few days. Some people will require the higher doses more typically used to treat depression; this doesn't mean anything except possibly that they metabolize the tricyclic rapidly or that they have comorbid depression and panic disorder.

Serotonin Re-Uptake Inhibitors for Anxiety

Sometimes an SSRI is the best choice as the first-line treatment for anxiety disorders. Some reasons that I would recommend an SSRI first include having a blood relative with a similar illness who responded to a SSRI, past personal response to an SSRI, past lack of response to a tricyclic, and any condition that would make the side effects of a tricyclic dangerous or intolerable. For example, a young woman in my practice had suffered multiple episodes of bladder infections. A tricyclic could cause the bladder to empty less effectively, which might increase her already high risk of recurrent bladder infections.

Your doctor may prefer an SSRI if you have heart disease, are not young (most doctors routinely obtain an EKG in women older than thirty-five or forty prior to starting a tricyclic), or have glaucoma, low blood pressure, severe constipation, or are at risk for interactions with other medications you are taking. Fortunately, the low doses of tricyclics that usually are effective for panic disorder very rarely cause appetite increase or weight gain, both of which are common at higher doses. (See Chapter 8.)

Kristy, the woman who was unable to drive by herself, was a good candidate for an SSRI.

> Kristy had two reasons for me to recommend an SSRI for her agoraphobia: She had a sister who had responded to Zoloft (sertraline), and she hadn't responded to a tricyclic in the past. She wasn't the least bit concerned about the possibility that she would have to work with her husband to overcome sexual side effects, but she was very concerned that any medication I give her not interfere with her ability to wake up at night if a child needed her. Zoloft fit her individual needs perfectly, and I started her at 25 mg per day (half the usual starting dose for depression).

After a week, Kristy felt no different: not better, no side effects. By two weeks, she felt a little better, still markedly agoraphobic, but less fragile inside. I recommended upping the dose to 50 mg per day, which caused her first side effect: vivid dreams that didn't particularly bother her and mild headaches that went away if she took ibuprofen. I asked her to stay at this dose for a month, at which point she noted gradual but very significant improvement, and the side effects became less bothersome. She could now occasionally drive a mile or two in her neighborhood by herself, and she didn't fall apart when her husband traveled out of town overnight. She had no panic attacks, and she felt that she could gradually expose herself to a progressive self-help plan in which she pushed herself to overcome her phobias, first by running into the grocery store by herself for milk, then for a few things, hoping that eventually she'd regain her ability to grocery-shop on her own.

Many psychiatrists prefer Paxil (paroxetine) for anxiety disorders, but there is no solid evidence to say that it is better tolerated or more effective than its counterparts. Prozac has advantages in that it is the easiest SSRI to take when very small doses are needed. (See p. 272.) If Serzone (nefazodone) or Effexor (venlafaxine) is the drug of choice, only a tiny once a day dose may do the trick, rather than the usual twice-daily dose used for depression.

SSRI Overstimulation

Many anxiety-prone individuals (and some who have never had even a twinge of anxiety in their lives) experience a transient stimulation from SSRIs, often described as feeling speedy. This can even precipitate a panic attack, which pretty much guarantees that a patient will detest the idea of taking it or any other medication in the near future. Not all general doctors are as familiar with this potential side effect in anxiety-prone individuals as are psychiatrists, so make sure you and your doctor discuss this before you start an SSRI. This tendency toward transient stimulation is best managed by starting at very low doses and adjusting upward. It's prudent to try a tiny dose first to test how your body responds.

Daily Tranquilizers for Anxiety Disorders

Kristy was adamant that she did not want to become addicted to a benzodiazepine, which I would have recommended next had she not done so well on an SSRI. Most anxious patients are anxious about everything and anything that involves loss of control: Addiction ranks high on the list of easily imagined catastrophes. It is wise for patients with anxiety disorders to avoid alcohol, because comorbid alcoholism is more common in individuals with panic disorder, perhaps because alcohol does appear to reduce anxiety when taken in small doses. However, rarely do people become addicted to therapeutic use of a tranquilizer for anxiety.

Individuals at risk of becoming addicted to a benzodiazepine often have one or more typical warning signs: a family or personal addictive history, past abuse of other drugs including illicit drugs or prescribed sedatives, a tendency to request more and more of the benzodiazepines (as opposed to taking less than I recommend, as many of my patients insist on doing!), and an enjoyment rather than abhorrence of the sedative effects.

Regular daily use of Klonopin or Xanax is an appropriate option for many women, either as a single medication or in combination with a tricyclic or a SSRI antidepressant. In fact, because of the tendency of SSRIs to cause temporary anxiety or insomnia, some doctors routinely coprescribe a tranquilizer or sleeping pill for use at bedtime during the first few weeks or months of SSRI treatment. Taking one of these tranquilizers may cause the fewest side effects, if you slowly build up tolerance to its sedating effect.

Only Xanax and Klonopin have been proven to be effective when used daily to treat panic disorder and agoraphobia. Some doctors feel that high doses of Ativan may prevent panic attacks, but the studies favor Xanax and Klonopin. Unlike panic disorder, benzodiazepines for GAD are clinically interchangeable in terms of effectiveness.

The most common side effect of benzodiazepines is sedation, which can make driving hazardous. When taking these medications, you should never drive until you are certain that you are fully alert, *never* drive after so much as half a beer (or other alcoholic beverage), and avoid alcohol in general because it interacts with benzodiazepines. These medications may cause subtle learning or academic/intellectual performance problems, although some individuals report improved concentration due to diminished anxiety. Besides alcohol, sedative side effects may be amplified by any other sedating medication: The sum of the parts may be greater than the whole.

Buspar for Generalized Anxiety Disorder

One medication that is effective for GAD but does not work for panic disorder is Buspar (buspirone). This nonaddictive medication is approved by the Food and Drug Administration specifically for GAD and is many doctors' first choice for this condition. It is nonaddictive and doesn't cause the sedation effect of benzodiazepines. (See p. 286.) It has few side effects, if any, compared to antidepressants. The usual starting dose is 5 mg three times per day, but a new formulation allows for twice-daily use. The usual daily maximum is 60 mg.

Can I Take Buspar as Needed?

Because it isn't in any way chemically related to Xanax-type drugs, Buspar is not effective taken on an as-needed basis; it takes two to four weeks to kick in. If you are accustomed to having medicine for anxiety work right away, you may be discouraged by Buspar's apparent lack of effectiveness. Don't jump ship prematurely: Give it time, that's just how it works. Buspar is sometimes prescribed for premenstrual depression, and it is an especially good choice for women suffering from GAD and premenstrual depression simultaneously.

How Long Do I Need Medication?

Many women wonder how long to take a medication to treat anxiety. This decision is highly individual, depending on how many bouts of anxiety disorder you have had and how much stress it took to develop the disorder. In general, once I feel that medication is an appropriate intervention for one of the anxiety disorders, I recommend a full year of treatment. After a year, I taper the medication slowly. If the disorder comes back quickly, then I usually recommend resuming medication for two years, when we will try again to stop it gradually.

Panic disorder waxes and wanes: It may plague you for a few months, then not come back for five years. Going off medication doesn't seem to cause any harm; if you must resume it, medicine that worked before will usually work again.

Because of the chronic nature of GAD and agoraphobia, and of panic disorder that has been present for a long time, usually it is wise to take medication longer to treat them. Taking the medication for two years to let its chemical effects settle in your brain gives you plenty of time to develop new coping skills and new ways of viewing your ability to handle stress and fear. Chronic anxiety disorders creep into your lifestyle, your personality, your expectations for yourself and the world. Taking medication for an extended period of time lets you build up your confidence, which may make it more likely that you will be able to get off the medication eventually.

Will I Need More Medication Later?

In general, effective antidepressant doses remain fixed: If 35 mg Adapin does the trick, it is likely to do so indefinitely; likewise for SSRIs. However, over time, you may need more benzodiazepines in order to obtain the same clinical effect, a phenomenon called tolerance. This is one of the reasons why tricyclics and SSRIs are better first-line treatments.

Whichever medication you are taking, especially if you are taking a tranquilizer, when it comes time to stop, taper the dose slowly. **Abrupt discontinuation of a benzodiazepine is extremely uncomfortable and may even be life-threatening because it can cause a seizure.** Do not stop a benzodiazepine on your own, without medical supervision. Tolerance and the need to taper off benzodiazepines do not mean that you are "addicted," but do indicate that your body has become accustomed to the medication, as happens to anyone who takes a benzodiazepine daily.

CONCLUSION

Women with anxiety disorders often feel that no one understands what it's really like. The very word "anxiety" doesn't begin to express how awful it feels. If your friends or family think that you are just being self-indulgent or aren't trying hard enough, they certainly won't support your taking medication to feel like yourself again. You can be sure that someone who is telling you to just relax hasn't ever had a panic attack. No one but you is in your shoes. One thing that I see over and over is that women who recover through medication for anxiety disorders are as amazed at the transformation as I am. Trust in your own judgment, and take care of yourself. Let others think what they think.

Chapter 5

WHY CAN'T I STOP WORRYING?

Obsessive Compulsive Disorder

KEY POINTS

- Do not let embarrassment about your symptoms keep you from getting help for obsessive compulsive disorder (OCD).
- Cognitive and behavioral therapy are much better talk therapies than traditional psychoanalytic psychotherapy for OCD.
- Serotonin-enhancing antidepressants are much better medications for OCD than other types of antidepressants.
- Medication for OCD markedly relieves symptoms but usually does not take them all away.
- Relapse after stopping medication for OCD is common.

Like most women with obsessive compulsive disorder (hereafter OCD), Holly has a very active imagination.

Not only can she picture one catastrophe after another in her head, if there is a one-in-a-million chance that it could happen, she knows with a deep conviction that she'll be the one. She constructs possible scenarios in her head over and over again, even though these images leave her terrified, feeling helpless, and very, very anxious.

Holly recalls always being what she calls "tightly wrapped" as a kid, the child who never had to be told to wash her hands before dinner, the one who never had a single school paper returned with the words "good job but messy," who insisted on the yellow shirt with the yellow shorts before she could talk. She was a self-described "anal-retentive" person, the one who drove every college dorm roommate up the wall by straightening out the closet. But prior to the birth of her first child, Holly's attention to detail, her perfectionism, her ability to anticipate and thereby avoid disasters had served her very well.

She was at the top of her profession, the head emergency room nurse at a large metropolitan hospital, where running a tight ship was a wonderful asset. Her ability to imagine the worst, to head off unlikely tragedies, was part of what made her so competent. But when she got pregnant at age twenty-nine, she went from being a good worrier to a woman overwhelmed by anxiety.

Holly couldn't find peace thinking about all the healthy pregnant women she had seen. Instead she could focus only on tragedies, the horrible pain that she felt when a baby was born with devastating birth defects, when two parents brought in a sudden-infant-death-syndrome baby, when a pregnant woman suffered a stillbirth after being in a car accident. She began going to great lengths to protect her own baby from the one-in-a-million chances, even though in her heart, she knew she wasn't being rational. She stopped driving on the highway to get to work, taking side roads through a dangerous neighborhood just to prevent a highway accident. She left the room when one of the doctors used a cellular phone, because you just never know. Her heart raced every time someone took an X ray anywhere in the ER, even though she knew in her head that the technicians were always careful to clear the area. She lay awake at night worrying about accidentally sticking herself with a contaminated needle and getting AIDS. She could play out the whole scene in her mind: She would get AIDS, her baby would die of AIDS, and her husband might get it from her too. She even wanted him to wear condoms so that he wouldn't catch it from her—even though she hadn't had an accidental needle stick in well over a year. She kept thinking that maybe the scientists weren't right, maybe there were ways of picking up AIDS that hadn't been identified yet, maybe she could still be carrying a virus from a year ago no matter how unlikely that was. She knew that she was driving her obstetrician crazy asking for reassurance over and over again, but she couldn't stop.

No one at work knew how consumed with anxiety Holly felt. They knew she was going a little overboard with the X ray thing, but they basically thought it was cute, a sign of how much she loved her baby. They knew she was exhausted, but they wrote off her fatigue to pregnancy, never suspecting that she was suffering from night after night of painfully obsessive insomnia.

She started counseling, with a therapist who focused on what she called Holly's codependency. You're a caretaker, he said, like many doctors and nurses, and you're terrified that you won't be the perfect mother. He taught her relaxation techniques, how to breathe deeply, meditate, encouraged her to pray more, and used creative visualization to help her replace the frightening images with mental pictures of a happy, healthy, strong baby who would adore its mom.

The therapy helped Holly take the edge off the anxiety. She went back and forth trying to surrender some control to God, asking God to give her the strength and courage she needed to get through this. The cynical ER nurse part of her kept shouting that God isn't a vending machine who can provide healthy babies if you just pray hard enough. At other times, she found some spiritual peace that eased the anxiety. She did get through the pregnancy, taking it literally one day at a time.

When her baby was born, a full-term, healthy seven-pound girl, the most beautiful baby Holly had ever seen, she felt high for weeks. The minute her head hit the pillow, she slept. She was euphoric, wonderfully happy and in love with her baby, her husband, with life itself.

At three weeks postpartum, she had a terrifying image out of the blue. Unlike the tragedies that she had imagined during her pregnancy, this time she pictured actually hurting her baby herself. She was running down the stairs from the nursery to get a bottle when she flashed on a mental picture of dropping her beloved baby, of seeing her daughter lying on the hallway floor, her tiny bones broken, after Holly had let her slip through her hands. That night she hardly slept.

The thoughts got worse and worse over the next few weeks, and she was flooded with horrifying images of harming her baby. She worried about accidentally leaving a pillow in the crib and causing her baby to suffocate, even though she'd never even had a pillow in the baby's room. Still, just to be sure, she brought all the pillows into the garage for safekeeping. She couldn't take her eyes off the baby, and she wanted someone with her at all times so that she couldn't accidentally hurt her. She threw out all the sewing needles in the house, just to be sure that she didn't accidentally leave one out somewhere where it could poke the baby in the eye and blind her. She cleaned her refrigerator at least six times a day and panicked that unseen germs might contaminate the formula. She felt ridiculous: She was responsible for hundreds of babies at the hospital, she knew infection control backward and forward, yet she couldn't find a moment's peace unless she acted on the worries. Even then, the peace was momentary, a temporary haven until the next wave of anxiety rushed in.

It didn't take long for Holly to become severely depressed. She felt so terribly afraid and out of control that she cried almost all the time. She couldn't eat, couldn't sleep, and couldn't shake these thoughts, even though she knew they were ridiculous and not going to result in harm to her baby. She told herself over and over that what everyone was telling her was true: She's a good mother, her baby is thriving, relax, for heaven's sake. By two months postpartum, she actually had lost so much weight that she was much thinner than the day she got pregnant. She called her obstetrician, who told her that she probably had postpartum depression and suggested that she call me for help. Her therapist agreed that it made sense to find out about medication, if for no other reason than to get some sleep before she had a complete nervous breakdown.

I told Holly that I thought her main problem was obsessive compulsive disorder, not postpartum depression. Yes, she had gone on to have many symptoms of clinical depression, but the anxiety disorder had been in charge for months. Holly soaked up information; she couldn't get enough. Her style always had been to dig for information, to master problems by really understanding them intellectually. As I often do, I pulled out my *DSM-IV* and showed her the diagnostic criteria for OCD. Good heavens, she said, that's what's been wrong all these months. That's me they're describing.

YOU ARE NOT THE ONLY ONE

Contrary to what psychiatrists once believed, OCD is far from rare. Current estimates are that one in forty women will suffer from OCD in her lifetime. If you take a cross-section at a single point in time, one in sixty-five women meets diagnostic criteria for OCD. The illness usually begins by age thirty.

Studies indicate that OCD occurs at the same frequency in men and women. This is remarkable, since most mood and anxiety disorders are more common among women. However, childhood onset of the disorder is more common in men, and many women first experience the illness in the context of childbearing, either during pregnancy or shortly after giving birth.

When I was learning psychiatry, I rarely diagnosed OCD because only a decade ago, the disorder was largely ignored. The neglect of this serious illness actually didn't much matter, since there was essentially no progress in treating it since the days in which Sigmund Freud attempted to treat OCD using psychoanalysis.*

I had my eyes opened to OCD as a result of my interest in postpartum depression (PPD), since postpartum OCD often masquerades as PPD. The introduction of Prozac (fluoxetine) and Anafranil (clomipramine) also helped all mental health professionals become more aware of the illness—finally we could do something useful. With the discovery that behavioral therapy was highly effective for OCD, suddenly there were helpful words *and* helpful medications.

OBSTACLES TO CARE

One reason why this disorder lurked undetected in the background is that people with OCD are often extremely competent in many areas. Women with OCD usually hide the illness, and often they function extremely well professionally and in caregiving roles, where an orderly and thorough nature is helpful.

The symptoms of OCD may be very bizarre, yet the sufferer is not delusional or hallucinating. Since a woman who has OCD doesn't think forces from an alien planet are invading her brain, she is aware that the horrifying images or irrational behaviors are a product of her own mind. Images may center on a loved baby or child, and many women are loath to describe these symptoms. Shame and secrecy are the rule for OCD: The average sufferer experiences the illness for seven years before asking for help.

OBSESSIVE COMPULSIVE DISORDER: THE DIAGNOSIS

Holly saw herself most clearly in the obsessive subtype of OCD. She clicked with the description of having intrusive, terrifying images and impulses that were deeply disturbing, even though she knew that these thoughts came from her own head, knew that she was, in a sense, doing this all by herself. She clearly didn't have postpartum

---

* The case published in 1909 as "Notes upon a Case of Obsessional Neurosis," described by some as "The Rat Man."

psychosis; she had no sense of being controlled by others; she was very anxious but not paranoid; and she hadn't lost contact with reality. The following box presents the diagnostic criteria for OCD.

DIAGNOSTIC CRITERIA FOR OBSESSIVE COMPULSIVE DISORDER

Obsession: one or more of the following mental phenomena:

• Repetitive, senseless thoughts that provoke anxiety (such as excessive fear of contamination by germs, toxins, chemicals, or AIDS)

• Repetitive, senseless urges that provoke anxiety even though you know that you won't act on the urges (such as graphically violent impulses even though you are a very peaceful person, or sexual fantasies that you would never act out)

• Repetitive images that provoke anxiety or even horror (such as having harmed a child or having accidentally and unknowingly hit someone in traffic)

• Massive doubt and indecisiveness for fear of making a bad decision (such as taking hours to choose what to wear)

Compulsion: one or more of the following repetitive behaviors:

• Repetitive checking (such as checking locks or the gas stove over and over)

• Cleaning rituals (handwashing until your skin bleeds)

• Ordering or symmetry rituals (such as attempting to line up towels in your closet until they are perfectly aligned)

• Compulsive mental rituals (counting or repeating words to yourself silently, saying a single prayer hundreds of times, or repeatedly demanding reassurance)

• Other ritualistic acts that are similarly of a driven, compulsive quality (these may include sexual compulsions)

Obsessions are defined as repetitive thoughts that cause anxiety, much more anxiety than the situation merits. Like Holly, the person suffering makes extraordinary efforts to stifle or mentally neutralize the obsessions. Compulsions are defined as repetitive behaviors, actions that are designed to minimize fear or worry or to prevent an imagined catastrophe. The actions must be irrational or unrealistic or extremely rigid. In both instances, the person suffering is painfully aware that these urges and ideas are a product of her own mind, even though they are typically experienced as ridiculous, "not me at all." In Holly's case, obsessions were the main problem, but her repeated cleaning of the refrigerator (up to an hour a day) is an example of a compulsion.

Regardless of your individual symptoms, the diagnosis of OCD is made only if you recognize that the worries and behaviors are fundamentally unreasonable and if they cause great distress; interfere with your ability to play, love, work, or study; or are so time-consuming that they impinge on your ability to function as usual.

Is There More Than One Kind of OCD?

Sometimes OCD is purely obsessive or purely compulsive in nature. Most typically, women with OCD have both obsessions and compulsions. Usually, however, one or two symptoms dominate. Some women are "checkers" while others are "washers." Some are "doubters" while others are most troubled by contamination fears. You may have panic attacks due to OCD, but, unlike panic disorder, the attacks are precipitated by a specific worry or situation. Panic attacks caused by OCD do not come out of the blue.

The concept of "obsessive compulsive spectrum disorders" is gaining strength. This model proposes that a number of emotional illnesses that have a compulsive or obsessive quality are actually variants of OCD. The idea of a spectrum is based in part on the fact that these illnesses respond to serotonin-enhancing medications. Also, they cluster in families, which suggests a genetic factor. The following disorders ultimately may prove to be closely related to OCD and may respond to the same medical treatments: binge overeating, body dysmorphic disorder (an abnormal belief that you have a physical defect, especially in your appearance), compulsive shopping, hypochondriasis, pathological jealousy, sexual addictions, and trichotillomania (compulsive pulling out your own hair from your head, eyebrows, or eyelashes).

Comorbidity with OCD is common. The majority of women who suffer from OCD will experience at least one episode of clinical depression. Panic disorder, bipolar disorder, and substance abuse occur more frequently in those suffering from OCD.

WHAT CAUSES OBSESSIVE COMPULSIVE DISORDER?

Biological Causes

The evidence for a major biological cause of OCD is quite strong. While early theorists, including Freud, attributed OCD to childhood developmental blocks, especially conflict and anxiety about toilet training and anal eroticism, few modern clinicians believe these old models anymore.

The first evidence that OCD has a basis in the brain (rather than in the psyche) was seen in the 1920s, following an encephalitis epidemic. Encephalitis is a brain infection that may leave survivors with residual neurologic abnormalities, such as epilepsy. After this particular epidemic, survivors had a higher than average rate of OCD, which indicated that the brain infection had caused a physical abnormality. Higher than expected rates of OCD also are seen in survivors of head trauma and birth injury, which provides further evidence that OCD is a brain disorder. (See p. 252.)

But most people with OCD do not have a history of a specific brain injury, and the disorder clusters in families, which suggests a genetic basis. Other evidence indicates that OCD is a brain disorder: Individuals who suffer from either the neurologic conditions Sydenham's chorea or Tourette's syndrome have much, much higher rates of OCD than either the general population or people with other neurologic conditions. Conversely, as many as one in five individuals who have OCD also have the motor or vocal tics seen in Tourette's syndrome. (This situation is more common in men, however.)

The Basal Ganglia and OCD

Until modern brain scanning techniques, the specific location of OCD dysfunction wasn't known. Now it is generally recognized that the basal ganglia, including the caudate nucleus and the front part of the cerebral cortex (popularly called gray matter), are abnormal in OCD. In fact, what appears to link OCD, Syndeham's chorea, and Tourette's syndrome together is the brain's the basal ganglia structure.

Prior to the technological breakthroughs that have dramatically increased scientific knowledge about the brain, illnesses with motor symptoms (chorea and Tourette's) were classified as neurologic disorders (brain illnesses). Illnesses such as OCD, with behavioral and mental symptoms, were classified as psychological (viewed as emotionally caused). This historical brain-vs.-mind or neurological-vs.-psychiatric dichotomy not only contributes to stigma but irrationally forms the basis of discriminatory insurance coverage for mental illness.

Evolutionary Basis of Obsessive Compulsive Traits

According to the leading theory about how these abnormalities translate into the specific symptoms of OCD, one function of the basal ganglia is to screen danger signals. In OCD, the screening function doesn't work correctly. It's a leaky sieve, allowing danger signals in too easily, setting up a feedback loop with the gray matter that perpetuates itself endlessly, resulting in OCD. Since receptivity to danger enhances survival of the species, OCD may represent the extreme continuum of a useful trait.

We are all faced with "worry messages" all day long: Watch out for that car coming, be sure to avoid germs, don't drop the baby, be careful, be careful, be careful. These worry signals could inundate us, yet they are absolutely necessary for survival. However, some automatic mechanism by which we screen out big danger warnings from little danger warnings must exist, or we would be immobilized by fear. To use compulsive handwashing as an example of the leaky sieve, first it must be recognized that cleanliness is an instinctive urge; mammals, including humans, groom themselves as part of automatic behaviors. If the brain is not filtering out excessive urges to wash, if the gray matter doesn't guide us to respond appropriately when we are sufficiently clean, the brain signals contamination worries, leading to excessive handwashing, and the loop of worry-wash is endless. Instead of appropriate, safe cleanliness, the OCD sufferer is literally receiving brain worry messages to wash over and over, even though she knows it's excessive and often even though her skin is raw or even bleeding. She knows it's ridiculous, but she can't stop herself due to the anxiety.

Understanding the potential benefits to the species may provide insight into why pregnancy and childbirth often trigger OCD. It is quite easy to imagine that one of the miracles of human design would be to make childbearing women unusually able to anticipate and imagine disaster. Imagine how the species would thrive were the primary caregivers of the most vulnerable members unusually cautious, protective, and vigilant. The design isn't without glitches: Some women are already such good worriers that the complex brain-hormone changes of pregnancy and childbirth turn them into painfully, futilely unproductive worriers, washers, and compulsive "checkers." Sleep deprivation (which any pregnant woman will tell you begins in pregnancy; it isn't just because the baby wakes you) may be the specific biological trigger for increased worrying. Prehistorically, adolescent males were the primary warriors, the defenders of the tribe. OCD in young men may have served a useful evolutionary function, and thereby been preferentially transmitted to the next generation.

Serotonin and OCD

Serotonin is clearly the most significant neurotransmitter that is dysfunctional in OCD. (See p. 253.) It is not likely that the serotonin imbalance of OCD is identical to that of clinical depression and panic disorder, since those illnesses respond to a wider variety of medications than does OCD. This fact is indirect evidence that OCD is more of a "pure" serotonin deficiency than are other mood and anxiety disorders. Since there are over fifty different subtypes of serotonin receptors in the brain, OCD may turn out to involve a different set of serotonin receptors than, say, those that are dysfunctional in agoraphobia.

WHAT ARE THE TREATMENTS FOR OCD?

Talk Therapy

Traditional psychotherapy and psychoanalytic treatment are ineffective for OCD. Fortunately, two relatively new forms of psychotherapy called cognitive and behavioral therapy are highly effective. These two forms of treatment often are combined, abbreviated "CBT" for cognitive-behavioral therapy. In general, studies indicate that behavioral therapy in combination with medication therapy is the ideal treatment for OCD.

Behavioral therapy has an advantage over medication therapy, because its benefits persist long after treatment is completed; medication therapy works only while the medication is in the system. Unfortunately, behavioral therapy is not widely offered to and/or utilized by women suffering from OCD. Psychotherapists tend to offer patients traditional talk therapy, and many therapists (including psychiatrists) simply haven't been trained in cognitive-behavioral therapy. Medical doctors (including psychiatrists) are often quick to jump to medication, especially since it usually is well tolerated and often is quite effective.

But some women will choose medication as a sole treatment because the very idea of cognitive-behavioral therapy is anxiety provoking. Dropout rates are high in behavioral therapy, because initially the treatment increases anxiety.

One of my patients recently went through behavioral therapy for OCD.

Maggie was terrified that something would bring harm to her beloved baby. She was especially worried about honey, because she knew that botulism toxins had been found in honey and that this might lead to sudden infant death syndrome (SIDS). But rather than merely avoid honey, Maggie washed and washed herself, her clothing, and her baby's clothing, and she worried incessantly that she might accidentally touch honey in public and then transfer it by mistake to her baby.

Maggie underwent a three-week intensive behavioral therapy program, which involved high-anxiety-provoking situations, such as touching a honey jar in a grocery store and working her way up to touching public trash cans. The treatment caused her extremely intense anxiety, but she found that she survived it. She felt absolutely miserable, but each time she walked into the fire, she came through it with less residual anxiety. She put herself through hell for three weeks. At the end of it, she told me, she got her life back. Maggie got back the ability to relax with her daughter, to play with her without the immobilizing fear, to walk and breathe and smile outside of the isolated cocoon she had built to protect herself from her fears. "Tell your readers it was worth it," she said. "Make sure they know that it's awful to feel this anxious, but then you get yourself back." She had developed elaborate rituals in order to keep her anxieties about her baby's health at bay, and the treatment helped her walk through the anxiety, emerging a loving, cautious, protective mother who could function in the real world.

Behavioral therapy for OCD requires the sufferer to jump right into the anxiety-provoking situation, and a high number of patients won't consider doing so or immediately drop out. The treatment is very time consuming and expensive at first, often requiring several hours of therapist-accompanied treatment per day for a few weeks. (Some behavioral specialists don't rely as heavily on a therapist-companion, relying more on "homework" assignments, but the accompanying therapist model is common.) The basic premise is to repetitively expose the person with OCD to an escalating set of anxiety-provoking situations, with progressively longer periods of time in which the typical maladaptive response is prevented. This is called response prevention, exposure, or desensitization therapy. As another example, a pregnant woman with severe avoidance of cellular phones might first look at a picture of a cellular phone, work up to being next to one that is turned off, and finally make a quick call on one. Of course, adaptive coping skills for anxiety are part of the treatment, including relaxation and self-talk.

A related model of talk therapy uses a more cognitive approach for OCD. The premise is to interrupt the worry-response feedback loop by first labeling the thought. For example, instead of thinking "What if I drop the baby?" you say to yourself, "I'm having an obsessive thought." Then you try essentially to unskip the record by engaging the brain in some other type of activity, which you have planned before the symptoms flare up. For example, you might put photographs in an album, pull weeds, make lasagna, chat on the computer, run to the grocery store, or change your car's oil. The key is to have a planned activity ready, because it's too easy to lose perspective and become helpless when the symptoms are really flaring up.

An individual with OCD often incorporates her partner or other family members into the rituals; in such cases, some family therapy may be helpful. For example, Holly regularly asked her husband to reassure her that she didn't have AIDS. He became a font of knowledge about the risks of infection, and could and did cite study after study to his wife, indicating that she didn't have AIDS more than a year after being stuck by a needle in the emergency room, since she had undergone many HIV tests since the incident. He'd tell her over and over that he hadn't had an affair, that he had not exposed her to the virus through extramarital sex. I advised him to stop reassuring her and to remind her that I had asked him to no longer participate in her rituals, because she needed to let go of the obsessing rather than depend on her husband for temporary relief.

Cognitive-behavioral therapy is not clinically appropriate for patients who are: suffering from severe depression along with OCD; actively abusing substances; or on such a high dose of a tranquilizer (benzodiazepines, such as Xanax [alprazolam], Klonopin [clonazepam], or Valium [diazepam]) that their ability to learn and really work with their own anxiety is affected.

Behavioral therapy is an especially good idea during certain special circumstances, such as pregnancy and breast-feeding, or because of intolerable medication side effects, such as the sexual dysfunction that is so common with the class of medications used for OCD.

When Words Are Not Enough: Medical Therapy for OCD

Because of the nature of the illness, the decision to take medication may be especially burdensome for women with OCD. It isn't uncommon for me to see a patient for her first follow-up appointment (when I am expecting to find out how it's working and whether she has side effects) only to learn that she still hasn't started the medication because she is ruminating about whether to do so or not. You are entitled to make this decision carefully, but try to avoid getting hung up about the decision.

Many women suffering from OCD opt for medication readily, relieved to learn the good news that the new serotonin-enhancing antidepressants (p. 268) are highly effective. They may choose medication because cognitive-behavioral therapy is not universally available in all parts of the country, and, as mentioned, it is time-consuming and expensive. It is perfectly valid to opt for medication as the least intrusive, most convenient, or least stressful form of treatment. Others turn to medication only after words have not helped. Do consider combining talk therapy with medication. The two treatments are complementary and do not interfere with one another.

Holly, the ER nurse whose OCD started in pregnancy, responded to Luvox (fluvoxamine).

> Since Holly had come to see me specifically to find out about medication, she had already worked through the issues in her mind. She was feeding her baby formula but mentioned in passing that she wouldn't have even considered taking medication if she had been breast-feeding. I started her on 50 mg Luvox at bedtime, increasing over the next several weeks to 150 mg.
>
> I explained that about one in five women taking Luvox got insomnia, one in five felt sleepy, and the rest noticed no difference. Holly found that the Luvox made her a bit sleepy, but she wasn't too "drugged" to get up when the baby woke at night.
>
> Holly's depression started to get better before the OCD improved; within a month she felt better than she had since she got pregnant. By three months she had a few scary images, but she found that the techniques her therapist had taught her were far more effective once the medication was in her system.

Serotonin-Enhancing Antidepressants and OCD

The specific role of serotonin has important treatment implications, because unlike medication for clinical depression and panic disorder, for OCD, only antidepressants that selectively affect serotonin are effective. Traditional antidepressants, including tricyclics and monoamine oxidase inhibitors, have little or no effect on and do not help OCD.

The FDA has approved five medications for OCD: Anafranil, Luvox, Paxil, Prozac, and Zoloft. While not specifically approved for OCD, other serotonin-enhancing antidepressants may be equally helpful. (See p. 268.) A doctor may prescribe a medication approved by the FDA for depression rather than for OCD because she believes that it may be equally helpful or better tolerated.

Sometimes a person tolerates or responds to one medication better than to another. Medication side effects are especially problematic for patients with OCD because usually the doses are higher than for panic disorder and depression.

Serzone (nefazodone) and Anafranil are different from the other serotonin-enhancing antidepressants in important ways. First, Serzone (the newest antidepressant on the market) does not cause sexual dysfunction, such as loss of sex drive or inability to climax. Serzone is approved for depression, but may prove to be effective for OCD. Because it is the newest medication, less information about it is available. It may be more sedating at first than the other SSRIs, and it must be taken twice a day, instead of just once. Many women are only too happy to take a medication twice a day, or to build up the dosage slowly while waiting for the sleepiness to wear off, in order to be free of sexual side effects. Sexual side effects from all other serotonin-enhancing medications are common in the relatively high doses needed for OCD.

Anafranil is chemically related to traditional tricyclic antidepressants. Although it increases serotonin activity, it also has many of the side effects of other tricyclics: weight gain, dry mouth, constipation, sedation, and tremor, and serotonergic side effects including sexual problems and diarrhea or nausea may develop. However, some studies indicate that Anafranil is slightly more effective than other SSRIs. It also causes less sleep disruption than other SSRIs. A reasonable approach is to start with an SSRI such as Luvox or Prozac and switch to Anafranil only if it doesn't work well.

Will Medication Make It All Go Away?

Regardless of which medication is used for OCD, it is unlikely that medication alone will cause a complete remission. While a full remission is common with panic disorder or depression, only about a seventh of women who take medication for OCD lose all symptoms, although three-quarters will have some response and about half have a moderate or good response. In general, compulsions respond somewhat better to medication than pure obsessions.

Although the effectiveness of medication for OCD is far from dazzling, even a moderate medication response may help people to use nonmedical strategies better. For example, my patients often tell me that the medication takes away the wildly escalating anxiety, letting them mentally shake off the smaller stuff. A frightening image, for example, is transformed from being crippling to merely annoying.

Combined Medication for OCD

Because the response is not usually dramatic, augmentation of SSRIs with other drugs is common. In augmentation, a full dose of a serotonin-enhancing medication is combined with a smaller dose of a second medication. Medications used to augment standard OCD medications—including Klonopin, Buspar (buspirone), lithium, or Desyrel (trazodone)—may be recommended. Tiny doses of a tricyclic antidepressant such as doxepin may be recommended either for augmentation or to reverse insomnia induced by a selective serotonin re-uptake inhibitor (SSRI). Specialists may combine a low dose of Anafranil with an SSRI such as Prozac, but doing so requires expertise. While this combination often is more effective (and low doses of Anafranil usually cause few if any side effects), the two medications can interact in dangerous ways. If you are combining medications for OCD, **ask your doctor whether a blood test is a good idea,** and **seek emergency medical help if you develop signs of serotonin syndrome: muscle jerks, profuse sweating, mental confusion, abdominal cramps, or vomiting.**

Comedication for sexual side effects (p. 158) may be especially helpful for women with OCD, because they don't have the option clinically depressed women have: switching to another type of medication. If the medication doesn't enhance serotonin—the chemical that can suppress sexual drive or pleasure—it is not likely to help OCD.

Usually treatment for OCD is also effective for women with comorbid depression or panic disorder. In rare instances, a comorbid illness might respond better to a different type of antidepressant medication. Also, if you responded to behavior therapy and didn't like the side effects of the SSRIs, you might prefer to use a different kind of antidepressant if you become clinically depressed, while relying on therapy to control the OCD.

How Long Do I Need Medication?

Unfortunately, OCD is a chronic disorder that usually recurs when medication is stopped. As many as 85 percent of women will relapse within the first few months of stopping medication. I generally recommend continuing medication indefinitely, with some exceptions.

First, since some women with postpartum or pregnancy-induced OCD may not develop chronic OCD, I like to try to stop medication at about a year postpartum. Also, it is reasonable to stop or wean medication after completing cognitive or behavioral therapy for OCD. Lifelong medication is a major commitment that few women are willing to make until they are absolutely convinced that it is necessary.

CONCLUSION

Some of my patients have never told anyone about their symptoms, including lovers and husbands. You may tire of keeping your secret: If so, consider asking for help. There isn't a quick-fix solution, but if you open yourself up to possibilities, you may find that life can be much less burdensome.

Chapter 6

WHY CAN'T I GET A GOOD NIGHT'S REST?

Sleep Disturbances

KEY POINTS

- Sleep changes are common symptoms of depressive and anxiety disorders.
- Insomnia can make you moody or anxious, or can make anxiety or mood disorders worse.
- Not all medications used for insomnia are potentially habit-forming.
- Antidepressants may cause insomnia, nightmares, or daytime sleepiness.

Since she's always been a sound sleeper, Mercedes can't figure out why she can't get a decent night's sleep anymore.

After two months of intermittent insomnia, Mercedes finally made an appointment with her internist, Dr. Taylor. "I can't sleep," she said. "This isn't like me at all." He asked her to describe her difficulty in more detail. She told him that she hadn't had more than a few hours' sleep at night for weeks, and things were getting worse and worse. She seemed to fall asleep okay, but she would wake up way too early. Bone weary, she would toss and turn for hours, lying there fuming. She was mad at everything: mad at her roommate, who slept like a log; mad at herself, certain that she was doing this to herself; mad at her boss, who wrote her up if she got to work eight minutes late. She tried warm milk, two glasses of wine, and an over-the-counter sleeping pill the pharmacist recommended, but nothing worked. The sleeping pill was a disaster: She buzzed that night until 3 A.M., groggy but just as wired as usual.

Dr. Taylor gave her one of the most popular new sleeping medications: Ambien (zolpidem). He told her to try a half a tablet. She did and, as usual, fell asleep well. Unfortunately, that night she still woke at 2 A.M. and didn't fall back asleep until an hour before her alarm went off. She called the doctor's office; the nurse advised her to increase the dose to a full tablet. That night, Mercedes actually slept for five and a half straight hours, a record for her lately. She continued to take the medication at 10 P.M., usually fell asleep by 10:30, and was up by 4:30 most mornings. She thought she shouldn't really complain: Compared to what she had been through, this was heaven.

But she didn't feel good during the day. She was draggy and irritable, and couldn't complete projects at work. It seemed that she was no longer capable of remembering to pick up everything she intended to get at the grocery store, and she found herself worrying about whether she would sleep that night almost from the minute she awoke.

Mercedes made another appointment to see Dr. Taylor. He scheduled some extra time for her, since he said that the fact that the Ambien didn't do the job completely was a sign that they needed to spend some more time trying to figure out what was going on.

YOU ARE NOT THE ONLY ONE

Mercedes is one of 10 million Americans who saw a doctor this year because of difficulty sleeping. Most women who seek medical attention for sleep problems are unable either to fall asleep or to remain asleep (insomnia). A smaller but significant number are sleeping too much (hypersomnia).

Sleeping problems may be the whole problem, the only thing wrong. This is called primary insomnia. Commonly, however, sleeping problems are a symptom of something else that is wrong. Sleeping problems often are due to an underlying mood or anxiety disorder. This type of insomnia is called secondary insomnia.

Nine out of ten women with clinical depression have changes in how they sleep. Poor-quality sleep is an everyday side effect of most of the new antidepressants. Women with anxiety disorders are exquisitely sensitive to insomnia as a side effect of these selective serotonin re-uptake inhibitors (SSRIs).

OBSTACLES TO CARE

If you aren't sleeping well, knowing where to turn for help is the first hurdle to get over. Women with insomnia often self-select which type of clinician to see based on what they believe is wrong. Psychiatrists almost never see women whose biggest complaint is trouble sleeping, because our patients usually identify the other emotional symptoms as the major problem. In other words, they come to us noting that they feel sad, worried, anxious, and, perhaps incidentally, can't sleep.

The reverse is often true for women who turn to a primary care physician for insomnia, thinking that the solution will likely be a sleeping pill. Indeed, many women with temporary insomnia do not need to see a psychiatrist or sleep specialist. Stress is the most common cause of transient primary sleep disorder, and chances are excellent that the disorder will pass whether you take a prescribed sleeping pill or not. But many women with highly treatable secondary insomnia never have their mood or anxiety disorder properly diagnosed and treated.

Depression and anxiety may disrupt sleep so profoundly that many women feel that everything would be okay if they just got a good night's rest. They attribute their emotional symptoms to the sleep disturbance: They feel that just getting some sleep would solve their mood symptoms or make the anxiety go away. They don't know to tell their primary care physicians about their emotional symptoms, and, in the typical rushed doctor's office visit, the true diagnosis may be missed.

It is perfectly fine to see a general practitioner, if she is skilled at evaluating the possibility of underlying depression or anxiety and if she is able to take enough time to sort it out with you. Many GPs are increasingly sensitive to emotional disorders that masquerade as physical ailments or sleep disturbance. Unfortunately, as Mercedes discovered, if the sleep problem is a symptom of another illness, it won't go away with a sleeping pill. The prescribed sleeping pill improved the quality of her sleep, but it did not improve the quality of her life. Mercedes's doctor took a very reasonable approach: He assumed that her insomnia was a temporary, just-one-of-those-things problem, and took a closer look as soon as it was clear that that wasn't the case.

Sometimes the stigma of depression interferes with self-identification of the problem. It may be more socially acceptable to view oneself as stressed out or as an insomniac than as depressed and thereby to minimize the emotional symptoms. But some women simply do not feel the emotional symptoms of anxiety or depression. The extent to which an individual experiences the subjective emotion of sadness, depression, or being on edge influences whether she believes she can't sleep because she is depressed or is depressed because she can't sleep. Older women, women of lower socioeconomic status, and women who have recently immigrated to the United States may be more inclined to experience insomnia than a sad mood or an anxiety attack when suffering from an emotional illness.

Finally, fear of addiction keeps many women from even discussing sleeping medication with their doctors. **Often insomnia can be treated without habit-forming medications.** Don't put off getting help for fear that the cure will be worse than the disease.

INSOMNIA: THE DIAGNOSIS

The list of emotional problems that may cause sleep disorders is lengthy. Getting the proper diagnosis may be especially challenging because many medications for depression and anxiety affect sleep. However, before assuming that your sleep problem is due to an emotional problem, you should know that there are physical causes of sleep disturbance also.

One important cause is sleep apnea, which is actually a problem of breathing (either an obstructed airway or a brain sleep-drive problem). Sleep apnea is often but not always associated with obesity and snoring. If you have morning headaches, daytime sleepiness, poor concentration or memory, or your sleeping partner has noticed that you gasp or flail about at night, be sure to tell your doctor. She may wish to obtain a specialized test called polysomnography. Proper diagnosis is extremely important, because sleep apnea can cause heart rhythm problems, and sleeping pills can be deadly in this condition.

Other physical causes of sleep disruption include over- or underactive thyroid hormones, alcohol or substance abuse or withdrawal, dementia, excessive caffeine intake, epilepsy, or side effects from a wide variety of nonpsychiatric medications (including over-the-counter or prescribed diet pills).

This Too Shall Pass: Stress-Induced Insomnia

Transient insomnia is triggered most commonly by stress. Hardly anyone alive hasn't experienced occasional sleeplessness due to worry, grief, anxiety, financial problems, or job stress. Missing sleep once in a while is normal, and you shouldn't jump in with a pill if real-life problems are the issue.

Widows often suffer temporary insomnia, and concerned family members or friends may be quick to suggest a call to the doctor for sleeping pills. Don't be too quick to medicate stress-induced insomnia, especially when it is part of a normal grief reaction. A few weeks of poor sleep is expectable and won't harm you. Instead of jumping to a pill, try natural remedies. (See p. 131.) If you aren't sleeping at night because you feel devastated by your loss, understand that you need to go through this. There is no shortcut out of the pain of bereavement. Your mind is running through painful memories for a reason; don't medicate them away.

I've Always Been a Terrible Sleeper: Primary Insomnia

Theresa has chronic insomnia.

> Theresa tells me that she's always fought for a good night's sleep. She is thrown by any change in her routine. If it thunders, she's usually up for the rest of the evening. If she has so much as a diet cola after lunch, if it's hot, if someone honks the horn down the block, if a child wakes her for a drink of water, if she is even slightly worried about the next day's schedule, she doesn't sleep.
>
> She tosses and turns in bed over and over. Sometimes she has a war with the clock. She turns it around, frustrated by the late hour. She stews, flops around in bed some more, then checks it again. This time she moves the clock across the room so that she can't keep looking at it. She hates to take a sleeping pill, and usually, by the time she admits that she can't stand it another second, it's too late to take one since she has to get the kids ready for school the next morning.

Theresa has a very typical pattern of primary insomnia. Always a light sleeper, she has developed a self-fulfilling prophecy. She is so worried that she won't sleep that she gets anxious the minute she gets in bed. She has developed conditioned insomnia, unknowingly giving herself the message night after night that she won't fall asleep easily. She often feels tired during the day, but she doesn't have waves of anxiety any other time of day, and she hasn't lost her enjoyment of life.

Depression and Sleep: Secondary Insomnia

Many women develop insomnia due to clinical depression. Most typically, depressed individuals fall asleep okay, but they are unable to remain asleep. The classic depressive sleep pattern is called early-morning wakening, characterized by waking somewhere between 2 or 3 A.M. and 5 A.M., usually without falling back to sleep. This particular pattern suggests that antidepressant medication is necessary because it indicates a chemical imbalance in the brain.

Even more commonly, depression causes women to wake feeling as if they didn't sleep at all, even if the hours "clocked" were normal. Sleep quality is as important as duration, so be sure to let your doctor know if you find that sleep is not refreshing or restorative.

Mercedes's doctor diagnosed clinical depression in her second appointment.

In retrospect, Mercedes saw that she had actually started to feel fatigued and bluesy before she developed her sleeping problem. Dr. Taylor reviewed other symptoms: Yes, her self-esteem was more or less shot, she felt overwhelmed and hopeless much of the time, and she couldn't remember the last time she laughed out loud. Mercedes was a bit surprised to hear that his diagnosis was clinical depression. She just didn't think of herself that way. But she trusted Dr. Taylor's opinion, and she accepted his advice that she take an antidepressant.

Mercedes's sleep problems were so severe that she thought the insomnia was making her feel down in the dumps. If you haven't slept more than a few hours at a stretch for weeks, it is natural to conclude that the sleeplessness is the cause of what's wrong rather than a result of the underlying emotional illness. Don't overlook the emotional symptoms. Lack of restful sleep and/or early-morning awakening due

to depression almost always go hand in hand with other symptoms.
(See p. 281.)

Depression and Sleep: Hypersomnia

Some women sleep too much when they are depressed; this situation
is called hypersomnia. Hypersomnia tends to cluster with the tendency to overeat. If you have hypersomnia, you may sleep ten or
twelve hours, then take a nap in the afternoon, and still never wake
feeling refreshed or energetic. Women are more likely than men to
have hypersomnia when depressed, and women with bipolar depression or seasonal affective disorder are also more likely to have
hypersomnia.* Hypersomnia also usually indicates that biological
treatment—medication or perhaps light therapy—is necessary.

The amount of sleep needed diminishes gradually as we move
from infancy into maturity. Sudden bursts of daytime sleepiness in a
woman in her late teens or early twenties may be left over from adolescence. Regardless of age, if you are experiencing this, it may suggest that you aren't clocking enough sleep hours: You may need eight
and a half hours to feel refreshed, but you only squeeze in seven and
a half. If so, once in a while your body will tell you to nap. This is
readily distinguished from depression-induced hypersomnia in that
the sleep is eventually restful and restorative, and it is not accompanied by other symptoms of depression.

Anxiety Disorders and Sleep: Secondary Insomnia

Anxiety disorders are another common cause of insomnia. (They
don't cause hypersomnia.) As a rule, women with anxiety-induced insomnia can't fall asleep, the reverse of depression. When your system
is revving along from a previous panic attack, when you just experienced a burst of adrenaline, it is understandable that it is hard to relax. The sleep problems caused by anxiety disorders (especially

* Women with bipolar affective disorder who are entering the manic phase almost always have bursts of decreased need for sleep. The symptoms are reversed: Despite little sleep, energy and activity levels are higher than usual, way out of proportion to
the few hours actually slept.

generalized anxiety disorder; see p. 87) often look just like primary insomnia: you toss and turn until you eventually fall asleep.

The presence of other symptoms of anxiety, such as panic attacks or daytime anxiety, distinguishes difficulty falling asleep due to anxiety from primary insomnia. Anxiety-induced insomnia is distinguished from depression-induced insomnia because **anxiety causes problems falling asleep while depression causes problems staying asleep.**

Some women have nocturnal panic attacks or are more susceptible to panic attacks as they fall asleep. Drowsiness may trigger a panic attack because the brain falsely perceives that you are under attack, and therefore sleeping is not in your best interest. Understandably, having even a single panic attack as you fall asleep quickly sets off secondary anxiety about falling asleep. A mild sedative such as Benadryl (diphenhydramine) actually may make matters worse.

Some women with OCD develop obsessions about not sleeping. Typically, they will see the insomnia as the problem, but the tip-off is that they have other symptoms of OCD, such as ritual behaviors or obsessive thoughts. Bedtime rituals or magical thinking about sleep ("I can only sleep exactly fifteen minutes after *Letterman* starts, wearing my Bulls T-shirt, with two pillows lined up") is another indicator that OCD is the problem.

Posttraumatic Stress Disorder and Insomnia

Restless, interrupted sleep with nightmares and flashbacks is typical of posttraumatic stress disorder. The most common cause in women is sexual or physical assault. The nightmares may be actual mental repetitions of the attack, or they may be more diffuse. Sometimes it seems that the brain is telling you that suppressing the memories, as you do in order to get through the day, isn't working when your defenses are down during sleep. The nightmares may be telling you that you have to find a new equilibrium, perhaps through community support or psychotherapy.

However, the most common comorbid illness associated with posttraumatic stress disorder is clinical depression. (See p. 34.) Don't overlook an easily treatable sleep disruption just because having trouble sleeping after a traumatic event makes sense.

Sleep Changes Induced by Antidepressants

While antidepressants typically reverse sleep problems by correcting the underlying mood or anxiety disorder, they also can cause sleep problems. Typically, tricyclic antidepressants (see p. 266) range from mildly to extremely sedating. Daytime sleepiness usually resolves within a few weeks. The tricyclics Norpramin (desipramine) and Vivactil (protriptyline) may cause insomnia or may have no adverse effect on sleep.

Serotonin re-uptake inhibitors are more likely to cause insomnia than tricyclics. These include Effexor (venlafaxine), Luvox (fluvoxamine), Paxil (paroxetine), Prozac (fluoxetine), and Zoloft (sertraline). Wellbutrin (buproprion) is also somewhat stimulating and may cause insomnia. Many women have vivid dreams (and occasionally nightmares) while taking SSRIs. Others have trouble falling or staying asleep. Taking these medications first thing in the morning instead of at night may help you sleep better (although this is not an option for Wellbutrin). Often the insomnia wears off within a month or two even if you do nothing. SSRIs may improve sleep by correcting the underlying problem.

Antidepressant Effects on Sleep in Bipolar Depression

Antidepressants may precipitate bouts of hypomania or mania in women who have bipolar affective disorder. Often the first signal that mania is about to occur is a sudden decreased need for sleep. An abrupt need for less sleep accompanied by bursts of energy, especially during the night, may indicate that the depression is switching into a manic episode. **If you have a personal or family history of bipolar disorder and you suddenly feel energized despite getting much less sleep, notify your doctor immediately.** You may urgently need a mood stabilizer, or you may need to stop your antidepressant.

WHAT ARE THE TREATMENTS FOR SLEEP DISORDERS?

Nonmedical Therapy

Regardless of the cause of insomnia, a wide range of treatments are likely to help most people sleep better. Nonmedical techniques are not appropriate as sole treatment for secondary insomnia or for medication-induced hypomania or mania. However, I encourage most of my patients to try nonmedical means first, especially those with primary or stress-induced insomnia.

Developing new sleep habits break the worry-can't-sleep conditioning that insomniacs experience. These effective sleep habits usually are helpful for anyone experiencing difficulty sleeping, and they may help ward off chronic insomnia for those going through temporary sleeplessness. Since women with chronic primary insomnia are likely to need medication indefinitely once they start it, it is especially important to try aggressive behavioral-relaxation therapy before committing to lifelong medication.

These techniques don't work on the first night. Conditioned insomnia has taken months or years to develop, and reversing long-standing habits will take a few weeks of practice. The box on page 131 lists some effective sleep habits.

The self-help techniques described may be sufficient. However, professional treatment also may be very helpful. Some types of therapy that are highly effective for chronic primary insomnia include biofeedback, relaxation training, meditation, and hypnosis.

You may be advised to try something called sleep consolidation or sleep restriction therapy. This therapy consolidates the amount of time that you spend in bed. Let's say you slept from 1 A.M. until 2:30, then again from 4:00 until 6:00, then from 6:30 until 7:15. Your total sleep time was four hours and fifteen minutes. With sleep restriction therapy, you would be instructed to go to bed at 3 A.M. and set the alarm for 7:15. My patients look at me like I am completely bonkers when I suggest this, but it quickly enhances sleep quality and helps them overcome conditioned insomnia. You gradually increase your sleep time until you are sleeping enough to feel refreshed during the day. Don't assume that you need eight hours. The amount of sleep that you need depends on how refreshing your sleep is. Obsessing about getting a certain amount of sleep aggravates anxiety about not sleeping.

If life stress is causing significant insomnia, open yourself up to what this is telling you. Some causes of stress-induced insomnia may just need to run their course: bereavement, divorce, sickness in a family member, for example. But consider whether you can do something to feel better. This is the perfect time to see a professional ther-

EFFECTIVE SLEEP HABITS

1. Do not toss and turn in bed. If you are not asleep within fifteen minutes, get out of bed and do something else for thirty to sixty minutes. Then try again if you feel sleepy. You should not watch TV, read, talk on the phone, stare at the ceiling, watch the clock, or stew in bed. Have something boring planned for when you get out of bed: paste photos in an album, read the encyclopedia, make school lunches.

2. Wake up at the same time every day, even if you are tempted to sleep late after a bad night. Routine waking times will help you get on schedule the next night.

3. Exercise daily if possible, but not later than early evening.

4. Have a snack rich in complex carbohydrates (see p. 68) just before bed. Avoid fluids if they are likely to make you wake up, and avoid caffeine (coffee, tea, cola, Mountain Dew or other caffeine-containing sodas, chocolate, and some headache remedies) after lunch.

5. Don't fall into the alcohol trap. A glass of wine or another alcoholic beverage may help you fall asleep, but you will pay the price later by being more susceptible to waking up after an hour or two. Abstinence is advisable for insomnia sufferers.

6. Get a "white noise" machine. A loud fan or vaporizer that drowns out background noise will also work.

apist for supportive psychotherapy. Talking over your problems, developing new coping skills, and paying attention to feeding your spirit will be much more helpful than a sleeping pill.

Proper nonmedical treatments for secondary sleep disorders due to depression or anxiety target the underlying disorder rather than the sleep disturbance. (See pp. 42, 90.)

Hypersomnia that serves as a means of escape from reality may get better once you face the issues. However, hypersomnia caused by clinical depression, winter blues, or bipolar disorder often indicates a need for medication. Severe sleep disorder is a rough marker of depression severity: When oversleeping or insomnia is bad, usually the depression is too. Because of this, women with severe sleep problems secondary to depression are less likely to respond to talk therapy alone.

When Words Are Not Enough: Medication for Sleep Disorders

If changing your sleep habits doesn't work, or helps a little but not enough, you may benefit from medication. Usually women with chronic insomnia do not do well taking medication intermittently. Because the sleep problem *is* chronic, many women go through an anxiety-plagued ritual about whether to take medication or not, much like the clock-staring routine. Do I take a sleeping pill tonight? Is it too late? Okay, if I'm not asleep by ten minutes, I'll take a pill. But if I take a pill, will I get up in the morning? Obviously, this worrying is not conducive to good sleep.

Many women are relieved to know that with all of the contemporary medical options, taking a regular sleeping pill does not mean that you are on your way to the Valley of the tranquilized Dolls. Usually it is not necessary to have to choose between getting hooked on pills or sleeping well. Terrific new medication alternatives don't carry the risk of tolerance, the phenomenon in which some individuals need a higher dose over time in order to have equal effectiveness, or rebound insomnia, the phenomenon of actually sleeping worse than you did before you starting taking tranquilizers for sleep.

Medication may be the appropriate course when the insomnia is causing poor daytime concentration, if you begin to worry that you aren't driving safely due to exhaustion, or if reducing stress and getting counseling isn't doing the trick.

Nonaddictive Remedies

Some women are more comfortable taking an over-the-counter medication than a prescription drug. It seems less "drastic" than a prescription. Over-the-counter medication such as Tylenol-PM, Unisom, or Benadryl are actually sedating antihistamines also used for allergies. These mild medications work well for most people, and they may even be strong enough to reverse SSRI-induced insomnia. However, elderly people do not tolerate antihistamines well, and they sometimes cause even young women to feel groggy the next morning.

Ambien, the medication that only partly helped Mercedes, is a wonderful new option for women with insomnia. For years, doctors and patients alike have known what the perfect sleeping pill would be like: quick-acting, nonaddictive, gone from the system by morning. Ambien has all of these features. No wonder prescriptions skyrocketed when it was approved by the FDA a couple of years ago.

Ambien is very popular with doctors, because it works well and is usually well tolerated. From time to time, a patient will have a bad reaction, usually related to the drug's rapid onset. Because Ambien may kick in much sooner than other sleeping pills, some women are surprised by its powerful effects the first time they take it. One of my patients told me she took an Ambien, went to fold laundry, and promptly went to sleep on the basement floor. Others have had conversations they do not recall. If you take Ambien, respect that it has a quick onset. Take it and go straight to bed.

Over the last ten years, doctors have turned to prescribing tiny doses of nonaddictive sedating antidepressants in place of tranquilizers. The three most popular are Elavil (amitriptyline, 10–25 mg), Sinequon (doxepin, 10–25 mg), and Desyrel (trazodone, 25–50 mg), usually taken an hour before bedtime each night. These medications also do not cause rebound insomnia when they are stopped. Women with chronic insomnia can expect that a dose that is effective today will continue to be effective for years.

Tranquilizers for Insomnia

Finally, tranquilizers, also called benzodiazepines, may be helpful for chronic insomnia. You can probably see my bias; these are not my first choice. Benzodiazepines such as Dalmane (flurazepam), Halcion (triazolam), Klonopin (clonazepam), Prosom (estazolam), or Restoril (temazepam) pose some unique problems for women with insomnia. While they may be perfect for occasional use, if you take a tranquilizer every day, soon you can't fall asleep without it, and you may become tolerant to the effect. Getting off these sleeping medications can be brutal. These drugs are best reserved for conditions where the insomnia is likely temporary: secondary insomnia and medication-induced insomnia, or when used as treatment for a primary anxiety disorder.

Antidepressant-Induced Insomnia or Nightmares

Some doctors routinely prescribe a sleeping pill during the first few weeks of starting a stimulating antidepressant such as Wellbutrin or an SSRI. Others commonly do so for those who develop insomnia or nightmares. It may seem confusing: Why is it more acceptable to take a sleeping pill regularly along with an SSRI or Norpramin than to take it for chronic insomnia? There are a few reasons why doctors are more comfortable giving a tranquilizer along with an antidepressant. One is that the insomnia is caused by the mood or anxiety disorder and/or the antidepressant. Unlike chronic primary insomnia, this is not a lifelong problem. Most women recover and discontinue the antidepressant eventually; therefore, most will find it easy to discontinue the sleeping medication once the depression is over or when the SSRI or Norpramin effect wears off.

Sometimes a low dose of an antidepressant is also prescribed for SSRI-induced insomnia. However, many antidepressants interact with each other. Combining a sedating tricyclic such as Elavil with an SSRI is potentially riskier than adding a tranquilizer.

Finally, SSRI-induced dream changes may respond to comedication. Usually having vivid dreams is not problematic enough to warrant comedication. One of my patients, who had recurrent dreams of being taught by nuns as a child, didn't mind this side effect. But another patient found her dreams of being attacked by terrorists intolerable. Nightmares often improve if the SSRI dose is adjusted downward. Sedatives that deepen sleep (such as Desyrel or Klonopin) may help. Some doctors have found that a medication usually used for high blood pressure—clonidine—suppresses nightmares.

Precautions

Older women do not tolerate full doses of any sedating medication. With age, the brain is more sensitive to sedation, and the body clears medications more slowly. Being sleepy during the day is especially risky for older women, because falls and hip fractures due to thinning bones can be devastating. Women over sixty or sixty-five generally should take half the usual dose of any sedative medication, with very gradual upward dose adjustments if needed. As a woman reaches her seventies, eighties, or nineties, further downward dose adjustments are prudent.

Women with stress-induced insomnia should not take habit-forming sleeping pills (barbiturates or tranquilizers/benzodiazepines such as Dalmane or Halcion) regularly. If they do, they may come to depend on them in order to fall asleep. While taking sleeping pills regularly may be fine in some circumstances, it is senseless to replace a temporary bout of insomnia with a difficult-to-break sleeping pill habit. Taking one or two sleeping pills per week is not habit-forming.

Finally, women with a personal or family history of addiction to alcohol or drugs are wise to avoid tranquilizers for sleep. Don't hesitate to tell your doctor if addiction is a personal or family problem before taking sleeping pills. You may be physiologically programmed to respond to these medications with the brain signal to take more. (See "reinforcement" on p. 95.) **Barbiturates (Seconal [secobarbitol] or Miltown [meprobamate], for example) are rarely, if ever, a good choice for anyone with insomnia due to their high potential for addiction.**

Secondary Insomnia Due to Depression

Until the depression is treated, a sleeping pill is not the solution. In fact, tranquilizers can aggravate depression. Taking a sleeping pill for secondary insomnia is like putting a blanket on a fire: It slows things down a bit, but sooner or later the fire erupts again. Antidepressants correct the sleep problem while they lift the depression; usually they take a few weeks to act. However, tricyclics and certain serotonin-enhancing antidepressants (Deseryl, Serzone [nefazodone], and perhaps Paxil, occasionally the others too) may help people rest better right away simply as a side effect rather than through neurotransmitter changes.

Mercedes's insomnia got better with an antidepressant.

> Mercedes's doctor gave her a prescription for Pamelor (nortriptyline), beginning at 25 mg at night. He instructed her to increase the dose to 50 mg three days later and to go up to 75 mg at bedtime after a week. Once she got up to 50 mg, she no longer needed the Ambien to fall asleep. At a follow-up appointment a month later, Mercedes reported that her mood, her energy, her concentration, and her insomnia were "90 percent better."

Secondary Insomnia Due to Anxiety

Tranquilizers also have a role in the treatment of primary anxiety disorders. (See p. 100.) Tranquilizers have a beneficial effect on anxiety *and* insomnia. Nonaddictive sleeping pills, such as Ambien and Benadryl, for example, don't help anxiety one bit. Depression is often mixed with anxiety, and the combination of an SSRI and a tranquilizer may be more therapeutic than adding Ambien to an SSRI.

A Word of Caution About Melatonin

Melatonin is a natural hormone that many women have taken for insomnia. Since it is classified as a dietary supplement rather than as a medication, it is not subject to the rigorous scrutiny that the FDA requires for both prescription and nonprescription medication. While melatonin does help jet lag, it isn't established as a sound long-term solution for chronic insomnia.

Do not assume that "natural" hormones are any less powerful or any safer than medications. Melatonin's safety has never been established, and it may have powerful effects on the body, including affecting women's fertility. **Do not take melatonin if you are pregnant.**

CONCLUSION

Sleep problems are a common reason for seeing a doctor. Restful sleep is a wonderful blessing and makes the difference between enjoying life to its fullest and just going through the motions. Many women are especially sensitive to fears of being overmedicated or becoming hooked because the so-called Mother's little helpers of the 1950s and 1960s were powerful and addictive medications that were much worse than the disease. While individuals may need to undergo a period of trial and error to determine which medication works best, most women are able to find the balance between effective sleep medication and waking without a persistent drugged feeling.

Part Two

SOLUTIONS AND THEIR PROBLEMS

Understanding How Medical Treatment for Depression and Anxiety Affects Women's Bodies

Chapter 7

WHAT HAPPENED TO MY SEX LIFE?

Sexual Side Effects of Medications

for Depression and Anxiety

KEY POINTS

• Sexuality may be enhanced by treatment of depression or anxiety.

• Unfortunately, sexual side effects are common with antidepressants.

• Changing how you make love and how you talk about making love may be an effective way to counteract sexual side effects.

• If sexual side effects are troublesome, your doctor may advise switching medications or changing the dose of your antidepressant.

• Your doctor may advise adding a second medication to restore sex drive or orgasm.

If you are lucky, treatment for depression or anxiety will restore your interest in and enjoyment of your sexuality. You may find that the medication restores your interest and pleasure in life, whether it is pleasure in your work, enjoyment of family life, or sexual enjoyment. You may not have sexual side effects from the medication. Unfortunately, however, many women experience significant sexual dysfunction due to medications for depression and anxiety.

Suzanne's problems were due to Prozac (fluoxetine), but they could just have easily happened with many other antidepressants.

Suzanne began taking Prozac two months ago when she couldn't pull herself out of a depression that started a month after she got laid off as a legal assistant. She felt so humiliated: In a town the size of Spring Valley, everyone knew she was out of work practically before she did, and she knew people were talking about her. Of course, depression ran in her family, so she wasn't too terribly surprised by the illness.

Suzanne's husband, Mike, kept after her to go see their family doctor, and she kept promising to get up the energy to call for an appointment. One day Suzanne's sister dropped in and announced that she was dragging her to their family doctor. "I won't take no for an answer," she said. "I've been there, and I know you aren't going to get any better until you do something about it," she declared.

The truth is, Suzanne was relieved to have someone take charge. Dr. Ford was Spring Valley's own Marcus Welby; he had actually delivered Suzanne and her sister almost thirty years earlier and taken care of her ever since. He went through a checklist of symptoms and told her that she was suffering from acute clinical depression. He prescribed Prozac, one 20 mg capsule per day.

Dr. Ford had said that the Prozac wouldn't take effect for at least two weeks, but Suzanne felt better almost immediately. She didn't have any of the side effects he warned might happen: no insomnia, no nausea, and no headache. By two and a half weeks, she was almost back to herself. Reality hadn't gotten any better, but she sure felt like she could face things again.

When Mike came home from work that Friday night with a bottle of wine and a bouquet of flowers, Suzanne knew just what he had in mind. She was embarrassed to realize they hadn't made love in ages. Things started out great. Unfortunately, nothing happened for her. No matter what. Mike practically stood on his head for her, but no go.

Things got more frustrating over the next few weeks. Suzanne didn't know who felt worse about it, Mike or her. Her depression was so much better that she didn't think it could be the illness, so she started to wonder whether the Prozac could be the problem. No way she was calling up Dr. Ford to ask though. First of all, you never got past his nurse, Lisa, and Suzanne was not about to describe this to anyone else. That left describing it to Dr. Ford in person, about as attractive a proposal as talking about her sex life with her dad.

YOU ARE NOT THE ONLY ONE

Sexual side effects are common in women, yet information about women's sexual problems caused by antidepressants hit the women's media before the medical literature gave it much attention. Women's health reporters knew how important this issue was before many doctors did.

When I lecture to doctors about women and depression, I often say that my goal is to make my audience as knowledgeable about women's treatment issues as Oprah Winfrey is. They laugh, not believing me that women's media serve as sophisticated sources of information for many of their patients. So, for those doctors who have never so much as glanced at *Good Housekeeping, Glamour,* or *Family Circle,* or who have never spent a day in bed watching daytime talk shows, I display a sampling of slides from articles taken from women's magazines.

I saved the best for last: *Elle* magazine's article on the sexual side effects of antidepressants. The title always gets a laugh: "Not tonight dear, I had a Prozac." The subtitle evokes more laughter: "Do mood altering drugs like Prozac and Zoloft suppress your libido? Or make you so happy you stop looking for love in all the wrong places?"

I'm crazy about this slide for several reasons. First, I think it's important for doctors to know that women's magazines (even teen magazines) are full of detailed information about medication for anxiety and depression. Doctors should know that their patients are knowledgeable consumers too. Many are especially surprised to know that this article appeared well before mainstream medical literature started to address the specific issues of the sexual side effects of antidepressants for women. I also like the slide because, just as many patients need permission to talk about sex with their doctors, many doctors need to get over the hurdle of discussing sexuality with their patients. I want them to know that if they bring up orgasms, their patients may not automatically faint, or vice versa!

Your Doctor Might Think You Are the Only One

If you are wondering what happened to your sex life, you should know that you are far from the only one suffering sexual side effects. It may be especially important to know this because the *Physician's*

Desk Reference seriously underestimates the incidence of sexual dysfunction caused by antidepressants, especially the new group of serotonin-enhancing antidepressants. (See p. 268.)

Suzanne found that her doctor wasn't aware of how common sexual side effects are.

> After months of no sex followed by weeks of bad sex, Suzanne's husband confronted her. They hadn't had sex for the whole time she was so depressed, and now that she couldn't have an orgasm, it was almost worse because he felt so guilty and selfish. I'll call Dr. Ford, he said, and he did. Dr. Ford pulled out his *PDR* and read Mike from the list of side effects. "Sexual dysfunction, 2 percent," he said. "That sure seems rare, but I guess rare doesn't mean much if it's happening to you. Have her cut back her pills to every other day. If it's not gone by a few weeks, call me back."

Dr. Ford read the *Physician's Desk Reference* (PDR) correctly. It does say that "sexual dysfunction" occurs 1.9 percent of the time, with loss of sex drive occurring at a rate of 1.6 to 11 percent. The *PDR* also mentions male impotence and abnormal ejaculation, but you won't find the statistic you want to know: how many women who were having orgasms before Prozac can't have them after. You also won't find that under other the descriptions of other selective serotonin re-uptake inhibitors (SSRIs), which mention about a 2 percent incidence of sexual changes in women. (One uses the appalling term, "female genital disorders.")

The *PDR* is wrong. Difficulty reaching orgasm or complete absence of orgasms (anorgasmia) is very common in women taking certain antidepressants. A more reasonable estimate, based on more objective research, is that at least 30 percent of sexually active women will experience some change in sex drive or function. Loss of sex drive in the absence of orgasm changes also may occur, but it is just common sense to say that sexual interest declines when sexual pleasure is absent.

The *PDR* underestimates the incidence of orgasm changes for a few reasons. The numbers usually come from pharmaceutical companies, which have a strong interest in presenting minimal side effects of their new product. Also, researchers often exclude sexually active women from clinical trials, due to concern about a newly introduced medication's unknown impact on pregnancy. Volunteers for new drug studies may be eliminated if they take any other medication at all, including birth control pills. This leaves men, post-menopausal women, and sexually inactive women in the studies, which disproportionately eliminates the most sexually active women from the drug studies in which side effects are identified. No wonder the rates seem so low!

Moreover, volunteers in pharmaceutical studies have the same sexual hangups as the rest of us and either don't realize that the drug caused the sexual changes or are too embarrassed to bring it up. The researcher may get a very different answer to the usual question "Have you noticed anything different?" than to "Have you noticed anything different about your sex life?"

Why is the PDR's underestimation of the problem so important? Because the PDR may be your doctor's main source of information about the sexual side effects of serotonin-enhancing antidepressants, especially if the doctor is not a psychiatrist or doesn't prescribe these medications frequently. General doctors are most comfortable prescribing the new antidepressants, because they are safer and have fewer overall side effects. This trend is great in that more women are getting the help they need. The down side is that a generalist cannot know every medication as well as a specialist does. Your doctor may not know about all the alternatives available. Of course, there is no guarantee that a psychiatrist, even a female psychiatrist, will be knowledgeable about sexual side effects either.

OBSTACLES TO CARE: TALKING WITH YOUR DOCTOR ABOUT SEX

First: Convince Yourself It Is Okay

Open communication about sexuality is the first step toward resolving problems. This may be hard for you—as it was for Suzanne—or hard for your doctor. Women who love sex, who usually climax, who feel comfortable with being sexual are perhaps those least likely to have problems due to medication. They are definitely more likely to be aggressive about overcoming sexual changes caused by medication, more likely to demand that they be fixed. Women who tell me they can't make love without images of nuns floating through their head are both at higher risk for sexual difficulties due to medication and less likely to pursue remedies aggressively. Take charge!

There's no guarantee that your doctor is comfortable talking about sex, places a high priority on your sexual pleasure, or is knowledgeable about the alternatives. Don't decide that just because your doctor is a father figure like Dr. Ford, or from another cultural background than you, or seems too straight-laced he or she isn't prepared to talk about this issue. But . . . you might have to be the one to bring it up. If the conservative approaches I describe on pages 153 to 155 don't work, you will need to ask your doctor for help.

Why should you bring sex up and risk the embarrassment? Because, at last—some good news. You don't have to choose between sex and depression. It isn't a matter of feeling good mentally or feeling good sexually. There are a number of alternatives, which I will describe. First, you need to convince yourself that you are entitled to talk to your doctor about having orgasms, good, easy orgasms.

You may not be at all shy about this issue. This is terrific, but rare. Many women feel funny talking about sexual pleasure. You should know that no one has ever died of embarrassment talking about climaxes with their doctor. Do it for yourself, and do it for your partner, who should be as troubled by the difficulty as you are. Do not do it only for your partner: More than one of my patients has been forced to face deep-seated relationship problems when she realized that her partner cared far more about her sexual interest than he did her emotional well-being.

You might find it easiest to talk to your doctor's nurse, a midwife, or a nurse practitioner. If you are more comfortable with a younger person or a woman, see if your health plan will let you make an appointment with one of your doctor's associates. Better yet, just do it. Bring it in writing, bring this book with you, talk about it with your eyes on the floor, call on the phone, whatever. You will find a way.

It's Okay to Have Limits on What You Talk About

Talking about sexual pleasure doesn't mean you suddenly have to reveal all aspects of your sexuality to your doctor. For example, if you want to ask your doctor about lowering your dose because you can't have an orgasm, you can choose to keep private that you are dating his brother, that your partner is a woman, or that even your vibrator isn't doing the trick anymore. The details aren't relevant. If your doctor asks you something that seems off the wall, ask why he or she needs to know. If you aren't satisfied with the answer, you might need to consider another doctor.

SEXUAL PROBLEMS: THE PROPER DIAGNOSIS

Good doctor-patient communication is critical because the issues are often complicated. Sexuality issues for women with emotional illnesses sat on the back burner for many years, coming to the forefront only when it became clear that the newest group of antidepressants, serotonin re-uptake inhibitors, often dramatically interfere with sexual enjoyment. Because these drugs can thwart pleasure, it's necessary to discuss preexisting sexual concerns in order to sort through the biological impact of medical treatment for depression and anxiety.

Careful diagnosis will clarify whether the depression or anxiety is negatively affecting sexuality, whether the medication is the problem, whether both are, or neither. The first step is to identify baseline sexual dysfunction.

Sex Was a Problem in the First Place: Depression

Depression and sex are intricately intertwined issues for women. Men who have clinical depression rarely complain of loss of sex drive. Kimberly Yonkers, M.D., director of the Reproductive Mood Disorders Program at the University of Texas in Dallas, has found that even when men are severely depressed, unable to function at work, even contemplating suicide, their sex drive may be unaffected. Dr. Yonkers notes that this is quite untrue for women, for whom loss of sex drive is a common symptom of depression. (Another major gender-related difference is crying, which is rare in depressed men.) Acute clinical depression and dysthymic disorder are both associated with low libido.

Besides suffering loss of sexual interest or pleasure during an episode of depression, women with mood disorders may have yet another burden. Some recent studies indicate that sexual dysfunction, including low sex drive and inability to achieve orgasm, is more common in women with mood disorders even when they are not acutely depressed. It may be that sexual dysfunction is a subthreshold marker of depression, present as a precursor or residual symptom of major depression. Or it may be that depression itself interferes with achieving full sexual potential. For example, chronic low self-esteem may interfere with a woman's ability to communicate her sexual wants openly and assertively. Chronic pessimism may make a depressed woman decide, "What's the use, I probably can't climax anyway; if he knew what to do he'd have done it already; I'm just not meant to have orgasms."

Sex Was Terrific in the Past: Bipolar Disorder

Enhanced sexuality is a common symptom of a manic episode. When the episode is severe, it is usually obvious in hindsight that sexual impulsivity or activity was uncharacteristic or inappropriate. However, when the upward cycles are somewhat mild, as in hypomania, sexuality may be enhanced without being so clearly dangerous, impulsive, or reckless. If you have experienced mild sexual euphoria as part of a bipolar disorder, it may be difficult to come to terms with your sexual baseline. Be careful not to use the sexuality of a hypomanic spell as "typical" or "optimal"—it can make the sexual baseline of a normal mood state falsely appear to be dysfunctional.

Sex Was a Problem in the First Place: Anxiety Disorders

Sexuality may be adversely affected by anxiety disorders also. The ability to relax is part of making love, and baseline tension and edginess can interfere with sexual drive or pleasure for either gender. Men with anxiety disorders may find that anxiety about sexual performance contributes to baseline sexual dysfunction. The cultural pressures and biological reality of sexual intercourse make male performance a source of anxiety even in some men who don't have any anxiety about anything else. However, while anxious men may experience premature ejaculation, anxious women may find that anxiety about having an orgasm has the opposite effect, making it more difficult because of the pressure to climax.

On the other hand, from time to time my panic disorder patients will tell me that making love helps relieve anxiety, either by distracting them from their fears and worries or by providing a physical intimacy and closeness that is soothing and reassuring.

Women with obsessive compulsive disorder may experience sexual symptoms directly as a result of the illness, although this is less common than with depression. Most typically, concerns about sexual contamination with germs—AIDS especially—can interfere with sexuality. Nighttime rituals also can interfere, since OCD sufferers may avoid sexual relationships in order to keep their rituals secret. If a woman with OCD or another anxiety disorder has a significant drop in her sex drive, I am much more likely to look very closely for other symptoms of comorbid depression.

What Sex Was Like Before Medication

You and your doctor will need to figure out whether your loss of sex drive or changes in orgasm are due to the medication or to something else. Be sure that you are clear in discussing this. Not long ago, I asked a patient whether she was having difficulties with orgasm. She sort of said yes, and I thought she was another SSRI victim. As we talked more, she acknowledged that she had never had an orgasm, alone or with a partner. She had gotten herself into a terrible bind, to boot: She was faking it. By faking orgasms, she was depriving her partner of the ability to bring her pleasure and depriving herself of the emotional intimacy that feeds and is fed by sexual intimacy.

What Sex Is Like on Medication

Assuming you have a confirmed sexual change, the most important factor is timing. **If a change in sex drive or functioning occurs within days or weeks of starting a new antidepressant or dosage increase, chances are very good that the antidepressant is causing the problem.** If you have been on the same medication for several months and only then begin to have sexual changes, likely there is another reason, such as relationship changes, stress, physical illness, fatigue, or a different sexual problem. Sexual changes due to medication usually do not emerge after you have a steady amount in your system.

Be very clear with your doctor whether you are talking about problems with sexual interest or the ability or quality of orgasms. Some
women lose the ability to have a climax and only then lose interest.
Other women can have an orgasm once they get going, but they
never initiate making love and dread being invited to do so.

If you weren't having sex regularly before you started the medication, it may be hard to compare before-and-after medication. You
may have stopped having sex due to a physical condition that predisposed you to an emotional illness, such as recent childbirth or treatment for cancer. You may have stopped having sex due to the emotional illness itself, especially depression. By chance, you may have
become sexually involved with someone only months after starting
the medication. If you aren't sure, I would still encourage you to talk
to your doctor about it.

If you have had a recent physical change such as childbirth or gynecologic surgery, it would be wise to get things checked out physically. Sexual changes may be due to a wide variety of medical treatments (such as medications for high blood pressure) or medical
conditions (such as a hormone imbalance).

A COMPARISON OF SEXUAL SIDE EFFECTS CAUSED BY MEDICATION

Any effective prescription may enhance sexuality by removing the
negative effects of emotional illness. However, certain medications
for depression and anxiety are more likely to cause negative sexual
side effects than others. While the statistics are imperfect, it is clear
that some medications are worse than others. Most serotonin-enhancing antidepressants have the greatest negative impact, while tricyclics are intermediate,* and tranquilizers usually have no sexual
side effects. Two new antidepressants, Wellbutrin and Serzone, appear to be free of sexual side effects. Serzone is unique in that it is a
serotonin-enhancing antidepressant that does not cause sexual dysfunction. The next box lists medications and their side effects.

Since two antidepressant medications do not cause sexual side ef-

---

* Some doctors feel that the rates of sexual problems are comparable for tricyclics but
that arousal rather than drive and orgasm is the problem. In my practice, I see many
more sexual problems caused by SSRIs.

MEDICATIONS THAT CAUSE ANORGASMIA, CHANGES IN ORGASM, AND/OR LOSS OF SEX DRIVE AS A SIDE EFFECT

Common

Anafranil (clomipramine)

Effexor (venlafaxine)

Luvox (fluvoxamine)

Monoamine oxidase inhibitors (Nardil, Parnate)

Paxil (paroxetine)

Prozac (fluoxetine)

Zoloft (sertraline)

Intermediate

Elavil (amitriptyline)

Norpramin (desipramine)

Pamelor (nortriptyline)

Tofranil (imipramine)

Sinequon (doxepin)

Other tricyclics

Rare

Ambien (zolpidem)

Ativan (lorazepam)

Buspar (buspirone)

Depakote (valproic acid)

Desyrel (trazodone)

Klonopin (clonazepam)

Lithium

Serzone (nefazodone)

Tegretol (carbamazepine)

Wellbutrin (buproprion)

Xanax (alprazolam)

Other sleeping pills

fects, you may say, then why take anything other than Wellbutrin or Serzone? Why bother with the other medications? I hope that you have this discussion with your doctor at the outset, so that you can express your views about "picking your poison." There is no perfect antidepressant, but, for some women, Wellbutrin or Serzone might be a good choice. For others, it may not be. Although a long-acting formula has just been released, Wellbutrin is usually taken three times a day and people with an eating disorder can't take it. Also, Wellbutrin does not enhance serotonin; therefore, it is not as effective for premenstrual depression and is completely ineffective for obsessive compulsive disorder and panic disorder.

Serzone does increase serotonin without causing sexual side effects, but it has drawbacks too. It must be taken twice daily (unlike the other SSRIs except Effexor), and it is far more sedating than other SSRIs. Some of my most respected colleagues tell me that their patients are doing very well with Serzone, but I have not been impressed in my own practice. Several of my patients have refused to take it after a single dose because they felt weird, spacey, or like a zombie. These side effects tend to wear off, and perhaps small, slow dose increases will minimize them. The dosing strategy "start low, go slow" is most sensible when a slower clinical response is acceptable, such as for premenstrual depression. It is not sensible for a suicidally depressed individual.

WHY DO ANTIDEPRESSANTS CAUSE SEXUAL SIDE EFFECTS?

Serotonin is present in the small blood vessels that supply the clitoris, and serotonin specifically inhibits orgasm. Since SSRIs increase serotonin activity, they also lower sexual responsiveness.* Other neurotransmitters, including dopamine and acetylcholine, promote orgasm. Besides chemically affecting the clitoris, antidepressants affect the brain chemistry responsible for sex drive. The separate effects on brain and body chemistry account for the fact that a person may experience changes in orgasm but not libido, or vice versa.

---

* Serotonin-enhancing medications are now being used in men to reverse premature ejaculation. Unlike for women, delayed sexual responsiveness may be highly beneficial for certain men.

The situation is somewhat different for tricyclic antidepressants. Tricyclics are less likely to interfere specifically with orgasm, but occasionally they cause vaginal dryness (just as they cause dry eyes and dry mouth), which can make intercourse painful. Vaginal dryness is especially problematic after menopause. (Estrogen, which is no longer produced after menopause, also contributes to vaginal lubrication.) Through their action on the brain, tricyclics also may cause low libido or impair arousal.

Sexual pleasure is multidetermined, not simply biological or psychosocial. The effects of medication are a specific physiological alteration, but the biological impact occurs in a human being with a full set of beliefs and values about sexuality. However, keep in mind that the major human sex organ is the mind, not the clitoris. In other words, while serotonin matters, sexuality is also about love, affection, intimacy, romance, desire, and passion. Addressing this side effect will be most successful if you open yourself up to a variety of solutions and don't just focus on the medication.

WHAT CAN BE DONE ABOUT SEXUAL SIDE EFFECTS?

Conservative Measures

When I approach the problem of sexual side effects in my practice, I begin with the most conservative measures and move up. Everyone prefers not to take a second medication if possible. I prescribe a second medication to reverse sexual side effects only as a last resort. The most conservative response to sexual changes is to do nothing . . . if doing nothing is an active choice that makes sense for you. As an example, one of my patients rarely experienced orgasms with a partner, but usually only when masturbating. After starting Paxil for premenstrual depression, she was unable to have an orgasm at all. However, she was so delighted with the emotional stability that she got from the medication, she was unwilling to make any changes in the antidepressant. She told me she was a much happier person without orgasms, and she didn't want to take any risks by changing the medication. Doing nothing also may pay off in the long run, since anorgasmia sometimes spontaneously resolves within two to five months (although this apparently doesn't happen during treatment with tricyclics). Many sexually active women are unwilling to wait this long for the mere possibility of orgasm.

Make Sex a Priority Again

You also can make some changes that may increase either your sex drive or enhance sexual pleasure. This is a good time to look at whether you are in a rut. If sex has changed over the years from a passionate event at 2 P.M. on the kitchen floor to a five-minute quickie during *Letterman* after you fall into bed exhausted from work and kids, you may benefit from making some changes in your sex life. In my practice, women who have recently given birth or who are raising small children are the most likely to have loss of sex drive and anorgasmia from antidepressants. They don't have a lot of sexual reserve to begin with, and time and energy are very precious.

It's all too easy to neglect your sex life, especially if you are busy with a young family. A great way to help matters is to stop being passive about making love. Plan it, plan more time than you think you need, and plan to make love when you are at your best. If possible, try setting the alarm earlier than the kids wake up and making love then. Sexual responsiveness for women is highly linked to fatigue, so mornings are often the best time to make love. Or hire a baby-sitter to take your kids to the park or to an indoor playland. Drop the sitter off with the kids at 10 A.M. on a Saturday, go home, take the phone off the hook, and make love. You also can trade kids overnight with another couple, such as friends or a sister. These solutions won't solve day-to-day sexual dysfunction, but often knowing that ideal conditions can restore the sexual vitality of your relationship is helpful.

If you only wish that you were in a rut because that would imply that you once had a wonderfully enjoyable sex life, do not despair. Look at this time as an opportunity, the silver lining in an otherwise dark cloud. In her absolutely wonderful new book, *Seven Weeks to Better Sex*, Dr. Domeena Renshaw states that women who do not have orgasms "are not abnormal or 'frigid'; they have just not given themselves permission to be fully sexual. They may also lack adequate sexual information." Rather than discuss this issue further, I refer you to this book. Every woman can have a climax, period.

Take Time for Yourself

Sex drive is not just a matter of chemistry. I tell my patients that if they haven't dropped the kids off at Grandma's and gone to a downtown hotel on a Saturday night, we don't know if they have no sex drive from Prozac or no sex drive because of Prozac *plus* child rearing. If Mommy exhaustion is part of the problem, try a minivacation. Make a date with your husband. On Saturday afternoon, tell him the kids are all his. Do something relaxing, like reading the newspaper at a coffee bar, or getting your hair cut, or buying some lingerie. Don't come home until the kids are asleep. Go to a movie by yourself if you have to, just to stay relaxed. Contrary to what you might expect, alcohol may impair sexual responsiveness, so avoid all but a small amount. Then, taking plenty of time, try making love. Explain to your husband that you need more foreplay. Tell him what feels good and what doesn't feel so good. Be adventurous. Instead of viewing this side effect as a horrible curse, consider it as an opportunity to enrich your sex life.

Sexual energy is part of your general energy and physical health. If you are having diminished sex drive, you owe it to yourself to try a whole-body tuneup. Give yourself a two-month trial of things that improve energy overall: eating right, exercising, sleeping regularly, and cutting back on unhealthy habits. This is an ideal time to cut out excess sugar, caffeine, alcohol, cigarettes, and junk food. Increase your intake of fruits and vegetables, and have at least five servings of complex carbohydrates daily. Aim for twenty minutes of aerobic exercise three times per week, more if possible. When you have gone through the exercise wall to the point that you miss it if you haven't exercised, you are at the place you need to be in order to see its benefits on your sex drive. Add a woman's multivitamin and mineral supplement. Get a physical exam if you haven't had one lately, and try to get plenty of sleep every night.

Conservative Measures May Not Be Enough

Antidepressants have sexual side effects because of their biological effect. While I preach changing sexual behavior and communication as a first step to counteract these side effects, you must not feel like a failure if these measures don't work. Quite commonly, these changes aren't practical, aren't possible, or aren't enough. Just as words may not be enough to help you battle depression, words and behaviors may not be enough to overcome the powerful biological sexual side effects of antidepressants.

MEDICAL INTERVENTIONS FOR SEXUAL SIDE EFFECTS

Adjusting the Medication You Are Taking

If changing how you make love isn't enough, you will need to approach your doctor or nurse practitioner to take the next steps toward fixing the problem. Two relatively conservative changes your doctor could recommend are lowering the dose to the minimum effective amount and trying what is called a "drug holiday." I would be very cautious about using these methods for a woman who had not responded readily to an antidepressant. If you required more than one drug trial, needed more than one medication to boost effectiveness, or had any complications of antidepressant therapy, I would recommend a different strategy. I am equally hesitant to lower the dose of a medication if you have had multiple episodes of depression or a particularly severe or life-threatening bout.

At times, lowering the antidepressant dose without reducing effectiveness is possible. This is especially true for women who respond to Prozac within the first few weeks, because blood levels continue to build up for up to six weeks. With your doctor's approval, skipping a Prozac every second or third day may improve your sex life without increasing depression. One recent trend is to prescribe 60 mg Prozac once a week (Sunday, so it's at its lowest level for the weekend) after the initial depression resolves. This regime hasn't been studied systematically in terms of sexual side effects, but a few patients have noted that they feel more like their old sexual selves by the following Saturday night.

When Suzanne's doctor recommended cutting her Prozac dose in half, he stressed how important it was to watch carefully for any signs of depression.

About a week later, Suzanne felt physical sensations that had been gone for some time. "I got closer that time," she said. Two weeks after starting the lower dose, she had an orgasm again. It wasn't like before

Prozac—it still took a lot of work and wasn't as spectacular as she re-membered—but at this point she was so relieved she didn't care. She stayed on this dose for a total of a year, without breakthrough depres-sion. After she stopped the Prozac entirely, her sexual enjoyment went back to what it had been.

You should never skip days or lower the dose of your antidepres-sant without medical supervision. If you do so, you may have with-drawal effects or breakthrough depression. If you and your doctor de-cide to lower your regular daily dose, you must watch carefully for signs of relapse, which might happen weeks or months later. It is not always possible to find that perfect balance of an effective antide-pressant dose and no sexual side effects. In other words, in order to remain in remission, some women will need to take a dose of med-ication that results in a persistent loss of sex drive or inability to have an orgasm. Fortunately, even these women don't have to choose be-tween feeling good emotionally and feeling good sexually.

"Drug Holidays": Regular Skipped Doses

Many women have a regular sexual partner with whom they make love once a week or less. If so, a so-called drug holiday may be a good choice. This involves skipping your medication for two to three days before planning intercourse (such as taking it Thursday morning, tar-geting Saturday night or Sunday morning for making love). Doing so has been shown to increase sexual satisfaction about half of the time. While this will not work for Prozac, it may work for Effexor, Luvox, Paxil, and Zoloft. If you choose this route, there is a small chance that you might experience withdrawal symptoms, usually toward the end of the drug holiday. These withdrawal symptoms might include feeling dizzy or woozy, shakiness, sleep changes, and moodiness, none of which are conducive to good sex. If something in between helps, such as skipping a single day's dose, terrific.

Changing Medications

If the previous suggestions are not effective or not clinically appro-priate, it may make sense to switch to a medication that is less likely to cause anorgasmia, such as a benzodiazepine for panic disorder, or

Wellbutrin or Serzone for depression. While it may not be the best first choice for all women with depression, either Wellbutrin or Serzone may be the perfect second choice for those women with persistent troublesome sexual side effects. Likewise, a benzodiazepine such as Xanax or Klonopin may be a perfect second choice for panic disorder in this situation.

Clinically it is much easier to switch from an antidepressant to an antianxiety medication such as Klonopin for panic disorder than it is to switch from one medication for depression to another. This is because benzodiazepines work right away, and overlapping medications during a transition is usually safe. Taking two antidepressants simultaneously, even for a transition period, requires the doctor to be much more experienced; probably only psychiatrists should oversee such treatment regimens. Certain antidepressants may interact together in potentially dangerous ways. Antidepressants are not necessarily interchangeable, so a highly effective drug should not be changed casually.

Aside from recommending Serzone or Wellbutrin, your doctor might also recommend switching to a tricyclic antidepressant for panic disorder or depression. Some examples are Elavil, Pamelor, Norpramin, Sinequon and Tofranil. These drugs are usually taken only once daily, at bedtime, and are less likely to cause anorgasmia than the newer serotonin-enhancing antidepressants. These may be an especially good choice if you are having both sexual difficulties and insomnia from the more serotonergic drug. A significant minority of women experience weight gain on these medications. (See Chapter 8.)

Comedicating for Sexual Side Effects

I take one other major approach in treating sexual side effects: I add a second medication to reverse the problem. Each patient has her own individual preference, but often I feel that adding another medication, especially specifically to restore the ability to climax, is most prudent. Some women are willing to invest the time and risk of relapse in order to switch to a new medication, because they strongly prefer to take just one drug. Unfortunately, adding a second drug is not as likely to reverse a generalized loss of sex drive, although often it's worth a try, especially since sex drive diminishes in the absence of orgasm. If low libido persists after adding another medication, switching drugs makes sense.

Several medications have been reported to reverse anorgasmia, but no systematic research has compared their effectiveness. Most of what is known is based on small case reports and trial and error. You may need to undergo a bit of trial and error yourself, as you and your doctor search for a medication that restores sexual functioning without causing a whole new set of side effects. The following table lists medications that might be used to reverse anorgasmia and their common side effects.

Planning to have sex is very uncomfortable for some women, especially women who are not married. Many of us were taught that sex outside of marriage is okay only if you don't actually mean to do it, if you can't help it because you got swept up in the moment. Taking a pill before a date just in case is a lot like remembering to pack a condom or your diaphragm. One of the reasons birth control pills are effective contraceptives is that you take them every day and don't have to confront the fact that you are considering making love with someone. Also, some couples do not want their sex lives to become routinized or mechanical, dread getting stuck making love on the schedule of a drug holiday, or are inhibited by whether you remembered to take that orgasm pill two hours ago. So while it may be preferable to take a medication to restore orgasm only when you need it (the diaphragm model), there are advantages of comedicating on a regular basis (the birth control pill model).

Taking all these factors into consideration, I usually prescribe 75 or 100 mg Wellbutrin taken every afternoon for women with sexual side effects from an SSRI. There is no definitive guideline here; we just don't have enough information. Anita Clayton, M.D., director of the Psychiatric Ambulatory Care service and an associate professor at the University of Virginia Health Sciences Center, is a researcher who studies sexuality. Dr. Clayton takes a different approach. She reports success using Symmetrel, preferably on a regular dose but occasionally just as needed. Alternatively she prescribes 5.4 mg Yocon one hour prior to intercourse. She tends to recommend Yocon for women who have the flexibility to make love in the morning, so that the insomnia problem is avoided.

DRUGS THAT MIGHT RESTORE ORGASM

Medication	How Administered	Side Effects
Buspar (buspirone)	5–10 mg 3 times daily	Nausea, stimulation (feeling hyper)
Periactin (cyproheptadine)	4–12 mg 1–2 hrs prior	Severe sedation, rarely increased depression, weight gain (daily use)
Symmetrel (amantadine)	100 mg once or twice daily or as needed	Usually mild or none
Urecholine (bethanecol)	30 mg 1–2 hrs prior	Dry mouth, fatigue, blurred vision, constipation
Wellbutrin (buproprion)	75–100 mg daily	Usually none; unsafe for anyone with epilepsy, bulimia, or alcoholism
Yocon (yohimbine)	5.4 mg 1–2 hrs prior	Flushing, anxiety, palpitations, insomnia

Note: Other coadministered drugs that have been reported to reverse sexual side effects include Cylert (pemoline), Dexedrine (dextroamphetamine), Ritalin (methylphenidate), and Prostigmine (neostigmine).

What If the Comedication Doesn't Work?

Because many of these medications act differently chemically, you may have to try more than one. Symmetrel, Buspar, and Wellbutrin affect the neurotransmitter dopamine. Periactin reverses serotonin. (In theory, this could diminish the antidepressant effect.) Yocon acts on the adrenergic system. Urecholine acts on the cholinergic system. If a particular comedication isn't effective, your doctor may recommend one with entirely different neurotransmitter effects.

CONCLUSION

Finally, you may have seen the widespread publicity about the few cases in which Prozac and Anafranil resulted in spontaneous orgasm while yawning. In my opinion, this is about as likely to happen to you as finding a winning lottery ticket slipped into your bottle of Paxil.

If you are looking for a sexual miracle, look within yourself and your relationship. Amazing things can happen when you communicate and when you make your needs known. One of my patients told me that after she became anorgasmic from taking Anafranil, her husband bought a how-to sex manual. The techniques restored her sexual responsiveness and then some. For this couple, Anafranil was the best thing that ever happened to their sex life.

Chapter 8

WILL PROZAC MAKE ME FAT OR UGLY?

Medication Side Effects That Might
Affect Your Physical Appearance

KEY POINTS

Medications for depression and anxiety may have an impact on physical appearance.
Potential negative body image issues that may be caused by antidepressants include:

Common
- Weight gain, increased appetite
- Weight loss, decreased appetite
- Dry mouth, possibly leading to dental cavities
- Tremor (shaking hands)

Less Common
- Hair loss, thinning, or breakage
- Easy sunburning, other skin changes
- Excessive perspiration
- Reduced exercise capacity

Angelica and I spoke about the possibility of weight gain during her very first appointment. Since she was suffering from dysthymic disorder, she would likely require an antidepressant for two or more years. Usually it doesn't make sense to discuss rare but annoying side effects in selecting a particular medication. It does make sense to think about common side effects when considering alternatives before you take the first dose, especially when long-term use is likely.

Angelica had never been on any kind of medication before, and I explained to her that we had three groups of effective antidepressants from which to choose: tricyclics, selective serotonin re-uptake inhibitors (SSRIs), and Wellbutrin (buproprion).

I ran over my list of pros and cons of each: Was it important for her to take medication only once a day (ruling out some of the SSRIs and Wellbutrin), would weight gain be a disaster for her (steering us away from the tricyclics), or would sexual side effects be her own worst-case scenario (leading us away from the SSRIs)? Angelica understood that none of these effects was certain to happen, but we both wanted to avoid something that would be especially problematic for her.

She had no trouble stating that weight gain would be a catastrophe: Now an average-weight woman, she had been very overweight as a teenager and couldn't bear the possibility of losing control of her eating. She wasn't concerned about taking Wellbutrin two or three times a day, and I prescribed that since it doesn't cause weight gain or interfere with sexual pleasure.

OBSTACLES TO CARE

The Culture of Thinness

Like it or not, we live in an appearance-obsessed culture, and things are getting worse. You may have seen the reports that both *Playboy* centerfolds and Barbie dolls have had progressively smaller waists since the 1950s. The gap between real women's bodies and those that adorn the magazines, dance through the MTV videos, or hawk toothpaste gets wider and wider. While numerous body image issues may arise during antidepressant treatment (usually antianxiety medications don't raise body image concerns), the potential for weight gain is the single most common concern expressed by my patients.

Women are bombarded with images of perfect beauty wherever we go. We are blasted with thinness as the foremost ideal: If you aren't less than normal weight, you don't fall into the pretty category no matter what. But it isn't just weight that preoccupies our socio-cultural airwaves. Who among us hasn't plunked down some serious cash in the hopes of having smoother skin, better hair, longer eyelashes, fuller lips, rosier cheeks, whiter teeth? I know I have!

Knowing how women both judge ourselves and are judged by others makes me very aware of how important potential side effects that are detrimental to body image are for women. I hate the fact that my patient and I have to discuss which is worse: depression or ten extra pounds. I hate the fact that I may have to stop a wonderfully effective medication because it's making my patient's hair thin. I hate the fact that I have to worry about whether the avid golfer in my practice will sunburn too easily or lose the competitive edge that defines her love of sports.

The feminist in me doesn't want to acknowledge my own deep understanding of how appearances matter to women. The feminist psychiatrist wants to be able to surgically remove that awful sinking feeling my patient has when she looks in the mirror. The physician doesn't want to violate the Hippocratic oath: First do no harm. Powerful medications, whether they are aspirin or Prozac (fluoxetine), always carry the potential for harmful or annoying side effects. The dance of weighing side effects against the benefits of a medication is partly why doctors can't be replaced by computers. Sometimes it's easy: Chemotherapy often has horrible side effects, but most doctors and patients agree that almost any short-term side effect is better than letting cancer spread.

Doctor-Patient Communication About Physical Appearance

Women and their doctors often don't reach consensus easily about body image issues, especially relatively minor weight gains. It may be due to poor communication: Many women are too embarrassed to admit how appearance concerns them to their doctors. Sometimes it feels too silly: A woman feels she is too mature, too accomplished, too educated, too rational, too politically correct to worry about five or ten extra pounds. Sometimes it feels too shameful: She doesn't want to seem shallow or self-obsessed. Sometimes it feels too far past the cultural norm of youth and beauty: Won't the doctor think it's ridiculous that a grandmother cares about being too thin? Won't the doctor think a 200-pound woman has no business worrying about an extra few pounds?

Doctor-patient communication is, of course, a two-way street. Women need to feel comfortable caring about how they look, but doctors also need to appreciate how great a concern this is for many women. If your doctor is not listening well to your concerns, either you need to talk louder or you need to find a new set of ears. Sometimes you have to shout to be heard: I am stopping this medication because I will not accept ugly scrawny hair as the price of feeling good. What are my alternatives?

Doctors may not be able to hear your concerns because of their own blind spots. Sometimes women tell me that male doctors don't take these concerns seriously.

> Javette told me that when she talked to her doctor about Tofranil (imipramine) causing her to gain weight, that she hated being a size 10 instead of a size 8, he laughed and told her she was acting like a teenager. Needless to say, Javette never brought it up again. In fact, she stopped the medication on her own, didn't talk to her doctor about it, and was pleased when she dropped back down to her usual size 8. Unfortunately, she had been taking Tofranil only for three months, and she relapsed within six weeks.
>
> She decided to see a woman instead. Her first words to me: Fix this but don't make me fat again. Javette had no problem expressing her wishes, but she hadn't been taken seriously by her doctor.

Don't be too quick to decide that all female doctors are sensitive to body image issues and no male doctors are. Good doctor-patient communication has much more to do with the individual doctor's ability to put him- or herself in your shoes, to make your concerns about side effects his or her concerns too. In fact, some women have told me that they have had many more problems discussing these issues with female doctors than with males.

Some of the difficulties that female patients have talking about their appearance with female doctors or nurse practitioners has to do with the discomfort women have comparing their looks with one another. I have an absolutely gorgeous, size-4-on-a-bad-day actress in my practice who gained eight pounds while taking a middle-range dosage of Sinequon (doxepin) for agoraphobia. The medicine worked great for her, but she was absolutely unwilling to be, in her words, "fat." She and I both know that in my wildest dreams, I've never been and never will be a size 4, yet I cannot approach her concerns from a place of envy, or even "don't you know that thousands of women would kill to be as 'fat' as a size 6?" When she looks in the mirror, the only eyes she is using are her own, and she has an absolute right to be satisfied with what she sees.

Other women may feel that a woman who has never struggled with weight gain doesn't understand the horrible feeling of being out of control of one's eating. A female doctor who never misses her aerobics class and always leaves half of her slice of cheesecake on her plate may not be able to identify with your struggle. She may not comprehend why you can't just run a few miles every day or stop buying Oreos. However, you should be wary of the possibility of projecting your own shame on the doctor: Does she really think you are a lazy slug, or is that the harsh message you give yourself about your weight?

Good communication about the body image side effects of antidepressants is not gender based. It's empathy based. I'll say it again: You are entitled to be taken seriously, whatever your concerns are. There is no shortage of caring doctors and nurses, but you are the only one who can find a better match for yourself. As is true for other side effects, often it is not simply a matter of having to choose between a side effect that you hate and feeling like yourself again.

Look at the Big Picture

If you are having intolerable body image side effects, take another look at the treatment approach. For starters, you and your doctor should have already discussed how long you need to take the medication. If your doctor believes that you are a good candidate to go off the medication after a few more months, you may be willing to accept increased or decreased weight, knowing that you will most likely return to your pretreatment weight after the medicine is stopped. In any case, you should discuss your concerns with your doctor. You are the only one who can decide whether the side effects are unendurable, but she can advise you about what your risk of relapse might be, what other alternatives are available, and whether you may simply be exchanging one bothersome side effect for another.

If your doctor thinks that you should stay on the medication, it is well worth reconsidering whether a specialized form of talk therapy (which by definition doesn't alter your appearance) would be as effective as medication or might help you get by with less medication or get off it more quickly. For example, interpersonal or cognitive psychotherapy may be as effective as antidepressants for mild to moderate clinical depression. Likewise, behavioral therapy for obsessive compulsive disorder may be as helpful as Anafranil (clomipramine) without the appetite changes. However, do not stop your medication without talking with your doctor.

If staying on medication is the most sensible thing to do, you may be relieved to know that there are many options. Read on.

WEIGHT GAIN

By far, the tricyclic antidepressants are the most common cause of weight gain, usually with appetite increases or specific cravings for sweets, starchy foods, or high-fat foods such as ice cream. This is not an inevitable problem with tricyclic antidepressants, but in my practice, it is by far the most likely reason my patients do not tolerate these medications. This side effect seems to happen in the same way that sexual problems from the serotonin re-uptake inhibitors do: The rich get richer and the poor stay poor. Women who have really fought the weight battle, who have weighed at the upper limits of normal body weight or more all their lives, are more likely to have this side effect. It's not an absolute: Sometimes women who have always been able to eat anything they want and not gain an ounce get this side effect too. I warn all my patients about it, but I worry most about women who gain weight just by smelling brownies. Weight gain also may be a sign of an underactive thyroid gland.

Weight gain from a tricyclic definitely depends on the dose taken. At low doses, it virtually never happens. Depending on the individual woman, it starts to be a problem at tricyclic doses in the range of 40 to 50 mg Pamelor (nortriptyline) or 75 to 100 mg Tofranil (or roughly equivalent doses of other tricyclics; see p. 274). Usually it happens rather quickly on reaching a particular dose, yet if it wasn't a problem early in treatment, it doesn't seem to be something that will occur after months or years.

While most of my patients who have this side effect tell me that the worst thing is that they can't seem to stop eating junk food, some patients have sworn that they are gaining weight but not eating more.

Others tell me that they are exercising religiously but still gaining weight. I believe them all.

The reason I believe them is because this effect seems to be due to an adjustment of the brain's set point, its thermostat for what you should weigh. Variations in weight appear to be due to an inherited brain-mediated mechanism by which metabolic rates and appetite are regulated. Currently we believe that being markedly overweight or very thin is not due to inferior or superior willpower but to this set point for weight. It's why those last few pounds are the hardest to lose (the body fights back by slowing metabolism, making fewer calories "worth" more) and why so many people gain most of their weight back after dieting. Tricyclic antidepressants adjust the set point upward, telling your body to weigh more. This may result in increased appetite, cravings for high-calorie foods, modest weight gain despite maintaining your total calorie intake, or becoming less sensitive to the effects of exercise on weight.

Before discontinuing an effective tricyclic due to weight gain, I usually advise patients to get a simple blood test to measure the amount of medication they have in their system, which reflects how they uniquely metabolize the drug. If the level is high or high normal, lowering the dosage may curtail their appetite or weight gain without reducing its effectiveness.

Some side effects go away over time, but I haven't found that the weight comes off by itself unless the medication dose is lowered or stopped (unless exercise helps). This makes a wait-and-see approach problematic. The weight gain may plateau at five or ten pounds, a price that may seem well worth it. But no one is willing to gain five pounds a month and weigh sixty pounds more by the end of a year. For women who seem to have stabilized with a modest, acceptable weight gain, I check the blood level and advise a wait-and-see approach if the medication is working well otherwise.

Why Even Consider Taking a Tricyclic?

Even with the risk of weight gain, in many situations I feel that a tricyclic antidepressant is the best choice. Since weight gain is not inevitable, certain clinical situations make it more sensible to try the medication and switch only if my patient gains an unacceptable amount of weight (or has any other intolerable side effect).

For starters, I often prefer tricyclics for panic disorder and agoraphobia, since the low doses used generally do not cause any problems with weight or appetite changes. Women with anxiety disorders typically respond to much lower doses of tricyclics than do women with depression, so the issue of weight gain never comes up.

Sometimes my patient and I are desperate for her to gain weight. While many women experience cravings for chocolate while depressed or premenstrual, a significant minority of women lose weight due to clinical depression or anxiety. A healthy diet is critical to recovering from depression and anxiety, and a medication that increases appetite often improves nutrition while restoring a healthy weight. This is especially a concern in pregnant or postpartum women, some of whom come to me in such dire straits that they actually weigh less than they did before conceiving. It also may be true for a woman with breast or another type of cancer who has lost weight due to the illness and/or the effects of chemotherapy.

Low doses of tricyclics are also prescribed for augmentation, to squeeze more effect out of a previously prescribed antidepressant, usually an SSRI. (See p. 280.) A sedating tricyclic (such as Elavil [amitriptyline]) may be prescribed along with an SSRI in order to counteract insomnia. In both situations, doses of 10 to 25 mg are common; such amounts are extremely unlikely to cause weight gain.

But occasionally the situation does come down to solving depression or maintaining a comfortable weight. One of my patients suffers from very severe depression. She responded only partially to an SSRI, and we were able to get her depression in remission only after using a tricyclic antidepressant. Until she reached a dose of a tricyclic that caused weight gain, she continued to have crippling despair and hopelessness, with thoughts of suicide. She gained enough weight that her jeans weren't comfortable anymore, and she usually had to buy one size up. We tried lowering her dose by a small amount, and symptoms broke through quickly. Her weight gain did stabilize after about ten pounds, and she decided that feeling good was worth the price. She also described a common phenomenon: While depressed, she absolutely hated how she looked at even five pounds more. When her depression lifted, her self-esteem improved in many ways, and although she didn't like the extra weight, she no longer hated herself for it.

Do Other Kinds of Antidepressants Cause Weight Gain?

Wellbutrin* generally doesn't affect weight either way (a very small number of women lose weight on it), but as I'll discuss next, SSRIs quite often cause weight loss. However, scattered recent case reports suggest that a tiny number of individuals paradoxically gain weight on SSRIs. I can count on one hand the number of my own patients who have experienced this. Unlike the situation with tricyclics, where weight gain happens early on, this seems to be a delayed side effect, emerging after months or years. Since many women do not need to stay on an antidepressant for years, this is a doubly rare side effect. Some clinicians report that changing from one SSRI to another works (as I've seen in my own practice), while others raise the dose (the opposite of what works for a tricyclic) in order to counteract SSRI weight gain.

Finally, a word of caution about combining antidepressants with new weight-loss medications, Redux (dexfenfluramine) and Pondimin (fenfluvamine) plus Fastin (phenteramine).† These medications may interact in dangerous ways and result in an extremely serious condition called the serotonin syndrome. (See p. 119.) Dr. Bonnie Spring, professor of psychology at Chicago Medical School, notes that some women are embarrassed to tell their weight loss doctors that they are taking antidepressants or, conversely, reluctant to tell their psychiatrists that they are taking weight-loss medications. Don't let this happen to you. Grapefruit juice can increase the amount of SSRI in your system, so avoid a crash grapefruit diet when taking these medications.

WEIGHT LOSS

SSRIs may cause a number of welcome effects on eating and appetite. They may reduce your appetite, lead to weight loss, reduce compulsive eating binges, and reduce cravings for high calorie foods.

---

* Wellbutrin is potentially dangerous in women with active eating disorders (bulimia or anorexia) because these conditions may increase the risk of a drug-induced seizure.
† Called "phen-fen" by many clinicians.

Some doctors avoid these drugs in women who have lost a lot of weight due to their illness, although treating the underlying depression or anxiety disorder often restores a more normal appetite. The weight loss is usually temporary, reversed within six or nine months and upon stopping the medication.

Fortunately, if you always weighed 135 pounds until you got depressed and started eating all the chocolate chip cookies and ice cream you bought for your kids, and you gained twelve pounds, you probably will lose that weight relatively easily if you take an SSRI and will likely stay at your usual weight after you stop it.

While many of us would give anything to take off a few pounds easily, some women do not tolerate even small amounts of weight loss. People can, indeed, be too thin. Proper nutrition is important for many reasons, including emotional balance. A few of my patients feel very unattractive if their weight drops, especially because they feel like their bodies look like boys' bodies rather than women's. Weight loss can flatten your breasts or thin your hips and bottom to an unacceptable degree. This may be more of a problem for midlife to older women, who have suffered loss of breast tone due to child-bearing or aging, yet they may feel socially prohibited from talking about their appearance since we equate youth with beauty. In gen-

ALTERNATIVES FOR WEIGHT LOSS

Reduce the dose of the SSRI.

Switch to a tricyclic antidepressant.

Add a low dose of a tricyclic to stimulate appetite.

Add Periactin (cyproheptadine) to stimulate appetite (which may also reverse sexual dysfunction as an added benefit).

Supplement your diet with body-building products (such as Sustacal, Ensure, or products available at many pharmacies or health food stores).

Add fat and calories: Use real butter, stop buying "light" or low-fat products, drink milkshakes made from whole milk and regular ice cream, try to have two candy bars a day.

Wear a padded or Wonder bra if that's where being thin is most bothersome.

eral, due to concerns about cardiac side effects from tricyclic antidepressants, most doctors recommend an SSRI for women over forty
and are especially inclined to use these preferentially in women over
sixty-five. Regardless of your age, you are entitled to do whatever you
can do to be able to smile at what you see in the mirror and to be as
obsessed as any woman about your looks until the day you die! The
box on page 171 presents some medical and nonmedical options if
weight loss occurs.

TREMOR

I include tremor as a body image concern because women often experience it as embarrassing, a source of unwanted attention, or a sign
of aging. Your hands may shake from any of the three types of antidepressants: SSRIs, tricyclics, and Wellbutrin. Tremor often is a tran-
sitory phenomenon, disappearing or at least improving within a
month or two of starting the medication. If you can stand to wait it
out, the shakiness may become tolerable.

Certain conditions increase the likelihood that you will have a
tremor from an antidepressant. These include a condition called benign familial tremor (shakiness that runs in the family), underlying
medical or neurologic disorders such as Parkinson's disease, comedication with drugs that also cause tremor (especially lithium and antipsychotic medications), some antihistamines, and high caffeine
consumption.

If you have an intolerable tremor, you may be able to switch medications (even within a particular category, such as switching from
Paxil (paroxetine) to Zoloft (sertraline), or Elavil to Pamelor), can
talk with your doctor about taking a lower dose, or can comedicate
the tremor with Inderal (propranolol, usually 10 mg two or three
times per day) to reverse the tremor. At the low doses used for tremor,
Inderal usually does not cause side effects. However, women with
asthma and certain cardiovascular conditions, including low blood
pressure, cannot take Inderal, and it may reduce the ability to exercise aggressively. All tremors should be evaluated by a doctor.

HAIR LOSS

Hair loss is a very difficult problem to evaluate, but occasionally it can be caused by antidepressants (as well as lithium and mood stabilizers). Fortunately, the hair loss caused by medication is almost always reversible upon stopping the drug. One reason that hair loss is hard to evaluate is that we all lose hair on a daily basis, and just by worrying about it, it's easy to look at the same number of hairs in the shower drain that have always been there but agonize over whether there are more today. Reports of drug-induced hair loss are very much more common in women, although it's not clear whether it actually is more common in them or is perhaps underreported by men who don't recognize it as a possible side effect.

If you are concerned about possible hair loss, you can do an actual count. Brush your hair before and after a shower and several times during the day. Count the hairs. Loss (actually, technically the hairs are broken, not lost) of 100 or more hairs per day should be evaluated medically. Dermatologists often have special expertise in this condition. I also recommend an evaluation if someone else (such as your hairdresser) notices that your hair is thinning or if the hair loss is patchy or causes any bald spot.

Case reports indicate that mineral supplementation with zinc, selenium, or magnesium can reverse drug-induced hair loss, so it may be worth trying, with a follow-up hair count a month later. If you have rapid hair loss, consult a doctor soon. Hair changes also may warn of an undiagnosed thyroid condition.

Hair loss is a funny type of condition: It can happen due to a wide variety of causes, and the antidepressant may be a red herring. Even stress can cause it, and many women experience significant hair loss after childbirth. In some cases, I refer a patient to a dermatologist before changing medications. Other times switching to a different medication may be helpful, because the hair loss usually is idiosyncratic to a particular drug, not usually a sign of sensitivity to a class of medications. Sometimes the only way to know for sure whether the medication is causing hair loss is to stop taking it.

SKIN CHANGES

Most women taking medications for depression and anxiety have no rashes or skin changes of any sort. Among those who do have a problem, easy sensitivity to sunburn is perhaps the most common skin change. (This is known as photosensitivity.) Sunscreen (SPF 15 or higher), wearing a hat, and staying out of the direct sunlight usually will be enough to protect you. Of course, these are prudent measures for any woman, since they prevent the damaging effects of the sun and will slow down skin aging. Many over-the-counter moisturizers that contain sunscreen are now available. Keep in mind that photosensitivity may be a year-round phenomenon, equally problematic in the winter while skiing or playing in the snow. Women of color are not immune to photosensitivity. If you are brown-skinned and develop your first sunburn ever in your life, I would be especially suspicious of the antidepressant.

New prescription wrinkle removers or antiacne creams and lotions may increase the likelihood of sunburning. Always wear sunscreen, year round, if you are taking an antidepressant and Retin-A or using glycolic acids.

A skin rash that is itchy or has hives should be reported to your doctor immediately, since it may indicate an allergy to the medication itself or to the inactive ingredients (such as the dye on the pill coating). Rashes occur in 4 percent of women who take Prozac, but they can happen with any of the antidepressants or antianxiety medications. Allergic skin reactions should not be ignored or self-treated with antihistamines, because they can progress to more serious or even life-threatening allergic reactions. Your doctor may advise you to take an antihistamine once you stop the medication until the rash resolves. Usually an allergic skin reaction to a particular medication does not mean that you cannot take another drug with a similar action. For example, almost everyone who has a rash while taking Prozac can successfully switch to Effexor (venlafaxine), Paxil, Serzone (nefazodone), or Zoloft.

EXCESSIVE PERSPIRATION

Each antidepressant can cause excessive sweating, usually but not always only at night. It may be quite severe, literally soaking your bed sheets, or it may be mild. This may be extremely annoying, or it may be downright embarrassing in certain romantic or social encounters. Excessive perspiration may improve with a lowered dose, may be comedicated with Catapres (clonidine) or Hytrin (terazosin), or may be a cause for switching or stopping a medication.

DRY MOUTH OR DENTAL CAVITIES

Tricyclic antidepressants often cause dry mouth, through the same chemical mechanism that cold or allergy medications such as Benadryl or Contac do (called anticholinergic side effects). Dry mouth is much less common with the SSRIs, but it can happen.

An extremely dry mouth may affect your speech slightly. Usually it is not noticeable to anyone but you and your doctor, but if it is so severe that it is embarrassing, you may be able to reverse it fairly easily as described below. Besides altering how you talk slightly, severe chronic dry mouth may affect your dental health, which itself can adversely affect your appearance in the long run.

The biggest concern of chronic dry mouth is the fact that saliva serves a very useful purpose: It helps prevent cavities. A recent study indicated that people who take tricyclic antidepressants over a long period have more cavities.

Simply drinking nonsugary fluids often helps dramatically. Nowadays, carrying a bottle of water everywhere is common. Sugarless sour candy or sugarless gum will stimulate your natural saliva, and, if the candy contains sorbitol, it may have the added benefit of serving as a mild laxative. (Most women who have dry mouth also have constipation because these are both anticholinergic side effects.) I used to advise sucking on a small sliver of lemon, but regular exposure to its acidity may erode dental enamel.

Jill Baskin, a dentist from North Riverside, Illinois, believes that anyone with dry mouth due to antidepressant medication should use an over-the-counter fluoride rinse daily. Besides drinking extra fluids,

Dr. Baskin notes that there are also "saliva substitutes" that lubricate your mouth if you are having difficulty speaking or swallowing. Saliva substitutes—flavored rinses or sprays for rehydrating your mouth— may sound unappealing, but they are not someone else's spit! Some are available over the counter; others are available only by prescription from your doctor or dentist.

Another option, usually a last but typically effective choice, is comedication with a pilocarpine mouth wash or with Urecholine (bethanechol, (usually 5–10 mg twice or three times daily). Urecholine may kill two birds with one stone: It is also used to reverse sexual side effects.

Women who wear removable dental prostheses (dentures, partials, or orthodontic retainers) may find dry mouth debilitating. New sore spots may arise as a result. To alleviate the problem, Dr. Baskin again emphasizes the need to drink nonsugary fluids and use a saliva substitute while eating. Most important, she advises removing the dental prosthesis at night. Then your mouth gets a "rest" while you soak your appliance. Dr. Baskin reports that some women cannot sleep well without the prostheses; if you absolutely must sleep with yours, she advises removing it for a couple hours each day. If the sores persist, make an appointment to see your dentist.

REDUCED EXERCISE CAPACITY

On occasion, a particularly passionate exerciser (runner, dancer, aerobics teacher, etc.) finds that an SSRI takes the edge off her drive. For some women, this loss of drive may show up in other areas: being less aggressive at work or suddenly being satisfied with an A minus when you always had to have the top grade in the class. Very serious athletes (I don't mean exercise addicts, or eating disordered women who work out three hours a day in order to stay at ninety pounds) may find that they lose a little of the extra push that keeps them at the peak. You may be perfectly willing to trade this for feeling like yourself in other ways. If not, you may find that a lower dose or a switch to another medication is helpful.

Inderal may have been prescribed for a tremor caused by an antidepressant. Occasionally even small doses of Inderal cause my patients to feel reduced capacity to exercise, even those who run a mile or two or the equivalent level of exercise. Inderal may reduce your maximum cardiac output by blocking your ability to reach your target heart rate.

CONCLUSION

One of the messages that didn't get conveyed in the Prozac-is-great-let's-put-it-in-the-drinking-water craze is the reality that while antidepressants are well tolerated, they are far from perfect. They are not vitamins or placebos without side effects. Antianxiety medications have their own set of side effects, but they rarely affect how you feel about your body and do not change your appetite or appearance.

Sometimes these body image side effects aren't a big deal to you, but what bothers you is that someone notices and asks about it, and you don't want to say "it's my antidepressant making me shaky/thirsty/ravenously hungry." It's okay to want to keep this private—by taking an antidepressant, you did not automatically sign on to the campaign to reduce the stigma of mental illness. Of course, you may feel perfectly comfortable acknowledging side effects from an antidepressant.

If not, you will respond more comfortably and assertively if you are prepared for intrusive questions. You might be pointedly vague and nonresponsive: "Thanks for your concern, it's nothing serious." If necessary, repeat the exact same words if asked again until your intention not to answer is quite clear. Make a joke, or you might even tell a little white lie: "I'm just getting used to a new blood pressure medication." Be ready, whatever style is most comfortable for you.

Doctors and nurses tend to focus on dangerous side effects, even if they are quite rare, and easily overlook those that aren't risky to your health. Individuals taking medicine usually worry far less about theoretical concerns than things that are bothering them right now. Then sometimes we caregivers can't figure out why our patients aren't "following our orders," and patients can't figure out why their doctors aren't listening.

You must feel free to raise whatever concerns you have with your doctor, even if you feel ridiculous talking about body image issues. Believe me, thousands upon thousands of women share your concerns. Stopping your medication, especially without telling your doctor, is rarely the best decision, since many alternatives are available.

Chapter 9

IS THIS HORMONAL?

How Reproductive Hormones and Menstruation
Affect Prescriptions for Depression and Anxiety

KEY POINTS

- Natural metabolic variation due to menstrual cycling may cause changes in medication levels that appear to be due to hormone shifts.
- Medications for depression and anxiety may affect your menstrual periods, including sometimes helping cramps, or may cause hormone imbalances.
- Birth control pills may interact with medications for depression and anxiety.
- Progesterone may interfere with treatment of depression, so it is wise to avoid long-acting contraceptive hormones until you are sure that you tolerate them.
- Hormonal therapy for reproductive cancers may precipitate mood or anxiety disorders, as can any sudden hormone change.

Although data are limited, it is clear that some women are very sensitive to changes in their reproductive physiology.

When Helen went through a series of reproductive changes, her doctor wondered if she was suffering from "PMS."

At forty-two, Helen suffered an episode of clinical depression after she had her third miscarriage in five years. This one seemed to hit hardest, because it looked like eight-year-old Carter was the only child she and Dave would have. She had promised herself that this would absolutely be the last time she put herself through this; she simply could not bear the idea of another attempt at pregnancy.

Still, it took her by surprise when the heartache lingered on and on. When six months went by and she still felt like the miscarriage had happened yesterday, she asked her obstetrician gynecologist for advice. He said that she had something along the lines of postpartum depression and he prescribed Zoloft (sertraline), 50 mg per day.

Helen started sleeping better right away, and the anxiety lifted quickly. After three weeks, she started to feel much less depressed, and she thought she was out of the woods with this thing. But she crashed again a few days before her period and didn't feel better until it was almost over. Then it lifted again.

When the same thing happened the next month, Helen went in to see her doctor again. She reminded him that her cycles had gotten a bit irregular even before the last pregnancy. He thought that she might have "PMS," so he recommended natural progesterone tablets. She started taking the progesterone ten days before her period started, and this time she felt much *worse*.

Helen's doctor talked to a psychiatrist colleague he ran into at the hospital. The psychiatrist suggested that Helen's doctor prescribe a higher dose of Zoloft, explaining that 50 mg is on the low end. The psychiatrist encouraged the gynecologist to have Helen make an appointment to see him if this didn't do the trick.

The dose adjustment took care of the menstrual worsening, but it left Helen and her doctor puzzled. They both had a sense that the problem was "hormonal," yet the solution was not hormones. "Write this off to one of those things," her doctor advised. "Let's just be glad you feel like yourself again."

Not a week goes by that I am not asked about hormones and medications for depression and anxiety. Minh wants to know whether it's okay to take birth control pills, and Joan wonders whether the pill is what's making her anxious. Patricia has premenstrual depression, and she wants to jump start hormone replacement therapy because it feels like early menopause to her, even though her gynecologist said her blood tests were normal. Naomi has noticed that she gets hypomanic just before her period each month, and her doctor wants her to ask me whether Depo-Provera shots (a hormone used for contraception) would regulate her mood cycling.

OBSTACLES TO CARE

The major obstacle to care is the near absence of data. These are challenging clinical problems, with more questions than answers. What a surprise: Significant women's medical issues have been woefully neglected. With little systemic research, complex pharmacologic decisions about the possible benefits and/or the possible negative effects of reproductive hormones may be based on one or two published case studies. Since there are so many things we don't know about the powerful effects of hormones, I often discourage my patients from becoming medical guinea pigs until we get more information.

In the absence of information, many people are like Helen and her doctor, convinced that hormones are part of the problem but unable to do more than scratch the surface. Helen was lucky: When her doctor couldn't diagnose the exact nature of the hormone problem, at least he didn't tell her "nothing is wrong." He told her bluntly that we don't have the ability to pinpoint the hormonal nature of the problem.

MENSTRUATION AND MEDICATION

Menstruation May Affect Your Medication

The most likely cause of Helen's inconsistent response to the initial dose of medication is that she cleared the antidepressant from her system more rapidly during the last phase of her menstrual cycle. Clinically meaningful menstrual cycle changes affecting medication levels are unusual but not unheard of. The only way to sort out who is sensitive to menstrual cycling is to notice symptoms and side effects across one or more cycles and to get multiple blood tests when there seems to be a suspicious pattern.

Where you are in your menstrual cycle may affect how much medication you have in your system at a particular dosage. This can translate into clinical worsening when the amount of medication present in the bloodstream drops before your period or to problematic side effects when the level goes up after your period. Premenstrual drops in drug levels may result in premenstrual worsening of bipolar disorder (either hypomania or depression), increased vulnerability to panic attacks, or worsening depression. Even less commonly, a small number of women deteriorate for a day or two just at the time of ovulation.

If you have a mood or anxiety disorder but have repeated mini-crashes just before your period, you will almost certainly believe that you have "PMS," or premenstrual exacerbation, as Helen did. This cycling pattern of premenstrual worsening may also fool your doctor into thinking that "PMS" is the problem. However, instead you may have an easily correctable problem: menstrual cycle fluctuation in the amount of medication in your bloodstream.

How Does Menstruation Affect Medication Levels?

Many factors that affect a woman's drug level may vary across the menstrual cycle. Cyclic changes in stomach acidity may affect how much of the drug is absorbed at different points in the cycle, causing less medication to be transferred from the stomach to the bloodstream, where it is delivered to the brain. Because a woman's blood level of a medication depends on how much fluid she has in her system, premenstrual water retention may cause a drop in drug levels: Literally, the same dose is being dissolved in a larger amount of fluid. Also, many medications are carried in the blood by proteins, which vary across the menstrual cycle. Ovarian hormones also may influence how the kidneys and liver clear the medication from the bloodstream.

These factors may converge to lower the amount of medication that your brain "sees" during the premenstrual phase of your cycle. While these menstrual cycle fluctuations have not been studied systemically, there are many case reports of women with well-documented significant cyclic drops in their medication. This has been observed for lithium, tricyclic antidepressants, and serotonin reuptake inhibitors. Thus, most major medications used for depression or anxiety have the potential to fluctuate during your cycle.

When I suspect that this may be a problem in a patient, I may recommend a preovulation and premenstrual blood level. In this comparison, it is absolutely crucial to make the conditions on both days as similar as possible. Time everything as close to each other as you can: Take the test the same number of hours after your last dose, take it at the same time of day, eat breakfast the same time both days, and so on. The response is usually straightforward: When there is a premenstrual drop in your medication level, you probably need more medication during the last two weeks of your cycle.

Such a premenstrual drop in a drug level can masquerade as "PMS." But if the problem is not a premenstrual drop but a postmenstrual increase in drug levels, you may notice a problem that is equally difficult to detect: more pronounced side effects early in your cycle. If you have higher blood levels during the follicular phase (preovulatory phase, roughly days 1 through 14) than the luteal phase (between ovulation and the first day of your period), you may experience fluctuating side effects. This can be puzzling, since a menstrual cycle effect isn't usually suspected.

Women who sometimes have difficult side effects but other times tolerate the medication just fine should chart side effects for a month or two. If a cyclic pattern can be seen (for example, side effects build up on days 5 to 11, then they level out, dropping off beginning on day 20 of a twenty-nine-day cycle), the next step to confirm the diagnosis is to obtain blood tests during the two phases of the cycle. Assuming good response to medication, your doctor may recommend lowering the dose during the two weeks prior to ovulation.

Unfortunately, little is known about menstrual cycle effects on antianxiety medications, including benzodiazepines and Buspar (buspirone). Ordinary blood tests cannot test for these medications. In the absence of documentation, your doctor may recommend adjusting your medication across your menstrual cycle based on clinical judgment alone. Do not make any adjustments in your medication without consulting your personal physician.

Medications May Affect Your Period

Antidepressants occasionally alter the menstrual cycle. The most common effect is welcome: A few women report that the antidepressant reduces or even eliminates menstrual cramps. Antidepressants affect how the brain perceives pain (indeed, they are used clinically for chronic pain syndromes and migraines), so this isn't too surprising.

Rarely, SSRIs unmask a tendency to easy bleeding. If you develop heavy menstrual flow along with easy bruising or nose bleeds, notify your doctor.

If I Have Cramps Anyway, Is It Okay to Take Something?

The most effective medications for relief of menstrual cramps are called nonsteroidal anti-inflammatory agents. These include prescription and over-the-counter medications such as Advil or Motrin (ibuprofen), Aleve or Naprosyn (naproxen), and Orudis (ketoprofen). These medications are also called antiprostaglandins. Medications for menstrual cramps are generally compatible with psychiatric medication with one major exception: lithium. These medications may cause lithium levels to rise, which may increase side effects and even be dangerous. If you take lithium, be sure to check with your doctor or pharmacist about possible drug interactions with any medication for cramps. Certain water pills (diuretics such as hydrochlorothiazide), which may be given for premenstrual fluid retention, also may increase lithium levels and can be dangerous if not monitored closely.

Are There Other Effects on My Cycle?

Very infrequently, a patient will report that her period is lighter or heavier in flow. One study indicated that Prozac (fluoxetine) may slightly lengthen the time between periods, but this has not been replicated and is unlikely to make a difference in how you feel.

Could Medication Make Me Miss My Period?

Menstruating women who stop having periods have a condition called secondary amenorrhea. **The single most common reason why women taking medicine for depression and anxiety disorders miss a period is that they are pregnant.** Do not assume that you are not pregnant just because you are using birth control. Do not assume that you've missed a period because of the medication itself. Take a home pregnancy test or go to your doctor. Positive home pregnancy tests are usually reliable; however, if done incorrectly or too early in the pregnancy, they may register negative. Unexpected pregnancy is discussed in Chapter 10.

Rarely, antidepressants cause you to stop having periods because they cause a pituitary hormone called prolactin to rise. Prolactin then suppresses ovulation and menstruation (as in breast-feeding). It also may cause you to have a thin discharge from your nipples. Prolactin is the breast-feeding hormone, and when it is elevated, you get the changes that nursing women get: milk production, cessation of periods, and even infertility. Very rarely, prolactin is elevated due to SSRIs. (There are just a few case reports here and there.) More commonly, medications used for bipolar disorder (especially mania) cause this elevated prolactin; these include Haldol (haloperidol), Risperdal (risperidone), and Navane (thiothixene). Be sure to tell your doctor about any nipple discharge, because proper diagnosis is essential. Be sure to tell your doctor if you haven't had a period within three months, because you probably should take medication to induce one so that the endometrium (uterine lining) remains healthy. Prolactin levels can be measured in an ordinary laboratory test.

Depakote (valproic acid) is a mood stabilizer that may increase male hormones, a condition called hyperandrogenism. The condition may result in secondary amenorrhea (loss of periods), infertility, and masculinization (especially facial hair). If you develop any of these symptoms while taking Depakote, be sure to talk to your doctor.

WOULD HORMONES MAKE ME FEEL BETTER?

Postponement of pregnancy puts many women in between two powerful hormonal transitions: pregnancy hormone shifts *and* premenopause. It is common to wonder whether hormones would help.

Helen thought she might need hormones to feel better. Although she obviously wasn't menopausal, her periods had begun to change, so she knew her ovaries were different now that she was in her forties. She wondered if her hormones had already begun changing, even before the sudden hormonal drops caused by the miscarriage. She wondered if that was why the miscarriage hit her so hard.

Reproductive hormones may be part of the answer for some women; for others, they may be part of the problem. Helen, for example, felt much worse taking progesterone. However, she might have felt better taking a combination birth control pill that included estrogen. (See p. 258.)

A Warning About Progesterone

Progesterone is widely prescribed for "PMS" because the myth that it has emotional benefits still lingers. There is no scientific rationale for this, since progesterone has not been shown to be more effective than placebo. Question your doctor closely if she recommends progesterone for psychiatric purposes. While it may help a rare individual by suppressing ovulation and regulating menstrual cycles, it may make depression worse, or be an expensive placebo.

Preliminary Information About the Benefits of Estrogen

Eventually estrogen may play a significant role in the treatment of mood disorders, but the jury is still out. Recently estrogen has been shown to enhance cognitive activity and brain blood flow in post-menopausal women. Specifically, hormone replacement therapy may provide a protective effect against Alzheimer's disease. Whether a beneficial effect on cognition has any possible link to mood is completely unknown, but I expect that these findings will stimulate research into the effect of hormone replacement therapy on antidepressants.

Another related finding is one recent study indicating that estrogen skin patches were therapeutic for postpartum depression. (See p. 244.) This is intriguing, since the depressions that occur after miscarriage and close to menopause may be hormonally similar to postpartum depression.

Hormones for Abrupt Menopause

Women who have experienced an abrupt change in ovarian functioning and who suddenly develop emotional symptoms are most likely to benefit from prescribed hormones.

Sierra had a hysterectomy for uterine fibroids. Since she was only thirty-six, her doctor did not remove her ovaries, explaining that this would keep her from going through menopause so young. However, within a month of the surgery, Sierra felt terrible. She couldn't sleep, she cried over every little thing, and she was irritable and jumpy.

Her doctor told her that the problem couldn't be hormonal, because her ovaries were still working fine. She kept after him for a blood test, because her instincts were screaming that something hormonal was going on. Finally the doctor ordered a blood test for estrogen. Sierra was right: She had gone through an abrupt menopause. In retrospect, although the ovaries were left in, their blood supply had been accidentally interrupted as a result of surgery, and Sierra had gone through menopause overnight. The doctor put her on hormone replacement therapy immediately, and she felt like herself within weeks, without an antidepressant.

HOW DO BIRTH CONTROL PILLS AFFECT MY TREATMENT?

Chances are your doctor knows little about the interaction between birth control pills and medications for depression and anxiety. Don't blame her: Flip through a textbook on psychopharmacology and you will see how little attention this topic receives. Further clouding the picture, not only are antidepressants relatively new, but oral contraceptives also have changed quite a bit from a decade ago. Scientific reports on interactions between antidepressants from ten or fifteen years ago may not be relevant to current oral contraceptives, because much lower doses are used nowadays.

Most women taking birth control pills take medications that contain estrogen and progestin (progestin is the name for synthetic progesterone, the most common way progesterone is administered). The name of the pill may reflect the lower dose (Lo-Ovral, for example), but your doctor can tell you what type you are taking. These combination pills may contain a constant dose, or the amount of estrogen or progestin may fluctuate across the cycle. (Usually these types have the word "tri" in their names, or they have a series of numbers, such as "7/7/7" or "10/11.") Women who cannot take estrogen may be able to take the so-called minipill, which contains a constant amount of progestin taken throughout the entire cycle. If you are receiving your birth control pills from one doctor and your antidepressants from another, be sure that each knows about the other prescription.

Perhaps the most important problem to worry about is whether the medication for depression or anxiety might make the birth control pill less effective, resulting in unintended pregnancy. Especially with low-dose oral contraceptives, even a small decrease in the amount of contraceptive present in your bloodstream can increase the risk of pregnancy. This is most problematic for Tegretol (carbamazepine) because **interactions between estrogen and Tegretol make the Pill less effective.** Be absolutely positive that your doctor knows that you are taking the Pill, and assume that a low-dose contraceptive will not prevent pregnancy. If you are taking Tegretol, you need a different form of birth control or a high-dose oral contraceptive. Be sure to ask your gynecologist about how to know whether the oral contraceptive is effective. Be sure to tell your psychiatrist that you are on the Pill, and ask him to consider using lithium or Depakote (valproic acid) as a mood stabilizer (if clinically appropriate), which will not lower the effectiveness of a birth control pill.

Estrogen-containing birth control pills may cause heterocyclic/tricyclic antidepressants such as Pamelor (nortriptyline) and Tofranil (imipramine) to remain in your system longer. This means that the medication may become more effective if the dose has been too low, or you may experience more side effects, even toxicity as the amount in your bloodstream builds up. Reducing the dose of the heterocyclic in women taking oral contraceptives, especially the higher-dose ones, may be helpful. This is not necessary for progesterone-only pills and may not be an issue for low-dose pills. SSRIs appear less likely to interact with oral contraceptives.

Oral contraceptives may increase or decrease the amount of antianxiety medication in your system. Buspirone is not affected by OCs. However, Klonopin (clonazepam), Ativan (lorazepam), Sevax (oxazepam), and Restoril (temazepam) may be may be less effective when oral contraceptives are added. Other benzodiazepines, including Xanax (alprazolam), Valium (diazepam), Dalmane (flurazepam), and Halcion (triazolam), may be more active (including more sedating, a potentially dangerous effect) when birth control pills are added. Be sure to tell your doctor about any of the following changes after you begin a birth control pill: increased jitteriness or increased anxiety, excess sedation or poorer concentration or attention, increased morning sleepiness, or any confusion or unsteadiness on your feet.

A WARNING ABOUT LONG-ACTING CONTRACEPTIVE HORMONES

The two long-acting forms of hormonal contraception have different ways of delivering progestin. Depo-Provera is a shot taken every three months. It contains medroxyprogesterone acetate, which suppresses ovulation. Because progesterone may contribute to depression, I recommend that you try an oral form of progesterone (the minipill) before you commit to long-acting forms of progesterone. If your depression worsens (which may appear clinically as if the antidepressant has stopped working), you can immediately discontinue the progesterone pill. Otherwise, you may regret it if the long-acting form of progesterone exacerbates your mood disorder: Once the shot is in your system, it remains there for at least ninety days.

Norplant is the other means of delivering synthetic long-acting progesterone for contraception. The implants that are placed beneath the skin slowly release levonorgestrel, another type of progestin. Everything from mild mood changes to full-blown anxiety or depression has been reported with Norplant, although most women tolerate it just fine. Again, before starting a long-acting form of progestin, I highly recommend that *any* woman with a history of depression, especially if she is taking antidepressants and/or mood stabilizers concurrently, undergo a trial of an oral progestin to screen for individual sensitivity to progestin-induced mood disorder. Ideally, I recommend a three-month trial of oral progestin in at-risk women prior to Norplant. It's much easier to stop the progestin than it is to take the Norplant out.

SOME WARNINGS ABOUT HORMONE REPLACEMENT THERAPY

Postmenopausal estrogen/progesterone treatment is called hormone replacement therapy. Usually symptoms of menopause, such as hot flashes and vaginal dryness or painful intercourse, respond to estrogen replacement. Estrogen is also the active hormone that reduces the risk of thinning bones (osteoporosis) and heart disease (coronary artery disease, or atherosclerosis). Including progestin in the hormone replacement therapy appears to counterbalance the risk of endometrial cancer that estrogen taken alone causes.

Although the treatment varies quite a bit from one woman to another, most doctors prescribe some combination of the reproductive
hormones estrogen and progesterone; some add a third: testosterone.
Common estrogen-containing prescriptions include the pills Premarin, Estrace, Ogen, and Ortho-Est and the skin patches Estraderm
and Climara. Progesterone may be given as oral micronized natural
progesterone or as Provera. PremPro is a relatively new medication
that combines estrogen and progestin in one tablet. Small amounts
of testosterone in combination with estrogen may be especially beneficial to women with postmenopausal loss of sex drive. The most
common such medication is Estratest.

Women with a history of mood disorders may not tolerate progestin as well as other women. Combination pills tie the doctor's
hands to a particular ratio of estrogen to progestin, yet it is certainly
more convenient to take PremPro (a single pill) than to take both estrogen and progestin together. However, some depression-prone
women will do best on relatively lower doses of progestin, which will
require that they take less convenient single-hormone compounds.

As far as drug interactions with psychiatric medications go, the
same concerns hold for hormone replacement therapy as for oral
contraceptives. The mood stabilizer Tegretol (carbamazepine) may
lower the effectiveness of the estrogen component of the medication.
Thus, if you begin to take Tegretol, you may suddenly develop hot
flashes or other menopausal symptoms, and the effectiveness of hormone therapy in preventing bone loss or heart disease may diminish.

It may be advisable to lower the dose of a tricyclic antidepressant
when hormones are added or to start with lower doses in a woman
taking hormone replacement therapy. Postmenopausal women are
more susceptible to heart rhythm problems due to tricyclic antidepressants, so I recommend both blood and electrocardiogram
monitoring for them, regardless of whether they take hormone replacement therapy. Repeat monitoring is advisable when estrogen-
containing hormones are added or removed.

Older women are far more sensitive to the sedating and motor-im-
pairing effects of benzodiazepines. When they also take estrogen,
their need for much smaller doses of benzodiazepines may be even
greater. Middle-age and older women should be prescribed and take
sleeping pills and tranquilizers with extreme caution, regardless of
their hormone status. Progestins also may increase sedation.

Fossamax (alendronate sodium) is a new nonhormonal prescription medication for postmenopausal osteoporosis. It does not appear to have interactions with medications for mood and anxiety disorders, and it has not been reported to cause psychological symptoms as a side effect.

WHAT ABOUT CHEMOTHERAPY THAT SHUTS OFF MY NATURAL HORMONES?

Nolvadex (tamoxifen) is a form of chemotherapy often prescribed for women with estrogen-receptor positive breast cancer. It is antiestrogenic, which means it is the chemical equivalent of shutting down the ovaries. Women with cancer are already at higher risk than the general population for developing mood and anxiety disorders. Those who begin taking Nolvadex may have two unique physical factors that increase their likelihood of developing depression or anxiety. First, women with abrupt ovarian shutdown (as opposed to natural, gradual menopause) are more likely to develop acute depression, much like what Sierra went through. Second, Nolvadex and selective serotonin re-uptake inhibitors may interact in such a way as to lower the SSRI's activity. Clinically, a woman with a past good response to an SSRI may suddenly develop breakthrough depression or anxiety when Nolvadex is prescribed. If so, the doctor may increase the antidepressant dosage.*

CONCLUSION

It is common for my patients to ask me about taking hormones for mood and anxiety disorders, especially when a link to a reproductive event such as menstruation, menopause, or childbirth seems to be the cause. It certainly seems possible to me that hormones will turn

* There are unanswered questions and conflicting data as to whether antidepressants promote or inhibit tumor growth, or neither. An oncologist is more likely than a psychiatrist or primary care doctor to be up to date on the latest information about this. Women with cancer should be sure that their doctor has fully explored nonmedical treatments for depression or anxiety disorder and that the doctor is fully up to date on the latest risk-benefit analysis.

out to have a significant therapeutic role for some types of mental syndromes.

However, at this moment, we just don't have a solid enough scientific basis to recommend hormones as a first-line treatment for depression and anxiety disorders. We especially don't have a scientific basis for saying that hormones are as safe as ordinary antidepressants or antianxiety medications. While hormones may seem preferable because they are natural, they are also very powerful substances that may cause very significant side effects. Don't make the mistake of assuming that natural equals safe. And don't assume that responding to hormones makes your disease any more real than one that responds to antidepressants.

Chapter 10

OOPS! WHAT DO I DO NOW?

Accidental Pregnancy While Taking Medication

for Depression or Anxiety

KEY POINTS

• Insist on using consistent, effective birth control with your sexual partner. (Don't forget to practice safe sex too.) It is much better to prevent pregnancy than to find yourself agonizing about it too late.

• Monitor your menstrual cycle: Early detection of pregnancy is strongly advisable if there is any possibility that you would continue an unplanned pregnancy.

• If you choose to have an abortion, tell the doctor that you are taking medication for anxiety or depression.

• Do not assume that your medication has seriously damaged your fetus.

• If you wish to have the baby, insist that your doctor provide you with sound information, not unsubstantiated opinion, about the possible risks of accidental fetal exposure to medication.

• Consult your doctor before abruptly stopping medication.

Since depression and anxiety peak in women between the ages of twenty and forty-five, accidental pregnancy is a common concern for heterosexually active, potentially fertile women undergoing medical treatment for these conditions. Unplanned pregnancy may be a crisis for many reasons, or it may be a blessing in disguise.

While the meaning of every accidental pregnancy is highly individual, certain themes emerge in treatment. In this chapter, I discuss three potential immediate reactions to unplanned pregnancy: abortion, a transitional period of uncertainty and ambivalence, and continuation of the pregnancy.

Sometimes, as with Jennifer, the timing of a pregnancy is all wrong.

Jennifer is a twenty-nine-year-old secretary who has been dating Dan for almost a year. They aren't seeing anyone else and spend most weekends together from start to finish. Jennifer has started to wonder whether Dan might be "the one." At first, they used condoms whenever they made love, but after they both tested negative for HIV, Jennifer agreed to Dan's request to stop using condoms, and she dusted off her diaphragm.

Jennifer doesn't pay too careful attention to her cycle. She believes that she's pretty regular, but, when her period starts, it starts, that's it. She hasn't ever been pregnant before, and, unlike her sister who had an abortion before she was twenty, she has never in her life had sex without using birth control. Since she used birth control so religiously, she didn't wait in terror for her period each month.

Consequently, it took awhile for her to realize that her period was late. In the middle of August, she was rummaging through her medicine cabinet when she came across a box of tampons and suddenly remembered that she had her last period over the fourth of July weekend. She felt the room spin: It's been six weeks. She thought back, no, every time since then, she put her diaphragm in. No way, she said, maybe it's just the stress going on at work.

She put it out of her mind for another week, until she was lying in bed with Dan one morning and blurted out, "I might be pregnant." She couldn't have asked for a better response from Dan: She worried that he would be angry or blame her, but he just held her and listened. He offered to run to the drugstore and pick up a home pregnancy test, since, he said, "We need to know. I'll back you whatever you decide you want to do, but let's know one way or the other."

Unfortunately, the test was as plain as day: Jennifer was pregnant. She repeated it anyway: still pregnant. She felt so stupid; how could this have happened to her? She felt angry: It's not fair, she hadn't even made a mistake, and she was still pregnant. She felt guilty. She felt scared. She cried. She berated herself: Why hadn't she used a more effective method, like the Pill? Why hadn't they kept using condoms *and* the diaphragm? Why hadn't she noticed that her period was late sooner? Had she done something to deserve this? Was God punishing her for being so smug when her sister got pregnant?

YOU ARE NOT THE ONLY ONE

Accidental Pregnancy

Unexpected pregnancy is unbelievably common. In the United States, one-half of all pregnancies are unplanned. When I cite this statistic, I often encounter shock and disbelief. This is a well-kept secret, for a few reasons. One reason is that women don't advertise having had an abortion after becoming pregnant unexpectedly. Not too many years ago, the mysterious disappearance of unwed young women who reappeared six or seven months later, sadder but wiser, reminded observers that unplanned pregnancies did indeed happen, even to smart girls. Nowadays, access to abortion allows us to keep this information private.

Another reason is, of course, that unexpected pregnancies are not necessarily unwanted, either from the beginning or as time goes on. We idealize pregnancy and motherhood, and band together to deny the mixed feelings that often accompany an unexpected pregnancy. It is not socially acceptable to acknowledge that when you first learned that you were pregnant with little Johnny, you were really upset. It becomes a permanent secret: I love this child, but at first I was not overjoyed to become pregnant. Mother Nature is often both wise and kind, allowing many women the time they need to move from private despair to public joy.

Abortion

Women with depression and anxiety have higher than average rates of elective abortions, and many, many women undergoing medical treatment for anxiety and depression face and make this decision every day. This is your choice, and I hope to provide you with useful information that helps you to make the best decision for yourself.

Women who suffer from clinical depression may have higher rates of elective abortions for multiple reasons. Specific symptoms of depression—low self-esteem and disempowerment—interfere with negotiating for protected sex. Perhaps women with these illnesses feel less equipped to cope with an unexpected pregnancy or to raise a child in less than ideal circumstances. Another possibility is that the circumstances that may lead a woman to decide that she cannot have

a baby right now—poverty, divorce or abandonment by a partner, serious illness in a child or other family member, abuse—also increase
her risk of developing depression and anxiety.

Whatever the cause, the facts are clear: Abortion is the path taken
by many women who suffer from depression or anxiety disorders. We
live in a sexually active society, yet birth control options are far from
perfectly effective or user-friendly.

THE DOCTOR'S ROLE

In the case of an unwanted pregnancy, I provide my patients with the
information and support they and their families need to make the
best decision for themselves. Some readers will not see abortion as an
option; others will consider abortion but decide to continue the pregnancy. The concerns of these readers are covered in the second half
of this chapter and in the next chapter, which covers planned pregnancy. If you doubt that your doctor is able to be objective about
abortion as an option, be sure to ask. Ask that he or she give you information, not judgment. If he or she cannot be objective because of
personal feelings about abortion, you are entitled to have the doctor
help you find someone who can.

CHOOSING TO END AN ACCIDENTAL PREGNANCY

Like many women, while Jennifer never thought accidental pregnancy could happen to her, nonetheless, she had considered the unthinkable.

> When I prescribed Klonopin (clonazepam) for Jennifer's panic disor-
> der, we had talked about what she might do if she found herself un-
> expectedly pregnant while taking this medication. She had answered
> quickly: I'm not ready to be a mother. She wanted kids, she wanted to
> be a mom, but she wanted the whole package: a husband, a secure
> and stable home for children, and a set of parents who were ready to
> be parents. Like most women who have an unplanned, unwanted
> pregnancy, she didn't see giving a baby up for adoption as even a re-
> mote possibility. In her mind, the only choices were to marry Dan and

have the baby, which she wasn't yet ready to do, or have an abortion, end of discussion.

Since she decided quickly to end the pregnancy, she didn't give the Klonopin much thought one way or the other. She didn't even call me until she had already called an abortion clinic and set up an appointment to terminate the pregnancy. She had expected to be able to walk right in, have the abortion, and begin the work of making peace with herself. She was shocked to discover that she had to wait almost a month until the abortion could be performed safely. The wait was so stressful that her panic attacks got worse, and she wanted to increase her Klonopin dose.

I asked her about whether she had told the clinic doctor that she was taking Klonopin. No, she said, it's bad enough that they think I'm so stupid that I got pregnant, do I have to tell them I'm psycho too? She was trying to make both of us laugh, but we both knew that she was seriously mortified. I responded in kind: Undoubtedly, she was the first woman in the city of Chicago who had an anxiety disorder and an unwanted pregnancy. I was positive that she would be kicked out of the clinic if she told them she took Klonopin, that the clinic staff would probably talk about her for months, because they performed abortions only on little old ladies who never took anything stronger than a Tylenol once in a blue moon.

Okay, she said, I know I have to work on this shame thing, I know it's really about the abortion more than it's about the Klonopin, but do I really have to tell them? Yes, I said, you really have to tell them.

Tell the Clinic About Your Medication

The chances of the clinic doctor giving you anything that would interact with the your medication or, heaven forbid, of you having an unexpected problem are very slim, but they aren't nonexistent. **You must tell any doctor who is prescribing medication for you or performing any type of surgery, including minor or outpatient surgery, that you are taking prescription medication.** This advice is true for *all* psychiatric medications: antidepressants, antianxiety medications, lithium or other mood stabilizers, and **especially for those few women who take a monoamine oxidase inhibitor (MAOI) type of antidepressant or having general anesthesia.**

Not telling a doctor that you are taking other medication could result in dangerous drug interactions or could lead to withdrawal if the unimaginable happens: You end up with general anesthesia, and no one knows to continue the medication after you come out of surgery. These are, fortunately, very rare complications of any outpatient surgery, including abortion, but why take any unnecessary risk?

The most common reason my patients don't want to tell another doctor that they take medication for depression and anxiety is that they are embarrassed or afraid of being judged. I'd like to promise you that all doctors and nurses will be nonjudgmental, but of course that's not true (although I can assure you that there is almost no chance that taking an antidepressant or antianxiety medication will so much as raise the eyebrow of a staff member at an abortion clinic). I can tell you that you have an absolute right to be treated with respect by your doctors and that you probably should change doctors or speak with the clinic administrators if you feel that the doctor assigned to you has archaic attitudes toward medication for depression and anxiety.

Is It Okay to Take More Medication During the Crisis?

Jennifer, like many women with anxiety disorders, is sensitive to stress. She experienced an increase in symptoms during the crisis of an unwanted pregnancy and found that taking more Klonopin during the weeks just before and after her abortion helped her focus on working through the painful reality rather than getting buried in an avalanche of panic attacks. However, I would have discouraged her from taking more medication if she was uncertain what direction she was heading in. Never take more medication without your doctor's advice. Be sure to talk to your doctor about tapering back down to your previous dose when you feel more settled.

Take Advantage of Painful Lessons

Jennifer had what I think is the best possible emotional outcome from such a crisis.

> She and Dan used the experience as a watershed, a unique moment that allowed them to reflect on who they were together and where they wanted to end up. Jennifer decided to take birth control pills, which have a much lower rate of failure. She and Dan got engaged six months after the abortion and made plans to establish the financial

security they would need in order to raise a family together after they were married.

I'D NEVER HAVE AN ABORTION

Jennifer is single, but since many of my patients first come to see me for postpartum depression or anxiety, I have many mothers of young children in my practice. Many of us have a stereotype about who gets pregnant unexpectedly: poor, urban teenagers. In fact, white married women with children have the most unanticipated pregnancies. Unplanned pregnancies are not rare in my patients' lives; pregnancy doesn't discriminate on the basis of education, income, marital status, or extreme youth. I used to ask my heterosexually active patients whether they used birth control. Now, when I start medication in a woman of childbearing age, I also ask: What if you got pregnant now? What if the birth control didn't work?

Some tell me what Laura said: "Don't you dare even think that. That would be terrible, I can't have a baby right now . . . but, if I did, of course I would keep it." Laura points out that an unplanned pregnancy is often not unwanted. She wouldn't choose to get pregnant, but neither would she really consider an abortion. She knows that she would make a quick decision to continue the pregnancy but would want to know if she might hurt the baby by taking medication when she didn't realize that she was pregnant. I talk more about this issue in Chapter 11, but I do notice that many of my patients assume incorrectly that psychiatric medications are highly damaging drugs.*

Did I Hurt the Baby?

The issue of whether the medications you took when you didn't know that you were pregnant are damaging to the fetus may be absolutely crucial in your decision on whether to end or to continue a pregnancy. If you feel that you have not harmed your fetus by taking the medication, and have more or less the same chance as everyone else of having a healthy baby, your decision is grounded in the mean-

---

* Most antidepressants have not been shown to cause birth defects. However, mood stabilizers do raise the risk somewhat, and tranquilizers may do so slightly.

ing of the pregnancy to you and your partner or family, not on worries or a sense that it would be unfair to the baby.

But women often make different choices about abortion when the baby's health is in question. If you feel that you would not wish to continue a pregnancy if your medication caused a birth defect, I caution you against jumping into an abortion without all the facts. Do not assume that these medications usually cause birth defects. You must get this information from your doctor, or from a consulting doctor if your doctor is not well informed about the risks of your medication in pregnancy. As described in Chapter 11, a maternal fetal medicine specialist (an obstetrician with advanced training) can provide the latest scientific information about the specific risks of your specific medication at your specific stage of pregnancy.

Monitor Your Cycle

Because Laura knows that she would continue an unplanned pregnancy, I advised her to pay close attention to her periods, so that we could take her off the medication right away, if feasible clinically. Many—not all—women with depression and anxiety will be able to go off medication for either the first trimester (when the fetus's major organs are formed) or for the whole pregnancy. It is often—not always—a good idea to try stopping the medication, even if resuming it becomes necessary. Thus if you would likely continue an accidental pregnancy, it is especially important to watch your cycle carefully and figure out as soon as possible if you are pregnant.

Early detection of pregnancy will allow you to taper off this and any other medication under medical supervision as early in fetal development as possible. Since Laura is using birth control and not expecting to become pregnant, it makes sense to us both to treat her as a nonpregnant person. However, since she knows that she would continue a pregnancy, it also makes sense to have a contingency plan. Never stop medication for depression or anxiety without consulting your doctor.

Does Knowing I Would Continue an Unexpected Pregnancy Matter?

Knowing that you would continue an accidental pregnancy that occurred while you were taking psychiatric medication may influence the choice of a particular medication. I take this information into consideration in two situations. First, antidepressants are preferable to benzodiazepines (Klonopin, Xanax [alprazolam]) for potentially pregnant women with anxiety disorders because apparently they are safer for fetal organ development and much safer for mother and baby to taper rapidly in the case of accidental pregnancy.

The second circumstance has to do with whether to prescribe Prozac (fluoxetine) as compared to a similar SSRI. Since Prozac remains in the system for weeks after a person stops it, in theory it may be better to start with a similar but shorter-acting antidepressant, such as Zoloft (sertraline) or Paxil (paroxetine), if it may have to be cleared from your system as rapidly as possible. On the other hand, Prozac is the only SSRI that has been studied scientifically in pregnancy (see Chapter 11), and it is my first-choice SSRI when someone who is pregnant needs this type of medication (because it doesn't seem to raise the risk of major birth defects).

CONSIDERING ABORTION; CONSIDERING STAYING PREGNANT

Unlike Jennifer and Laura, some women need time to make up their minds about whether to continue an unplanned pregnancy. Weighing the pros and cons may be an extremely agonizing process. Sometimes the decision is easy for one partner but not for the other, a situation in which breathing space is absolutely essential.

During this phase of mixed emotions and uncertainty, it is common both to wish to continue the medication you are taking and to worry that it might hurt the baby if you decide to remain pregnant.

Lilly called me when she was about seven weeks' pregnant to ask whether she could stay on her Zoloft for a few weeks until she made up her mind. Lilly and her husband were seeing a marital therapist, and they wanted to process the decision together in therapy. She had tried going off Zoloft almost one year earlier, and she relapsed very quickly. She feared that a relapse of her depression would cloud her judgment, and she wanted to be "as much me as I can be" while working this out.

I told Lilly that there simply wasn't good scientific information on the safety of Zoloft for fetuses—very few drugs of any sort are unequivocally "safe" in pregnancy—but we didn't have reason to panic.

Despite its widespread use in the United States, including among women of childbearing potential, there were no spontaneous case reports indicating a higher than expected rate of birth defects. We couldn't conclude that taking it for two or three more weeks would have any clear-cut negative impact on her baby's health, and we might reasonably assume that it would be like other antidepressants that don't appear to cause birth defects.

I explained that the FDA considered Zoloft to be a Category B drug: "animal studies have not shown fetal risk, but controlled studies in women have not been conducted" because the possibility of subtle effects on the developing fetal brain simply could not be ruled out. (See p. 214.)

Even though Lilly had relapsed ten months ago when she tried to stop it, I reminded her that we had planned to try to wean her off the medication about this time anyway: Pregnancy would just move the timetable up a bit. I encouraged her to talk about the decision with her husband as actively as possible and to see if her therapist was open to scheduling two sessions a week until they worked it through. In the meantime, I lowered her dose from 100 mg to 50 mg, as a compromise that I felt would not cause a relapse but would get her started on tapering should she decide to have this baby. Ten days later Lilly called to say that she and her husband decided to have the baby, and we tapered her completely off the medication over the next week in the hopes that she would be able to avoid it as long as possible.

I gave different advice to Sarah, who was taking Prozac for panic disorder.

Sarah had gone on and off Prozac for years, and each time she had stopped it, she had been okay for six months or even more. Since Prozac has a long half-life, tapering it is not necessary, but it remains in a person's system for weeks. For both of these reasons, I felt certain that Sarah could and should stop the medication until she made up her mind about the pregnancy. I told her that if she did decide to have the baby, Prozac would remain in her system for several weeks after stopping it. Her past long bouts of being symptom-free off medication gave us every reason to believe that she wouldn't relapse suddenly now, and, indeed, she didn't. She stopped the Prozac, felt as well as she could have expected to feel during such a difficult time, and started it back up after a few more weeks when she decided to have an abortion after all.

CONCLUSION

Under any circumstances, unplanned pregnancy is often a serious crisis. When you add the unknowns of accidental medication exposure and throw in an illness that can significantly affect your self-confidence, the crisis is compounded. It's easy to freeze and to do what Jennifer did by ignoring the early signs. Denial is not helpful in this situation, because the clock is running. Accidental pregnancy is a reality of life, one that every woman of childbearing age should be thinking about just in case. Be a control freak here: Use reliable birth control, watch your cycle, and have a possible game plan in mind should the unthinkable happen.

Then, if it happens, seek help. Up-to-the-minute news about the specific medication or medications that you are taking is just part of the information you need to make the best decision for yourself. Part of what you need isn't medical at all. Seek wisdom; ask for help; open yourself up to spiritual, emotional, personal, and professional support and guidance to help you sort through the issues.

Chapter 11

I WANT TO HAVE A BABY

Guidelines for Medication Use During Pregnancy

KEY POINTS

• Do not assume that you must choose between your alleviating your illness and having a baby.

• Do not assume that your illness will get better during a pregnancy.

• Many medications for depression and anxiety do not appear to increase the baseline risk of physical birth defects.

• Scientific studies have neither proven nor disproven the possibility of harmful effects of medications on the developing fetal brain.

• The decision to take medication during pregnancy must be made on a case-by-case basis, taking into account the theoretical risks of medication use compared to the risks of untreated illness.

• You may be able to take active steps to minimize medication use during pregnancy or its risks.

Depression, panic disorder, and obsessive compulsive disorder peak during the childbearing years. Chapter 10 discussed the issues of accidental pregnancy when you are taking medication for depression or anxiety. This chapter addresses the very different set of concerns experienced by women who wish to become pregnant while taking these medications or who suffer from a severe depression or anxiety disorder while pregnant.

If you are taking medication and want to become pregnant, if an accidental pregnancy becomes welcomed or accepted, if you experience the illness for the first time or relapse unexpectedly while pregnant, or even if you experienced a past bout of depression or anxiety that required medication, you probably have already wondered about how you or your baby might be affected.

Even though she's not trying to get pregnant, my patient Emily is starting to think about it.

Emily has posttraumatic stress disorder (PTSD) and chronic depression, and she has improved remarkably over years of psychotherapy. However, although her PTSD is much better, she remains persistently vulnerable to clinical depression, which runs in her family. I have been seeing Emily since before Prozac (fluoxetine) was available, and she was the first patient for whom I prescribed this then exciting new antidepressant.

Emily has positively flourished on Prozac, which worked much better than a tricyclic antidepressant, and she and I both feel that it's been a significant part of her peace and well-being. I have moments where I feel that I witness miracles in my work: Emily is certainly someone for whom Prozac seemed a literal gift from God. By no reckoning could her childhood be viewed as blessed or even innocent: Her family wrote the book on dysfunctionality. Prozac not only treats the textbook symptoms of her depression—sleep disturbance, hopelessness, suicidal thoughts; it transforms how she views herself. Like many trauma survivors, she tends to view herself as inherently defective: unlovable, ugly, burdensome, and deeply undeserving of any goodness in her life. Over the years, we have attempted many times to stop or adjust the dose of the medication. Each time, before the full depressive syndrome emerges, she loses her grounding, seeing herself as a hurt child who is convinced that she deserves nothing but misery. The competent, caregiving, confident woman disappears, and she sees rejection in every encounter.

A few years ago, Emily married a man who, like her, deeply wants to have children. Emily adores kids, and she has worked for years to develop the skills and the confidence in her potential mothering to believe that she is not doomed to inflict the hardships of her childhood on her own children.

Recently Emily bemoaned how she could ever get pregnant if she can't get off the Prozac. She was surprised at my response: Who says you have to? I just assumed, she said, you can't take this stuff while you are pregnant.

This is a common assumption: a life-transforming medication surely must be way too strong to take during pregnancy. Often people believe that medication that is so personally powerful must be dangerous to a fetus. Actually, a relatively mild medication used for a mild condition, such as aspirin for a headache, may be quite risky to a developing fetus. Alternatively, a relatively strong medication such as thyroid hormone, used for a serious and even life-threatening condition, may be clearly safe for use in pregnancy.

YOU ARE NOT THE ONLY ONE CONSIDERING MEDICATION IN PREGNANCY

Common Questions

You may be wondering whether you will somehow miraculously improve during pregnancy. You may wonder whether your doctor, husband, mother, and neighbor would be horrified if you even raised the possibility of continuing your medication during pregnancy. You may wonder whether your are putting your own health and safety at risk by stopping medication in order to become pregnant. You may wonder if it's fair to your other children even to think about going off your medication. You may wonder whether your doctor really understands when she tells you "Of course you can't take this if you want to get pregnant."

Common Pain

Because of my specialized practice, I often evaluate and treat pregnant women. My typical pregnant patient is about as desperate as any woman can be. Because we are so culturally fixated on idealizing motherhood, I don't think that there is any greater added stigma for mental illness than pregnancy. Pregnant women put off seeking help much longer than anyone would believe: The shame and fear of being judged, being thought to be an inadequate mother, keep them in the closet. As if that weren't bad enough, they are all too often subject to poor psychiatric treatment. Many of my colleagues who specialize in treating pregnant women tell me that they too have patients who drive two hours just to see them, because the first four doctors they saw told them to try harder.

Of course, I don't see the patients who are being well cared for in their HMO, those who are responding to intensified psychotherapy, those who are struggling to stay off medication and making it one day at a time, those whose doctors have said "Hold off as long as you can but if you can't stand it, call me." The women I see have a deep sense that things aren't right, that they are being asked to do the impossible. Often these women feel that the doctor just can't be right, that it can't be good for their unborn baby to go night after night without sleeping, losing weight by the minute. Some of the women I see are so desperate that they have already decided to have an abortion if I can't help them or regret that it's too late to do so.

Won't I Feel Better When I'm Pregnant?

Many women, and many doctors, falsely believe that pregnancy makes you feel better, that it confers immunity to psychiatric illness or acts as a natural antidepressant. You may know someone who never felt better in her life than when she was pregnant. I regularly talk to psychiatrists who subscribe to the myth that pregnancy "hormones" confer mental well-being. This is a lovely idea that is often far from true.

Some of my pregnant patients aren't surprised by their depression or anxiety: The illness has been there for some time, and they knew that going off medication was risky. Others are shocked, perhaps because someone in authority had advised them that feeling so bad was unlikely. Others are sick for the very first time, and the emotional symptoms feel pregnancy-induced, as indeed they may be. Although most women who suffer from severe depression or anxiety during pregnancy were predisposed to it (due to a personal or family history of similar problems), some women have a unique sensitivity to the physiologic changes of pregnancy that precipitate changes in sleep and mood or peace.

While it is true that about one-third of women with panic disorder improve during pregnancy, one-third get worse; the rest stay the same. I can't predict who will fall into which group, with one exception: If you had panic disorder before a previous pregnancy and improved dramatically, it is reasonable to believe that this is likely going to be the case again, since it appears that you benefit from the physiologic changes of pregnancy. Yet it is not guaranteed. Unfortunately, pregnancy is a definite trigger for obsessive compulsive disorder. Some women have their first symptoms of OCD during pregnancy, and some have it only during pregnancy. The impact of pregnancy on generalized anxiety disorder has not been studied, but usually this illness is not so severe that medication is appropriate in pregnancy.

Major mood disorders, including unipolar and bipolar depression and mania, are not typically improved by pregnancy. In fact, pregnancy itself is an especially vulnerable period for depression. Progesterone shoots way up in pregnancy, and this hormone may act like a sedative for women with anxiety disorders while increasing vulnerability to low mood for those who tend to depression. Steroid hormones also increase in pregnancy, and these may aggravate or precipitate a depressive episode.

OBSTACLES TO CARE

Is It Safe to Take Medication While Pregnant?

Pregnant women (and those contemplating pregnancy) usually ask me whether medication is "safe." Likewise, almost every doctor who calls me to consult about using medication in pregnancy asks me "What is safe for her to take?" Unfortunately, I cannot answer this question. What I try to answer are the following questions: What is the wisest decision to make in this individual's circumstances? Is it safe to stop medication? Is it necessary to continue treatment, and if so, what is the safest alternative? I need to answer these questions whether the patient is considering a possible pregnancy or is suffering an acute illness or relapse during a pregnancy.

These are also the exact same questions that any doctor treating any pregnant woman with an acute illness must consider, whether the illness is epilepsy, diabetes, an infection, or migraine headaches. I don't believe that the average doctor treating a pregnant woman who is suffering a medical condition such as high blood pressure wonders whether treatment is "safe for the baby." Rather, the doctor and the patient must navigate the murky waters together: How inca-

pacitating is the illness for the woman? What are the alternative therapies, and what is safest? What happens to the baby if the condition
isn't treated? What happens to the mother if the condition isn't
treated?

Biases and Stigma

The very different ways in which doctors and patients alike think
about these questions for conditions that are considered purely "medical," as opposed to mood and anxiety disorders, indicates a deep mis-
understanding of the potentially serious, even life-threatening nature
of these illnesses. The automatic assumption that psychiatric medications should never be taken in pregnancy also may reflect deep biases against women with emotional illnesses becoming mothers: We
are culturally invested in believing that pregnancy is a blissful time,
that a pregnant woman should be so overjoyed, feel so personally
blessed that she is happy, no matter what.

Kay Redfield Jamison, in her elegant book, *An Unquiet Mind*, tells
of the harsh treatment that many women suffer at the hands of possibly well-meaning doctors.

> ... in an icy and imperious voice that I can hear to this day, he
> stated—as though it were God's truth, which he no doubt felt that it
> was—"You shouldn't have children. You have manic-depressive ill-
> ness." ... I asked him if his concerns about my having children
> stemmed from the fact that, because of my illness, he thought I would
> be an inadequate mother or simply that he thought it was best to avoid
> bringing another manic-depressive into the world. Ignoring or missing
> my sarcasm, he replied, "Both."

Jamison does what you should do at the hands of such cruelty: She
leaves. As she correctly notes, the doctor was at best misinformed:
Lithium is known to increase the risk of physical birth defects somewhat, but as is often the case, inappropriately withholding medication could place the woman and her fetus in grave jeopardy. Her
bold reply to the doctor brought to light his implied message that she
herself should not have been born or that psychiatric illness was in-
compatible with mothering. Do not accept these biases.

The Myth of the Perfect Mother

Despite all the evidence to the contrary, we persist in believing that perfection is a reasonable and achievable standard by which to judge mothering. But if only women with perfect genes had kids, we would soon become extinct! If only women with spotless mental health records were authorized to have children, we would deprive countless children of loving and nurturing homes. If the ability to endure incredible suffering through nine long unmedicated months was the only way to be pregnant, we would be placing many good mothers in the position of needlessly sacrificing the very emotional health that we believe to be in the best interest of their families, by risking their long-term mental health. (See p. 250.)

The Doctor's Anxiety

The automatic statement "You can't take that during pregnancy" also reflects the fact that doctors don't like to be agents of risk. We doctors are all too human and dread the possibility that we could harm your fetus or be sued for malpractice. Irrationally, it is tempting to let nature take its course, to let the untreated illness cause harm, rather than write out a prescription that we do not know to be "safe." Most doctors would feel more comfortable using medication for a condition (such as epilepsy) where the risks of withholding appropriate medication are clear-cut: The risks of the anticonvulsants can be directly compared with the risks of a seizure.

THE FIRST STEP: WEIGH THE RISKS OF THE ILLNESS

In considering medication for any condition in pregnancy, the first step is to be fully aware of the risks of not treating the mother's illness. Some risks are clear-cut, like an infection: Suicide, malnutrition, psychosis, dehydration, or the decision to terminate a wanted pregnancy because of excruciating emotional pain are examples of severe risk due to untreated illness. Many of the risks are less easily defined. These include subtle nutritional problems, difficulty following through on prenatal care, marital conflict, difficulty caring for your other children, diminished ability to abstain from tobacco or alcohol use, and the fact that nonspecific "stress" has been shown to increase prematurity and low birthweight.

One risk of untreated depression or bipolar disorder is the possibility that the mood disorder would become less treatable after the pregnancy, especially since the postpartum period is one of heightened vulnerability. In other words, if you somehow hang on throughout nine months of pregnancy depressed but not actually suicidal, you cannot assume that you will have the same response to medication that you did when you started medication earlier. This fact is most worrisome for women who have had multiple depressive episodes, since experiencing three or more bouts of depression makes stopping medication riskier, and for women with bipolar disorder. Just as the fetus of a diabetic mother has a stake in the woman's long-term medical condition, the fetus of a woman with a chronic mood disorder has a stake in his or her mother's lifelong mental health.

The possibility of coming through an unmedicated pregnancy with a more severe disorder is less of a concern for women with obsessive compulsive disorder and other anxiety disorders. These illnesses are far less likely than chronic, recurrent mood disorders to become potentially progressive if left untreated. In other words, without medication, these illnesses may be very distressing and hard to cope with during pregnancy, but the risk of coming out with a less treatment-sensitive illness is not great.

Common Sense

Maternal sacrifice is part of pregnancy, part of being a good mother. But we shouldn't lump medical treatment with cigarettes and vodka, which are never worth the potential risk to the fetus. I'm all in favor of maternal sacrifice, but I believe that there can be too much of a good thing. If maternal sacrifice is defined as not having children when you would be a terrific mother, that's too much. If maternal sacrifice means suffering such severe depression that you stop eating and your fetus doesn't grow properly due to malnutrition, that's too much. If maternal sacrifice means that you consider aborting a baby that you really want to have because you cannot stand another panic attack, that's too much. If maternal sacrifice means that you emerge from pregnancy with a less treatable mood disorder, that's asking too much.

THE SECOND STEP: EXPLORE NONMEDICAL ALTERNATIVES

All pregnant women considering or requiring medication during pregnancy should be doing absolutely everything that doesn't involve medication in order to feel well. If medication has worked well for you in the past, you may have gotten a bit lax about nonmedical therapies. Take a fresh look at what you can do to reduce stress, increase pleasurable activities, let go of unnecessary hassles, and generally treat yourself well.

If your illness is sufficiently severe that medication is appropriate during a pregnancy, you also should be undergoing psychotherapy. Pregnancy is an important time to emphasize short-term, symptom-focused talk therapies—cognitive and interpersonal therapy rather than psychoanalytically based therapy.

Margaret Spinelli, M.D., associate professor of psychiatry at Columbia University School of Medicine in New York City, recently presented results of a study she conducted indicating that interpersonal therapy, a highly specialized form of talk therapy that focuses on relationships, is as effective as medication for many depressed pregnant women.

Interpersonal therapy (IPT) is not available in many parts of the country, but most women can find another effective short-term therapy, called cognitive therapy, and many therapists center on relationships without having formal training in IPT. Cognitive therapy is an excellent treatment for panic disorder, agoraphobia, and depression. Behavioral therapy is the best alternative for obsessive compulsive disorder in pregnancy.

Creative solutions may well be worth trying. For example, Dr. Spinelli also reports that she has had some success using light box therapy for depressed pregnant women, even when they do not have the seasonal type of depression.

But words may *not* be enough. These treatments are superior to medication, and they are safe for the baby, if and only if they work. If you are not responding to words alone, allowing your illness to

progress may be unsafe for you and/or your baby. Words are especially unlikely to be enough for women with the most severe mood
and anxiety disorders, especially bipolar depression.

THE THIRD STEP:
CHOOSING THE BEST ALTERNATIVE WHEN MEDICATION IS NEEDED

If taking medication during pregnancy is the most appropriate thing
to do, the next question that must be answered is: Which medication
is the best choice? Especially when it comes to pregnancy, no book
in the world can substitute for careful, individualized, knowledge-
based medical advice. This information changes rapidly, especially
for the antidepressant drugs that have been available for only a few
years. You must seek individual information from a doctor who has
reviewed your individual history and examined you personally before
deciding that medication is advisable in pregnancy, and reviewed the
latest available information about the potential hazards of the suit-
able alternatives. Part of your job is to assess whether your doctor is
equipped to provide this information.

Many doctors, including general psychiatrists and obstetricians,
are no more informed than the average person on the street about
the specific risks of these psychiatric medications in pregnancy. However, some doctors seem incapable of admitting that they don't know
something. I see many patients who have been told "This isn't safe in
pregnancy" when their doctor should have said, "I don't know. I'll
find out for you," or "It's complicated. There are no easy answers." It
is equally wrong for the doctor to tell you that it doesn't matter that
you are pregnant.

How to Find an Expert

If you don't have access to an expert in the use of psychiatric medication in pregnancy, a psychiatrist or obstetrician at an academic
medical center or a maternal fetal medicine subspecialist (a type of
obstetrician) may provide you with the answers you need. Also called
geneticists, maternal fetal medicine specialists are experts in high-risk
pregnancies and in the use of medications during pregnancy. Often

a team approach is necessary since each physician may know only a piece of the puzzle. You should expect the specialist consultant (psychiatric or obstetric), your psychiatrist, and your general obstetrician to communicate about your treatment alternatives. Looking around and finding a sound answer really is worth the effort: A shoot-from-the-hip opinion is not good enough for such an important decision.

The Challenge of Interpreting the Available Information

Leafing through a general book on medications will not give you accurate information. The Food and Drug Administration has a system of categorizing medications for use in pregnancy, which is also listed in the *Physician's Desk Reference* (PDR), but the system is not perfect. Simple answers such as "Don't take while you are pregnant" are often highly misleading. Of course, no pregnant woman should ever take medication that isn't necessary, even if it is believed to be safe.

Unfortunately, significant unanswered questions about Prozac and other antidepressants make it impossible to say with certainty whether they are "safe" or "unsafe" during pregnancy. We do not know, and we may never know, whether such use may cause subtle changes in a developing baby's brain, such as learning disabilities or behavioral problems. One reason why we probably will never know this is because it is not ethical to give medications to pregnant women who don't need them in order to follow their children for twenty years to find out. Instead we have to piece together information based on animal studies and spontaneous reports of birth defects, which can be highly problematic to assess scientifically. Often it is impossible to look at the babies of mothers who took medication and say with certainty which caused the problem, the medication or the maternal illness itself.

It is much easier to determine whether antidepressants cause physical birth defects, such as damage to liver or kidneys or the heart, or cause extra or missing fingers, or lead to premature birth or harm the growth of the baby. In general, although there is no absolute scientific agreement, most evidence suggests that tricyclic antidepressants and Prozac are *not* likely to raise the risk of major physical birth defects.

Recent Studies About Antidepressants in Pregnancy

Since your doctor may be surprised to learn this, I've included on page 301 a few scientific references that may be helpful to professionals. Here I'll briefly quote recent discussions about the use of antidepressants during pregnancy taken from the medical literature.

My friend and colleague Laura Miller, M.D., associate professor of psychiatry and director of the Women's Inpatient Psychiatry Service and Parenting Assessment Team at the University of Illinois at Chicago College of Medicine, recently summarized the scientific literature on psychiatric medications in pregnancy. She concluded: "Studies conducted to date have found no increased risk of malformations after in utero exposure to tricyclic antidepressants."*

Similarly, a study published by A. Pastsuzak in the *Journal of the American Medical Association* noted that is it "very unlikely that fluoxetine [Prozac] is a major human teratogen [chemical cause of birth defects]."

In the fall of 1996, a study published by C. D. Chambers in the *New England Journal of Medicine* received widespread media coverage. This study also found that Prozac did not cause major birth defects, but unlike five other studies, the researchers found higher rates of minor birth defects and higher rates of complicated deliveries (such as premature labor). An accompanying commentary written by Elisabeth Robert, M.D., Ph.D., interpreted these findings: ". . . it seems unjustified to withhold fluoxetine from women who require an antidepressant drug during pregnancy." She concludes that while Prozac and tricyclic antidepressants have not been proven unsafe, "their use involves a calculated risk," given the inherent uncertainty.

As the first serotonin re-uptake inhibitor on the market, Prozac is the first such antidepressant to be studied in pregnancy. Animal studies for newer antidepressants are similar to those for Prozac, but these studies do not always translate perfectly to human beings. Also, Prozac is too new to rule out theoretical delayed effects. As an example of a delayed effect, you may recall the findings for DES daughters, for whom the risks of maternal use of the medication did not show up for over twenty years.

---

* For sources cited in this chapter, see page 301.

My Approach

For this reason, while some experts feel that Prozac is the "safest" alternative, I usually recommend the older tricyclics, which have been in use in the United States for thirty years, as the "safest" medication in pregnancy. If a tricyclic doesn't work or can't be used for a particular reason, then I believe that Prozac is the next best choice, given that several studies have shown no increased rate of major physical birth defects. Tricyclics are not effective for OCD, so Prozac makes the most sense for that disorder if medication is needed during pregnancy.

Uncertainty About New Antidepressants

Some doctors are willing to prescribe Zoloft (sertraline), Paxil (paroxetine), and other new antidepressants for the smaller group of individuals who either do not respond or cannot take Prozac and tricyclic antidepressants, but the newer the drug, the less confidence we can have about its use in pregnancy. The shorter-acting SSRIs may be a better choice in late pregnancy if a woman plans to breast-feed, since Prozac is not the best choice in nursing mothers, but none of the SSRIs is as well studied as Prozac. I strongly discourage taking new medications during pregnancy, such as Remeron (mirtazapine).

Alternatives for Bipolar Disorder

Women with bipolar mood disorder and their doctors have the most complicated decision to make about which medication is best. This is the most serious mood disorder, and the consequences of the illness can be very severe for mother and baby. Uninterrupted medication is optimal in theory, since the illness can become progressive or treatment resistant if a person goes on and off medication. Women are at higher risk for a particularly severe form of bipolar disorder called rapid cycling, in which they switch back and forth between depression and mania, and stopping a mood stabilizer may result in setting off a flurry of rapid cycles.

Unfortunately, all of the common mood-stabilizing medications—lithium, Depakote (valproic acid), and Tegretol (carbamazepine)—do raise the risk of birth defects when taken in the first trimester.

While most women who take these medications will have normal, healthy children, mood stabilizers do cause devastating types of birth defects, including heart defects and spinal cord abnormalities. At the same time, the illness itself may be very risky to a fetus, since the mother's judgment and impulse control may be affected. Alcohol increases the risk of lithium-induced birth defects. Ask your doctor about taking folate and vitamin K if you are on Depakote or Tegretol.

Some women with bipolar disorder will opt to continue their mood stabilizers as usual and will plan to have a specialized ultrasound (called a Level II ultrasound), usually at sixteen to twenty weeks of pregnancy. Some women decide that if a severe birth defect is found, they will terminate the pregnancy. An ultrasound also might reveal a surgically treatable birth defect and can be useful to ensure that any immediate medical attention that might be helpful to your infant can be lined up before delivery.

Other women will decide to taper the mood stabilizer upon becoming pregnant, planning to start right back up after the first trimester or at delivery, if they can wait that long. Some women will make it through three months without a relapse, but some will not. Your own personal history of mood stability without medication gives you a rough estimate of whether it is reasonable to consider a three- to nine-month medication-free period. Women who do relapse may opt to restart medication, undergo electroconvulsive therapy (shock therapy is actually a safer alternative than a mood stabilizer, and it works for either manic or depressive relapses), or be hospitalized in the hopes of avoiding medication. The National Institute of Mental Health is studying whether medications called calcium channel blockers are the safest alternative in pregnancy for mania. Some doctors recommend an antipsychotic medication (such as Haldol [haloperidol]) during the first trimester, but such drugs do not specifically treat the underlying mood disorder. If you do stop your mood stabilizer, it is absolutely critical to start it back again within hours of childbirth, because bipolar women are highly susceptible to postpartum depression or psychosis.

Alternatives for Anxiety Disorders

The safety of antianxiety medications such as Ativan (lorazepam), Klonopin (clonazepam), and Xanax (alprazolam) during pregnancy is somewhat controversial. Since these medications (benzodiazepines) may be used in situations that themselves increase the risk of birth defects (they are used medically for epilepsy, and women with alcoholism or drug abuse may abuse them), it is more difficult to know with scientific certainty whether they are safe or not. Some researchers feel that benzodiazepines increase the risk of cleft palate (an abnormal development of the roof of the mouth) or cleft lip, or other nonspecific birth defects. However, abruptly stopping these medications could cause withdrawal in yourself or your fetus, which may be extremely hazardous. You must not stop these medications without medical advice. If you become pregnant accidentally while taking an antianxiety medication, and there is any chance at all that you would want to have the baby, call your doctor immediately. In general, antidepressants, especially low-dose tricyclics, are a better choice than benzodiazepines if daily use is advisable in pregnancy.

THE FOURTH STEP: WHEN TO STOP THE MEDICATION?

When a woman decides to try to stop medication in order to become pregnant, When? is as important a question as Which drug? to take. Proper timing is absolutely crucial, since it may minimize the risk of first-trimester use. If your illness is likely to recur during a pregnancy, you increase the chances of remaining medication-free during the crucial first trimester if you remain on medication until you miss your first period. Since it may take months or even years to get pregnant, going off medication in order to get pregnant may not be a good choice for those women with the highest likelihood of serious relapse (in general, women with bipolar disorder, those with multiple previous depressive episodes, and those with moderate to severe OCD and panic disorder). In a sense, you may "waste" your symptom-free interval and increase the likelihood that you will need medication a few weeks into your pregnancy.

If you and your doctor decide that it's best to continue medication until you miss a period, you will need to monitor your cycle closely and have a pregnancy test performed at the earliest possible moment. Home pregnancy tests are reliable when positive. If you do a home pregnancy test and it reads negative, you may be pregnant anyhow. A blood test called beta-HCG is the earliest way to determine pregnancy, since it will be positive even before you miss a period.

Nature's Grace Period

Nature is very clever sometimes. While all medications do cross the placenta during pregnancy, Nature built in a grace period. It takes five weeks for the blood system that transports maternal substances to the fetus to develop. This translates into a grace period of a few weeks after a missed period. However, once placental transport is established, the fetus is very vulnerable developmentally. You do yourself and your baby a big favor by monitoring your cycle closely while trying to get pregnant.

Tapering After Ovulation

An alternative strategy to tapering on becoming pregnant is to take a full dose during the first two weeks of your cycle (after you have your period and know that you are not pregnant) and to taper or even stop the medication for the second two weeks of your cycle (after ovulation). In general, full-dose medication is more effective than partial dose, but this technique may be preferable for some women, especially those with mild to moderately severe disorders. Beginning to taper the medication at the time of ovulation (approximately day 14) will make stopping medication when you miss your period smoother and quicker, if that's the most appropriate thing to do.

Stopping Medication When You Stop Using Birth Control

Some women and their doctors are more comfortable stopping the medication before pregnancy, especially if the illness is fairly mild or doesn't recur quickly. This may be the optimal approach for women who have a personal history of becoming pregnant quickly and easily and least sensible for women undergoing infertility treatment. In this case, ovulation predictors (basal temperatures, home ovulation tests) may help accelerate conception and thereby reduce the medication-free period.

DOES PREGNANCY CHANGE ANYTHING ELSE ABOUT MEDICATION TREATMENT?

Often pregnancy changes how a doctor prescribes. As mentioned, pregnancy is not the appropriate time to try the newest pill on the market. Also, during pregnancy the goal of medication is far more modest than usual. Rather than aiming for total symptom resolution, it is most prudent to look for symptom relief. When you are not pregnant, you and your doctor will want to target all your symptoms, to enable you to feel as good as you can. During pregnancy, the aim should be to bring your symptoms under control, to make them bearable.

You May Need More Medication Later in Pregnancy

Your medication dosage may change over the course of a pregnancy. Dr. Katherine Wisner, Director of Women's Services, Mood Disorders Program at Case Western Reserve University School of Medicine in Cleveland, studied the dosage requirements of tricyclic antidepressants across pregnancy. She found that dosage requirements increase over pregnancy, on average just over one and one-half times. In other words, as pregnancy advances your system clears the medication more rapidly, so you will likely need more of a tricyclic antidepressant in order to have the same level of symptom relief. I've seen a similar need for more medication later in pregnancy for the serotonin-enhancing antidepressants such as Prozac.

Third-Trimester Concerns

Dr. Wisner and her colleagues were also the first to advise tapering a tricyclic antidepressant two weeks before anticipated delivery. This is done because newborn babies may not clear the medication as well, and medication actually can accumulate after the baby leaves the womb. Rarely, the opposite can happen: Babies have a mild withdrawal jitteriness. Lithium should be adjusted to half the usual dose two weeks prior to delivery and resumed at the prepregnancy dose immediately after delivery. Since Congress recently eliminated the so-called drive-through deliveries (discharge the same day as childbirth), you should take full advantage of the forty-eight-hour stay. This lets you rest and gives you and the doctors time to be sure that the baby shows no signs of reacting to maternal medication.

CONCLUSION

This book cannot and should not substitute for careful, individual medical advice. It may be easy for women and their doctors to sort out who clearly should take medication throughout pregnancy and who clearly should not. Usually it's not anything close to easy; it's a very complex decision that must be made with knowledge and wisdom. In the not too distant past, doctors simplistically viewed the placenta as a barrier and were far too quick to medicate any maternal ailment despite pregnancy. In today's culture (with fear of malpractice suits ever present in the doctor's mind), the pendulum often swings too far the other way. Don't settle for simplistic reassurances or doomsday predictions.

The decision to take medication during pregnancy is incredibly complex. If your doctor tells you that the answers are easy—including offering the simplistic "of course you can't take anything when you are pregnant"—get another opinion. You must be very aggressive about trying words, squeezing as much benefit out of talk and alternative therapies as you possibly can. But if words are not enough, if your health is at stake, if your baby's health is at risk because of your illness, or if you are suffering more than is reasonable, medications may be a better choice for you and your baby.

Medication use during pregnancy has some risks that have nothing to do with birth defects or how the baby develops. One is that you will blame yourself forever for any problem your child develops, physical or intellectual or emotional, if you have taken medication during pregnancy. Nature gives any pregnant woman a 2 to 4 percent chance of having a child with a birth defect (mostly minor, fortunately), whether she takes any type of medication or not. Given the possibility of a natural birth defect, you need to make your medication decision in part based on whether you would blame yourself for-ever if something goes wrong, since a healthy baby is not guaranteed. This is one of the strongest reasons I know to avoid medication in the first trimester if at all possible: Even though antidepressants do not appear to cause birth defects, a woman unfortunate enough to have a problem with her child will have a much easier time if she is ab-solutely positive it isn't her fault. A father whose child is born with a birth defect will have a much easier time if he is not blaming his wife.

I encourage both parents to communicate with all of the doctors, and especially with each other, when a woman is considering taking medication during pregnancy.

Chapter 12

HOW CAN I TAKE CARE OF THE BABY WHEN I FEEL THIS BAD?

Guidelines for Medication Use After Childbirth

KEY POINTS

• If you are suffering from depression or anxiety for the first time in your life and you recently gave birth, you probably have postpartum depression. Your chances of full recovery are excellent, but you may be predisposed to non–childbirth-related episodes.

• If you have experienced any prior episode of depression or anxiety (postpartum or prior to pregnancy), you are at much higher risk for another episode after childbirth. Make contingency plans, just in case.

• You may be able to minimize your risk of postpartum illness by taking medication immediately after childbirth. This decision is more complex if you plan to breast-feed your baby.

• Do not assume that you have to choose between feeling good and nursing your baby.

• The decision to breast-feed while taking psychiatric medication must be made on a case-by-case basis, taking into account the theoretical risks of medication use compared to the risks of your untreated illness or weaning your baby.

Rae was in her eighth month of her second pregnancy, scared to death about experiencing another bout of postpartum depression.

Three and a half years ago, Rae delivered a healthy, much-wanted baby girl. She felt great for about a month, considering that she hadn't slept longer than a few hours at a stretch. She had always looked forward to being a mom, so she couldn't figure out what was wrong when she started feeling so terrible.

Rae's first symptom was insomnia; anxiety followed close behind. She was weepy, completely overwhelmed by the smallest decisions, and she felt like the worst mother in the world. She was calling her obstetrician's office four or five times a day, convinced that she was physically ill. The sleeping pills she got didn't do a darn thing, and she started to wonder if she would ever feel like herself again.

Rae got on the road to recovery when she saw an article in a baby magazine about postpartum depression. She had all the classic symptoms: sad and gloomy feelings, inability to sleep even when the baby slept, and thoughts that maybe the baby would be better off without her. The article listed two national organizations for postpartum depression, and she got the name of a psychiatrist in her area who specialized in the field.*

Before she saw the doctor, her obstetrician had advised that she stop nursing, wondering whether the drain of breast-feeding was part of her problem. Reluctantly she weaned the baby, but it didn't make any difference. The psychiatrist confirmed the diagnosis of postpartum depression, and, with the help of some Xanax (alprazolam), Rae somehow got through another few weeks of hell until the Paxil (paroxetine) started working. Around the time of her daughter's first birthday, she easily tapered off the Paxil.

Rae was desperate to avoid going through that again. Unfortunately, in the middle of her next pregnancy, she and her husband were forced to relocate, and now she was in Chicago with no family, no friends, and no familiar doctors. She started to get "moody" in her last trimester, which scared her even more. She was already having trouble staying on an even keel, losing her temper too easily with her preschooler; how bad could things get after this next baby?

Rae assumed that she couldn't breast-feed if she went back on antidepressant medication. "I loved nursing so much, I can't stand the idea of not doing it at all with this baby," she said.

---

* These organizations are Depression After Delivery and Postpartum Support, International. See pp. 295–96 for more information.

YOU ARE NOT THE ONLY ONE

Despite the myths of mother-child harmony and bliss, emotional illness is common after childbirth. In the first few months after childbirth, you may experience postpartum depression (see p. 30), panic attacks, obsessive compulsive disorder, or even psychosis for the first time ever. Approximately one in three new mothers experiences clinical depression or anxiety in the year after giving birth. Half of all new mothers have at least two symptoms of clinical depression.

Classical postpartum depression—what Rae went through after the birth of her first child—is not the only syndrome that affects new mothers. Pregnancy and the postpartum period are also vulnerable times for anyone who has ever suffered a bout of mood or anxiety disorder. Relapses of preexisting illnesses or exacerbations of milder disorders are common. Rae became depressed during her second pregnancy, which many doctors would view as a recurrent depressive episode. And she's more likely than not to get worse once the new baby comes.

This chapter discusses common medication concerns of women who are about to or who have recently given birth. You may be thinking about medication because you are suffering during a pregnancy and wonder whether to start medication once the baby is born. Perhaps you are already taking medication during pregnancy, unsure what to do differently after childbirth. You might be hoping that medication will ward off a subsequent bout of postpartum depression. You may worry that your preexisting mood or anxiety disorder will get worse after childbirth if you don't take medication. You might be concerned about how the medication will affect you as your body works through a tremendous physical transition.

But the most common painful and complex medication dilemma of this period is usually: Can I take something while breast-feeding?

OBSTACLES TO CARE

The greatest obstacle to care for postpartum women is the extreme idealization of new motherhood. As a mother of three children and a psychiatrist who has treated countless women with childbirth-related depression or anxiety, I should know better sometimes. In my head, I know that the first few months after childbirth are the time a woman is most likely to suffer clinical depression, anxiety disorders, and OCD. In my heart, I *ooh* and *aah* over the idyllic image of a mother and newborn just like everyone else does.

I should know that women who have postpartum depression or anxiety (hereafter PPD, a catch-all term for obsessive compulsive disorder, panic disorder, and clinical depression after childbirth) fake it better than anyone else, often looking great on the outside while falling apart inside. I should know that having a baby compounds the stigma of suffering from an emotional illness and that part of the problem is that society's expectations of maternal bliss are crazy-making. I should bear in mind that many women are pressured to continue breast-feeding when they'd like nothing better than to stop, yesterday. But I confess, it's easy to forget how hard it can be. It's easy to forget how our culture glorifies this life transition.

Everyone Tells You How Great You Should Feel

The discrepancy between fantasy and reality is hard enough when things are going great. But women suffering an emotional illness after childbirth bear the added pain of stigma and shame because society insists they feel and act happy. It's bad enough when PPD makes a woman unable to sleep, unable to stop the flurry of fears and worries, leads her to cry all day, have panic attacks, or suffer terrifying images of harming the baby. It's bad enough for her to feel unable to really smile at her infant or help her older toddler make the transition to being a big brother. It's terrible to feel physically depleted: fat, forgetful, and bone-weary. But it is torture for a woman with PPD to be told over and over how great she *should* feel.

Everyone Tells You This Is a Weakness

Women who admit to suffering from PPD get insulted on top of the injury: Their motherly instincts are questioned. They are subject to intense scrutiny about their love for their babies, their fitness for motherhood, their maturity, their ability to cope, as if PPD were a mild stressor. Even if everyone you know feels you just aren't trying hard enough, honor your sense that something is wrong and seek professional help.

Everyone Tells You Good Mothers Nurse Their Babies

Another obstacle is the idealization of breast-feeding. Some women feel enormous internal and/or external pressure to nurse, which may have a major impact on getting the right treatment if women never consider medication because they feel pressured to continue nursing. These days it's politically correct to nurse. In some circles, nursing has become a litmus test: If you don't breast-feed, you don't really love your baby, you are selfish or lazy, or you have unconscious conflicts about having a baby. This is nonsense.

Some women with PPD feel that they are a personal battleground for the war between La Leche and the if-God-hadn't-wanted-us-to-use-bottles-She-wouldn't-have-made-Similac camps. The stigma of PPD makes it difficult to tell your critics that you stopped nursing because you needed medication for depression and weren't comfortable nursing while taking medication. It makes it difficult to say: I was too depleted to nurse. But note, choosing to feel good is a loving act for your baby. Choosing to wean, whether to take medication or for any other reason, is up to you.

The misconception that taking medication for depression while nursing is likely to damage your baby is another obstacle to getting good care. As I discuss later in this chapter, it is possible to take medication while nursing.

Taking Medication Doesn't Make You a Bad Mother

The decision to take medication, whether you are nursing or not, may imply to a woman, her husband, her mother, or her mother-in-law that she is a failure as a mother, although this mistaken belief is unspoken in many families. Since many women with PPD have never experienced any prior mood or anxiety disorder, being so symptomatic that medication is necessary may increase their sense of failing as a mother. Don't fall into the trap of believing that PPD has anything to do with maternal fitness or devotion. It doesn't. Deciding to take medication, especially when faced with subtle or explicit criticism for doing so, is a wonderful gift that you give yourself *and* your baby.

Maternal emotional well-being is as good for babies as it is for mothers. Most women with PPD and/or exacerbation of preexisting emotional illnesses go through the motions just fine: Their babies are fed, cleaned, attended to. But it isn't realistic to expect to be your best when you feel terrible inside. I never want to see *any* of my patients suffer another moment, but I feel a unusual sense of urgency about getting my postpartum patients on a quick road to recovery. PPD usually pushes families well past their natural ability to cope with the needs of a new baby.

Don't Put Off Asking for Help

Postpartum women often put off getting help until they are just shy of a full meltdown. The stigma of having emotional symptoms during a time that you and everyone you know expected to be so happy probably kept you out of the doctor's office for too long. Like my pregnant patients, new mothers usually come to me in bad shape: They have tried to shake it off, ignore it, take extra prenatal vitamins, wish it away for a long time, and seek professional help only when the situation is completely out of hand. Treatment for PPD— whether words or medications—is easier when you ask for help at the first sign that things are amiss. Don't put off asking for help another minute.

The same advice holds for women with preexisting depression or anxiety. Don't believe that the happiness of the moment will protect you from relapse. Have a plan, just in case. Have a plan that you devised during a moment of strength and calm, not during an unexpected relapse.

Make Getting and Staying Well a Priority

Besides the stigma of seeking help, it's just plain hard to manage the logistics of getting to the doctor when you have PPD. After you give birth, your time is unusually precious, and just getting through the day is already a huge effort. Try to keep in mind that everything, absolutely everything, will be easier when you feel like yourself. Getting help now isn't a luxury, it's a necessity. Make time. Go even if you can't get a sitter. It is okay to bring a newborn with you to the doctor's. Any doctor or therapist who objects is totally out of touch with the realities of having a newborn, and probably can't help you anyway.

I FEEL FINE NOW: AM I AT RISK?

Chances are, if you even ask the question, "Am I at risk for PPD?" you are. Women with a history of bipolar mood disorder are the single highest risk group; at least half will relapse after childbirth without preventive medication. Generally, the next highest risk group is composed of women with multiple past episodes of depression or anxiety, especially those with chronic forms of obsessive compulsive disorder, panic disorder, dysthymic disorder, and depression. Any episode of postpartum depression roughly doubles the subsequent risk, but women who are unusually susceptible to subsequent PPD are those who had very severe prior bouts, especially those with early-onset PPD (within the first few weeks of giving birth); were hospitalized for PPD, became suicidal, or became essentially nonfunctional; and those with two or more episodes of PPD.

From time to time, I hear that someone has told a woman that PPD is like being struck by lightning: a bizarre act of nature that won't happen twice. Not true! Statistically women with depression after past deliveries can expect to have much more PPD in future deliveries than others. Women with preexisting depressive and anxiety disorders are also at higher risk.

Rae experienced a common risk factor for recurrent PPD during her second pregnancy: increasing depression as the pregnancy progressed. Since society expects pregnant women to be "moody," it is easy to tell yourself that things will get better once the baby is born. Usually the opposite is true: Pregnancy-associated depression, OCD, and panic attacks typically get worse after the baby is born.

> Rae had mixed feelings when I told her that I thought she should start medication as soon as the baby was born. She was both scared and relieved. While she was sad about the possibility of getting worse, at the same time she felt more in charge. She felt able to get through the last few weeks of her pregnancy without medication, but she promised to call me if anything got worse.

Can I Do Anything About PPD If I'm at High Risk?

Finally, some good news. Yes, women can dramatically reduce their risk of postpartum illness by starting medication immediately after giving birth. This is the one time in a woman's life when it may make sense to take medication for anxiety or depression *before* any symptoms develop.

Taking medication before you develop symptoms is called prophylaxis. Prophylaxis is common in other medical fields; for example, people routinely take antibiotics after surgery to prevent infections, consume Dramamine before going boating to prevent motion sickness, or take prenatal vitamins to ward off anemia. What makes the postpartum period unusual is that it is a clear-cut vulnerable period for emotional illnesses, a time when certain women are sufficiently at risk that preventive therapy is appropriate.

If your doctor recommends that you take medication to avoid PPD, it is absolutely crucial that you begin the medication immediately upon giving birth, in the hospital, *not* after you get home. Ideally, women with bipolar disorder should take lithium or another mood stabilizer literally within hours of childbirth, but even antidepressants or antianxiety medications are best started in the first day. Your psychiatrist and your obstetrician should consult before the baby is born to make arrangements for prophylaxis.

Preventive therapy may include psychological treatment, of course, but only prophylactic medication has been documented to reduce the risk of postpartum depression and psychosis. Biological factors play such an important role for postpartum women that psychological work and social support often will not be enough for those at risk of severe postpartum illness.

When Is Prophylaxis a Good Idea?

Taking medication prophylactically is a good idea in the following circumstances: bipolar mood disorder, past postpartum psychosis, three or more episodes of past clinical depression (related to childbirth or not), chronic anxiety or depressive disorder, a tendency to develop rapidly progressive depression, and a history of suicide attempts or other life-threatening symptoms during even one prior postpartum depression.

The issue of prophylaxis is complicated by the risk-benefit analysis of breast-feeding. I am less comfortable prescribing medication preventively for women who are breast-feeding, because I think that medication use during nursing must be based on the type of maternal illness. I also tend to avoid prophylactic medication in women who are likely to respond quickly to a drug, although past quick response is not a guarantee that the same thing would happen again.

General doctors and even psychiatrists may not be aware of new research about the benefits of postpartum prophylaxis. You may wish to point out to your doctor Dr. Katherine Wisner's research on preventing postpartum depression. (See the references at the end of the book; Dr. Wisner also has a study funded by the National Institute of Mental Health under way.) She is one of the true pioneers in the field, who has shown that prophylaxis is an effective way to prevent subsequent bouts of PPD. Also, contact Postpartum Support, International or Depression After Delivery for a referral in your area to help you find a doctor who specializes in PPD and who will likely be aware of this approach. (See the Resources section.)

Is There a Middle Ground?: Early Intervention for PPD

If prophylaxis is not the best approach for you—for example, if you are not comfortable nursing while taking medication and would prefer to quit nursing in order to take medication only if you have no other choice—then early intervention may reduce the impact of the illness. Knowing that you are at risk helps you get back on track more easily if you do relapse. Part of why PPD is so devastating is that it may take months to figure out what is wrong the first time it hits you. Watch yourself carefully, and have a plan for what do to just in case. Figure out whom you can trust, and ask them to help you be on the lookout. Get help at the earliest sign of relapse. If you intervene quickly, the illness will almost certainly be less severe than it was the first time. Early signs of relapse include insomnia, crying, anxiety attacks, and inability to experience pleasure.

POSTPARTUM DEPRESSION: THE DIAGNOSIS

Classical PPD starts within a few months of childbirth. It seems clearly triggered by the unparalleled stress of giving birth: Hormone shifts, sleep deprivation, fatigue, financial pressures, isolation from adult company, and marital stress often peak after a baby is born.

These same stressors make any woman who has ever suffered significant emotional illness susceptible to a relapse after childbirth. Yet even if you have had prior bouts, often a relapse is as much of a shock as the first episode: You may have expected that the joy of the moment would sustain you, never expecting that a crash was coming.

I am not going to attempt to squeeze into this chapter all the information that Karen Kleiman and I included in our book *This Isn't What I Expected: Overcoming Postpartum Depression* (1994). Here I emphasize medication issues, especially for women who choose to breast-feed. For more details about PPD, refer to our earlier book.

First, a quick review of the diagnosis. The single most important symptom that distinguishes postpartum disorders from ordinary stress is the inability to sleep when the baby sleeps. Exhausted women usually fall asleep when their babies sleep. Women with PPD are exhausted too, but the PPD interferes with their bodies' attempts to become rejuvenated. Anxiety attacks (which interfere with sleep and yet which are made worse by sleeplessness) are common in all subtypes of PPD. Women with classic postpartum depression usually feel an unremitting sense of hopelessness and despair. They may have presuicidal thoughts, wondering whether the baby would be better off without them.

For women with pure postpartum anxiety disorder, periods of severe panic and anxiety usually are interspersed with times when they don't feel awful. Sometimes looking at a woman's genetic predisposition can clarify the diagnosis of anxiety vs. mood disorder: Does depression, panic disorder, OCD, or bipolar affective disorder run in the family? If so, the new postpartum symptoms may be the first sign that a woman inherited the familial tendency to that disorder. However, comorbidity is common during the postpartum period, and a patient may have postpartum depression and panic disorder, for example.

Postpartum OCD almost always causes terrifying images about harm occurring to the baby; women may even fear that they could accidentally hurt the baby themselves. This is very different from postpartum psychosis, because women with postpartum OCD would never actually hurt their baby and do not believe that there is any actual possibility that they would. While women with postpartum OCD may have bizarre images, they realize that these ideas are coming from their own mind, not put there by alien forces. In postpartum psychosis, thoughts about hurting the baby are accompanied by a loss of touch with reality. For example, the thoughts may seem to be secret messages that only they can understand.

Postpartum psychosis is, thankfully, rare, but it is an extreme emergency, because it interferes so much with a woman's judgment that her safety and/or that of her infant may be in jeopardy. Postpartum psychosis is not uncommon in untreated women with bipolar disorder. **Emergency symptoms that necessitate immediate medical attention include hallucinations, delusions, and suicidal thoughts or impulses.**

Will It Just Go Away on Its Own?

Because the precipitant—giving birth—is so dramatic, many women believe that getting over childbirth will cause the emotional problems to go away. This is more likely to be true for women with mild symptoms, such as occasionally not sleeping when the baby does or a mild depression.

However, postpartum mood or anxiety disorders may linger for a year or two if not treated properly.* And the untreated illness may permanently rob women of something they cannot get back: enjoyment of a once-in-a-lifetime moment. In severe cases, not getting help could have terrible consequences. If you choose to wait it out, decide on a time after which you will seek help if you are not back to your old self. If things get worse, get help sooner.

Women who experience a postpartum disorder only, with no prior symptoms, are in the best prognostic category; **full recovery is the norm,** treatment is effective, and many women go off medication without difficulty. Unfortunately, some bouts of postpartum disorder, while precipitated by childbirth, indicate a potential lifelong vulnerability to mood or anxiety disorders. This is especially true in women with strong family history of emotional illness and those with a personal history of vulnerability during other stressful periods. Postpartum psychosis may be the first sign of bipolar affective disorder.

---

* Postpartum psychosis is a medical emergency that must be treated immediately. The following information does not pertain to postpartum psychosis.

TREATMENT OPTIONS FOR DEPRESSION AND ANXIETY AFTER CHILDBIRTH

A Speedy Recovery

When you have a new baby to care for, getting well is especially urgent, whether this is the first or the seventh time you have suffered an emotional illness. What does this mean for your clinical treatment? For starters, unless a woman is breast-feeding, I prefer to prescribe a selective serotonin re-uptake inhibitor for postpartum depression, because often a therapeutic dose is reached on day 1. While these drugs still usually take two to three weeks to kick in, the extra time delay needed to build up tolerance to a full-dose tricyclic is avoided. (Women with postpartum panic disorder often respond quickly to low-dose tricyclics, without weight gain or extreme sedation.)

SSRIs generally take effect sooner than tricyclics because the medication doesn't need to build up in the bloodstream. However, if I feel that a tricyclic is the most appropriate prescription, I raise the dose very quickly and encourage my patients to be as accepting as possible of side effects, knowing that the dry mouth and other effects will improve soon.

Recently someone with classic PPD asked whether it made sense for her doctor to put her on a low-dose antidepressant and have her return in a month. No! Women with postpartum illnesses of any sort should have frequent medication checks, at least weekly in the beginning. One of the only balancing factors under your control during this time of great stress is pushing your doctor to treat you aggressively. A two-month-old baby whose mother has been depressed for a month has had a depressed mom for half of her life; both she and Mom deserve more. Don't be a "good girl" if you think your doctor is minimizing your problem.

Also, the incredible stress of this transitional period means that many postpartum women will deteriorate further if an overly conservative approach is taken. While my patients would attest that I don't usually jump to medication at the first sign of trouble, I am least likely to take a wait-and-see approach with new mothers. With the obvious exception of breast-feeding, I favor liberal use of medication because the demands on a new mother are so high, and I worry a good bit about small postpartum fires becoming raging infernos.

The urgency of postpartum depression also makes me more likely to comedicate. For example, anxiety is a common symptom of depression that resolves once the antidepressant kicks in. I am more likely than usual to add a second medication for anxiety in a postpartum patient, because although antianxiety medications do absolutely nothing for the underlying depression, any symptom relief is welcome. Likewise with sleeping pills.

Is Talk Therapy Effective?

While effective short-term psychotherapies for depression and anxiety (such as cognitive therapy) compare favorably with medication after a few months, in the early weeks of PPD, medication induces clinical improvement more rapidly than psychotherapy. Support groups and counseling are important pieces of postpartum wellness, but neither acts quickly. Not all doctors are fully aware of how extraordinarily difficult it is to care for a new baby (or a new baby *and* her siblings). Be sure that your therapist and/or doctor know how much responsibility you have at home and how rapid improvement is your overriding priority.

SIDE EFFECTS FOR NEW MOTHERS

Don't Make Me a Zombie

The most common concern about side effects that my postpartum patients express is worry that the medication will make them too sleepy to get up when the baby wakes. Sleep is a major concern for mothers of babies, who are damned if they do and damned if they don't. As mentioned earlier, inability to sleep when the baby sleeps is a hallmark of PPD, yet the reality is that women still shoulder the main or sole responsibility for nighttime feedings and can't function if they are excessively sedated. Initially selective serotonin re-uptake inhibitors may aggravate insomnia (but ultimately may correct sleep problems), but some tricyclic antidepressants can be so sedating that women find it impossible to drag themselves out of bed. All benzodiazepines are sedating, and even normal doses may be too sedating for new mothers.

Postpartum women also often do not tolerate full doses of the older, more sedating tricyclics, such as Sinequon (doxepin) and Elavil (amitriptyline) (although low doses of these medications are usually fine for panic disorder). However, usually they can tolerate less sedating tricyclics, such as Pamelor (nortriptyline) and Norpramin (desipramine). SSRIs are usually well tolerated, but a small dose of a mild sleeping pill may be needed if insomnia develops. If your doctor recommends a sleeping pill along with Zoloft (sertraline) or Prozac (fluoxetine), for example (as some doctors do routinely), make sure you remind her that you must not be too sedated because you need to get up at night. Don't assume that the fact that the doctor knows you have a baby means that she is attuned to how caring for a baby affects your tolerance to medication. Lower doses, milder sleep medications, or gradual dose adjustment may be necessary to strike the right balance between insomnia and oversedation. One practical strategy is to make upward dose adjustments of sedative medications on the nights when someone else can care for the baby, usually on the weekend.

I Want This Weight to Disappear

Another especially problematic side effect for postpartum women is antidepressant-induced weight gain. Almost none of us returns to our prepregnancy weight quickly, and, indeed, rapid weight loss after childbirth may be a sign of overactive thyroid or severe depression. The medications that are safest for women who breast-feed (more about this later) are, unfortunately, those most likely to cause weight gain or interfere with the ability to return quickly to prepregnancy weight. While plenty of women do not gain weight on tricyclic antidepressants (see Chapter 8), added weight is an especially troubling side effect for anyone who starts out wishing to lose weight.

If a tricyclic is recommended to you for PPD, consider trying it rather than deciding that you can't even think about gaining weight. If your appetite increases greatly or you begin to gain weight, the medication can be adjusted. My observation is that women with tricyclic-induced weight gain drop those extra pounds quickly once they stop the medication, and those pounds may be worth it if you can feel like yourself again. Many women are willing to risk gaining weight as long as they know it is reversible. Some women lose weight even taking a tricyclic because they are nursing.

I'm Already Constipated from the Iron

Tricyclic antidepressants aggravate constipation, a particular problem for a woman taking prenatal vitamins or iron while nursing. Constipation is especially problematic if you have stitches and/or hemorrhoids from childbirth. If this is a problem, increase fluids and fiber, and talk to your doctor.

Can't the Obstetrician Tell My Husband I Can Never Have Sex Again?

Sexual side effects of medication are another unique concern for postpartum women. SSRIs in particular may interfere with sexual interest or sexual pleasure. (See Chapter 7.) This is especially problematic for postpartum women for a number of reasons. First, by definition, chances are pretty good that if you are having babies, you have an available and interested sexual partner. Many women become less sexually active late in pregnancy and find that their partners are looking forward to resuming sexual relations after childbirth, waiting eagerly for that six- or eight-week go-ahead from the obstetrician. But childbirth tends to diminish women's sexual interest, PPD or not, since fatigue and hormonal changes (especially those in breast-feeding) interfere with libido, even for the entire first year. Sexually depleted women—new mothers head the list—are more susceptible to antidepressant-induced sexual changes. Treatment of PPD may restore sexual interest.

I won't repeat the discussion in Chapter 7 of what you can do about sexual side effects. I do wish to highlight one special concern for postpartum women when it comes to Wellbutrin (buproprion), one of the few antidepressants that causes no sexual side effects and that may actually enhance sexuality. Wellbutrin (and Ludiomil [maprotiline]) are contraindicated in conditions that increase the risk of drug-induced seizures: epilepsy, bulimia, or alcoholism, for example. Since sleep deprivation also increases your vulnerability to having a seizure, this contraindication is especially important after childbirth.

BREAST-FEEDING AND MEDICATION

When it comes to clear-cut answers about the potential risks vs. benefits of prescribing medications to nursing women, things have changed little in the last fifty years. I was astonished to find an article in the *Journal of Obstetrics and Gynaecology* from 1947 that noted the following:

> The fact that it is practically never necessary to remove the child from the breast when the mother is receiving drug therapy is borne out by the rarity of cases of untoward actions reported in the literature. Another important point that still holds is that it is rarely if ever desirable to treat a child with drugs given to the mother.

I was astonished to read this because now, fifty years after that article was written, the field is essentially in the same place. In the medical literature, "untoward" reactions—infant problems clearly attributable to maternal psychiatric medication—are extremely few and far between. However, it is equally true that it is never desirable to give any medication to a nursing mother.

Long-Term vs. Short-Term Effects

"Untoward effects" are, indeed, rarely described in nursing infants whose mothers are taking prescribed antidepressants. The problem is that we are much better at assessing immediate ill effects, such as changes in sleep, appetite, or temperament, than we are at assessing subtle theoretical risks of even tiny doses of medications that act on the brain in young babies.

Choosing the Right Medication

The medications that cause the clearest short-term problems are those that are highly sedating, because they may lead to poor weight gain in babies too sleepy to nurse well. Antianxiety medications are the biggest concern here, although low doses of short-acting benzodiazepines are usually fine, especially for irregular use. Either because of how they pass into breast milk or how they are metabolized, I recommend Restoril (temazepam) or Ativan (lorazepam) in nursing women, with Xanax (alprazolam) my third choice. Ambien (zolpidem) is a new chemically unique sleeping pill that is either absent or found only in extremely trace amounts in breast milk, and I am quite comfortable giving it to nursing women. Of all available sleeping medications, the American Academy of Pediatrics (see page 294) lists Ambien and chloral hydrate as "usually compatible with breast feeding." Unfortunately, while Ambien and chloral hydrate promote sleep, they do not treat an underlying depressive or anxiety disorder.

Most women at risk for PPD have depression, panic disorder, or OCD. Usually antidepressants are helpful for these disorders and cause no short-term ill effects. However, their long-term safety is neither proven nor disproven. When an antidepressant is desirable, I have a strong preference for tricyclic antidepressants, especially Pamelor (nortriptyline) and Norpramin (desipramine) for depression and Anafranil (clomipramine) for OCD. I also use low doses of Elavil (amitriptyline) or Tofranil (imipramine) for women with panic disorder. Even less long-term data about safety is available for the newest antidepressants, the SSRIs.

Dr. Wisner, who has studied prevention of recurrent PPD, is also a leading expert in the use of antidepressants in nursing women. Her research indicates that infants nursed by women taking therapeutic doses of Anafranil and Pamelor show nondetectable or very low levels of maternal medication.

Find Your Own Comfort Level

Given that infants are unlikely to have much of these tricyclics present in their system, individual women must decide whether to stop breast-feeding in order to take medication for depression or anxiety based on their own values, those of their doctor and the baby's doctor, and those of their families. This is a judgment call. Recognize that experts do not agree about whether it is advisable to take medication while nursing. I have patients who would never consider taking medication while nursing and others who would never consider stopping nursing unless their babies stopped growing and developing properly. I have colleagues who would never give medication to a nursing mother and others who would never advise stopping nursing in order to take medication. Most fall in between.

The Benefits of Nursing

I am rather liberal about using antidepressants in nursing mothers because I believe so strongly that breast milk is good for babies, it's good for women when it's the right choice, and feeling good makes all the difference in the world to you and your baby. Breast-fed babies have far fewer life-threatening infections, fewer milder viral and bacterial infections, fewer problems with obesity down the road, and their jaws develop more correctly anatomically. Breast-feeding reduces the risk of breast cancer for some women. Many mothers absolutely love nursing, saying that it's the one time they feel fully able to care for their babies. The attachment can be simply marvelous— for both parties. Oxytocin, a hormone released during lactation, promotes a sense of calm and well-being.

If you are faced with a decision about medication and breast-feeding, try to make it without giving in to social pressures. Some good mothers nurse their babies. Some good mothers bottle-feed their babies. I assure you, some bad mothers nurse their babies too. I strongly support breast-feeding, especially in the first few months. It is the preferred feeding method, and Mother Nature is quite wise. But it isn't the only alternative, and switching to a bottle because you are not comfortable taking medication while nursing is not the same thing as not using a car seat or forgetting to vaccinate your child.

Another Viewpoint

A wise and highly respected leader in women's reproductive mental health, Leslie Hartley Gise, M.D., clinical professor of psychiatry at the John A. Burns School of Medicine at the University of Hawaii, recently told me of her objections to maternal use of antidepressants while nursing. Unlike pregnancy, she noted, with nursing you have an alternative. You can treat the mother without exposing her baby to medication by having her wean.

Dr. Gise points out that we will probably never have good data about the safety of medicines for depression and anxiety in breast milk, so it's always a judgment call. She also points out that although the data indicating that infants have low blood levels of antidepressants are reassuring, unfortunately, that gives us no information about what is getting into the baby's brain, where it could accumulate.

Dr. Gise's position: Why take a chance? Why risk blaming yourself for anything that goes wrong with your child? Make sure that you won't regret this decision down the road.

The Unknown Rules of Medication

I respect Dr. Gise tremendously, but I disagree. I believe that the benefits of breast-feeding outweigh the theoretical risks for selected medications. Even more important, I know that many women will choose to remain significantly ill rather than give up nursing, and I know that this is not usually in the baby's best interest. The writer Somerset Maugham said that there are three rules for writing a novel: Unfortunately, no one knows what they are. This applies equally well to medication use in breast-feeding! I know that this puts a tremendous burden on you, the patient, since doctors cannot and should not tell you what to decide. But, truly, it's a decision so highly affected by values and feelings that it must be centered in your own values, in your own family. The good news is that if a doctor has told you that absolutely, positively you must give up nursing and so instead you are choosing to remain seriously ill because you just won't do that, you have some alternatives. Staying sick is the worst choice for you and your baby.

If You Choose to Take Medication While Nursing

Some medications should not be taken during nursing: lithium, antipsychotic medications, and phenobarbital generally should be avoided while nursing.

Otherwise, although the widely used contemporary medications released after Prozac have not been classified, all other antidepressants and antianxiety medications fall into the gray zone. Some of the medications classified by the American Academy of Pediatrics as "effect unknown but may be of concern" include Elavil, Anafranil, Norpramin, Sinequon, Luvox (fluvoxamine), Prozac, and Desyrel (trazodone). Also in this category: Valium (diazepam), Ativan (lorazepam), and Restoril (temazepam). I disagree a bit with this list. For example, I believe that Restoril, in moderate doses, is acceptable in nursing.

I also believe that Prozac is about the worst possible choice for use in nursing mothers. Prozac and its active metabolites remain in the body for longer than any other antidepressant.* Infants do not clear medication as well as their mothers. (Unlike in pregnancy, where the fetus relies on the mother to clear the medication, a baby must use its still-developing kidneys and liver.) Any medication, psychiatric or otherwise, has a tendency to build up in an infant. For this reason, I believe in substituting a shorter-acting medication, such as Effexor (venlafaxine) or Zoloft, if an SSRI is needed, since either drug is less likely to accumulate in the baby's system.

However, as in pregnancy, all else being equal, I strongly prefer to prescribe the traditional tricyclic Pamelor for nursing mothers when I need a full-strength dose. This is one of the times in which I feel tricyclics are more appropriate than the newer SSRIs, not because they work any differently but because they seem safer for the baby. I believe that other tricyclics are acceptable in small doses for panic disorder. If I anticipate that my patient is likely to end up requiring a full dose, I usually start with Pamelor. Other colleagues use Nor-pramin as a drug of first choice. Both drugs are usually well tolerated by postpartum women, because they usually don't interfere with sleep or affect concentration or energy, except to improve them once they kick in.

Rae took Paxil for her first episode of PPD, and it worked well for her. She really wanted to nurse, and I explained that since Paxil was so much newer than the old medications, I preferred to use a different medication. She was glad to learn that clinical effectiveness is comparable among the antidepressants, and since she had never tried anything else, we had no reason to believe that Paxil would be any better than another antidepressant.

I recommended Pamelor, starting at 25 mg at first, adjusting up by 25 mg every three nights if she could stand the side effects. When she reached 75 mg, I would send her for a blood test and adjust the medication after I had a sense of how she metabolized that dose. As it turned out, the blood test showed that she could get by on only 50 mg.

The baby thrived, growing and developing well. Rae's instincts were that everything was fine, and she did not want to put herself or

---

* "Active metabolites" means that the medication is broken down in the bloodstream to a chemical by-product that also induces brain chemical/neurotransmitter changes.

the baby through a blood test. Her pediatrician insisted, so Rae made her husband take the baby to the lab so she didn't have to watch. She hoped it was true when he told her that the baby just cried for a minute or two! After the results showed no detectable Pamelor, Rae was glad the test had been done.

The depression she felt during pregnancy resolved within a month postpartum, and it seemed that the medication averted a crisis. At four months postpartum, Rae felt so good that she decided to stop the medication. Although this is sooner than I advise stopping medication for "ordinary" PPD treatment, I explained that there wasn't much known about how long to treat preventively. Since Rae was nursing, she wanted to take as little medication as possible. Her instincts were right again; she did not relapse after she stopped the medication.

Women with OCD will not respond to Pamelor or Norpramin. In this case, Anafranil or a short-acting SSRI is preferred. However, many women with OCD don't consider continuing nursing while taking medication because they may become obsessed about the ambiguity of taking medicine while nursing. Most of my OCD patients elect to wean. I support this; no woman should be coaxed into taking medication while nursing if she is not totally comfortable with the decision.

The American Academy of Pediatrics does classify the mood stabilizers carbamazepine (Tegretol) and valproic acid (Depakote) as "usually compatible with breast-feeding," so these are much better alternatives than lithium for women with bipolar disorder. However, postpartum psychosis and/or a manic-depressive relapse is so very devastating that I urge women to put their health first and foremost above nursing if they are preferentially responsive to lithium. Nursing isn't worth a potentially catastrophic relapse.

Monitoring Mother and Baby

If you are nursing, it is best to take as little medication as possible. Your dose of medication can be adjusted after you take a simple blood test for a tricyclic antidepressant.

It is also important to monitor your baby carefully for any signs of side effects. Besides watching for changes in the baby's gastrointestinal system, sleep, and appetite, or temperamental difficulties, I often also recommend a blood test for the baby, to be sure that the medication isn't building up in his blood. Some hospitals can do a "screen" for a tricyclic using a heel stick alone; others will require a venipuncture (a regular blood test from the baby's arm). A urine test also might be considered.

Since watching your baby take a blood test is excruciating, you may wish to get a regular test only if a heel stick or urine screen detects medication in the baby's system. A regular blood test is needed for newer medications. **Any time blood is drawn from your baby, be sure that the technician has double-checked to find out the absolute lowest quantity that is needed.** Most labs routinely say that a whole teaspoonful is necessary but will accept less from a baby. I also recommend that you get the test done at a place with someone experienced with babies.

HORMONE TREATMENT AND PPD

It is natural to wonder whether estrogen or progesterone would be helpful for PPD. This issue is covered more fully on page 185, but I will touch on some of the issues here too. Some doctors prescribe progesterone for PPD, just as they have for premenstrual depression. There is absolutely no evidence that this is an effective treatment, and, indeed, progesterone may aggravate depression. So-called anecdotal evidence ("I know someone who took progesterone and it helped her") led to widespread use of progesterone for "PMS," but later it was shown to be no more effective than placebo. I encourage women to be careful to avoid the lure of "natural" hormones, especially since many safe and effective treatments for PPD are available.

One very exciting study published in 1996 did find that estrogen was an effective treatment for PPD. While this information is very preliminary, a team of British physicians used a form of estrogen skin patches (usually used for menopause) in women with severe postpartum depression, with excellent results. Many women who had not responded to ordinary antidepressants got better. However, much remains unknown. Time and time again, apparent medical wonders have not fulfilled their early promise, and women and their doctors would be wise to avoid nonchalantly jumping on any bandwagon, hormonal or otherwise.

This study raises fascinating possibilities for meaningful mind-body approaches to reproductive emotional health and treatment. But many questions are unanswered. The study did not compare conventional treatments for PPD to estrogen in a controlled, randomized fashion. It did not compare relative safety, and estrogen may be dangerous. Estrogen may be unsafe for women with a history of breast cancer (and worrisome in women with a strong family history), a history of or tendency to form blood clots, and in pregnancy. Also, the study addressed only PPD. At this point we know absolutely nothing about whether estrogen might be helpful prophylactically, whether it might help or prevent postpartum anxiety disorders, or if it could benefit women at risk of postpartum exacerbation of a pre-existing mood or anxiety disorder.

PPD and the Thyroid Gland

Postpartum thyroiditis, the most common hormonal imbalance that is associated with PPD, actually is not related to reproductive hormones. Postpartum thyroiditis is a transient thyroid inflammation that causes a temporary excess of thyroid hormone followed by too little. Classically, thyroid overactivity causes anxiety and insomnia, while underactivity causes fatigue and depression. Ordinary blood tests may not pick up postpartum thyroiditis, and it usually resolves spontaneously. Even when it is diagnosed, however, sometimes we just don't know for certain what role mild thyroid imbalance played in a particular woman's postpartum course. Because subtle ("subclinical") hypothyroidism may contribute to all forms of depression, especially PPD, I generally recommend tiny doses of thyroid hormone as the first-choice augmentation strategy (see p. 280) if regular antidepressants haven't worked.

HOW LONG DO I STAY ON THE ANTIDEPRESSANT?

Of course, how long any individual should take medication is a decision that should be made by a woman and her doctor. As a general guideline, I recommend that women experiencing their first or second bout of classic PPD remain on medication for the entire first postpartum year. Then I taper slowly, watching for the possible emergence of premenstrual depression, which can follow a bout of PPD (see p. 65) or be an early sign that the medication was stopped too soon.

The issue of how long to take medication prophylactically is unknown. The most vulnerable period for women is during the first three months postpartum, but no one knows whether mood stabilizers or antidepressants taken in the third through twelfth month are more effective preventive treatments. When I recommend tapering medication, I generally consider the counterbalancing stresses: Is the baby sleeping through the night yet? Is this an easy baby or a colicky, exhausting one? Is the woman getting help with household responsibilities? Are child care or other employment issues problematic? In general, I err on the side of continuing medication rather than risk stopping it too soon.

After three months of estrogen, progesterone should be taken for five to ten days to induce a period, since the estrogen can cause the uterine lining to become unhealthy.

CONCLUSION

It is terribly important to take good care of yourself after you have had a baby. This is a hard time to undergo medical treatment for depression or anxiety, because everyone in the world acts as if its the happiest time in your life. Reject the stereotypes. Do not buy into the myth that good mothers are immune to emotional illnesses. Do not buy into the myth that breast-feeding is the only way good mothers feed their infants. Good mothers take care of themselves and, in doing so, take care of their families.

Appendix A

THE BIOLOGICAL BASIS OF DEPRESSION AND ANXIETY

While I was writing this book, one of my patients reminded me how easy it is for women with depressive and anxiety disorders to blame themselves for their illnesses. This woman is a walking argument for the biological basis of depression. She has the genetic component: All of her siblings suffer from depressive disorders, and every distant branch of her family tree lights up. She has physical symptoms: extreme fatigue, sleep disturbance, sugar cravings, poor concentration. She responded to antidepressant medication in the past. She is blessed with a good job, good friends, a close-knit family, and no recent stressors. She has been happy and well adjusted in between depressive episodes.

But now she's depressed again. As happens from time to time, the medication she takes to ward off chronic depression isn't working as well anymore, and she and I are struggling to find a new biological treatment that will help her feel like herself again. Depression that breaks through formerly effective medication is a clinical challenge. While we search for a better solution than her old medication, she begins to doubt herself, to blame herself for her symptoms. "Maybe I'm just doing this to myself," she says. "Maybe I'm talking myself into this."

My heart breaks when I hear this. It seems the ultimate final insult that women with emotional disorders are so prone to blame themselves for the illnesses. Throughout this book, I have repeated that your symptoms aren't your fault. It isn't your fault if words are not enough. Sometimes a woman believes it isn't her fault only when the medicine kicks in. Try not to use this as a barometer. Not all women respond to medication, and those who don't are not to blame. Not all women respond to talk therapy, but those who do respond do not have any less real of a disease.

In the text, I briefly described what is known about the biological basis of anxiety and depression. This appendix is intended for readers who are interested in more detail. Here I describe the major biological findings in anxiety and depression: genetic studies, brain imaging, and neurotransmitters (the chemical messengers of the brain). While we don't know half of what we should know about women's reproductive hormones, I will discuss what some of the latest research tells us.

DEPRESSION AND ANXIETY ARE INHERITED

If an illness is genetic, then it should run in families, with closer blood relatives having more shared illness than distant relatives. Identical twins (whose genes are exactly the same) should have more shared illness than fraternal twins (who are no closer genetically than other siblings), and individuals who are adopted should suffer illnesses inherited from their biological families, not their adoptive families.*

Depression is a genetic illness by these criteria. As an example, having an identical twin with major depressive disorder doubles the already higher risk of having a fraternal twin with depression. The identical twin of an individual suffering from bipolar disorder is quite likely to also have the disease, while the identical twin of an individual with major depressive disorder has about a fifty-fifty chance. Bipolar illness is the single most clearly genetically transmitted emotional illness: If you have a parent, sibling, or child with bipolar disorder, you have a one in four chance of developing the disorder in your lifetime. As yet no specific gene or chromosome has been identified as causing depression or bipolar disorder.

The fact that identical twins do not have an identical risk for major mood disorder tells us that genes are not the only causative factor. Unlike shared eye color, which is solely genetic—all identical twins

---

* Any familial trait may be transmitted by nature or by nurture. Looking at illness in adopted children is the best way to sort out the contribution of nurture (environment) versus the contribution of nature (genetic predisposition).

have the same eye color—depression and bipolar disorder are best thought of as strongly genetically based illnesses that may remain latent, surfacing only if triggered by stress, other biological precipitants, or an individual's social and personal environment. Many familial diseases show this dual contribution of genes and environment: Diabetes, hypertension, heart disease, and cancer cluster in families but are not solely genetic.

Familial Affective Spectrum Disorders

An evolving concept based on genetic findings is that of affective spectrum disorders. Relatives of individuals with unipolar or bipolar affective disorders are at increased risk for a broad spectrum of psychiatric conditions: eating disorders, attention deficit disorder, premenstrual depression, and alcoholism. The genetic basis of various disorders may help explain why so many of these spectrum disorders respond to antidepressants.

Notice what is missing from the list of affective spectrum disorders: anxiety disorders, including panic disorder, agoraphobia, generalized anxiety disorder, and obsessive compulsive disorder. Anxiety disorders also cluster in families, but genetic predisposition to anxiety disorders is unrelated to genetic predisposition to depressive illness. We would expect this of genetic diseases: Relatives of individuals with diabetes are at increased risk for diabetes, but not for cancer. The specificity of familial predisposition to develop distinctive emotional illnesses is further evidence of the contribution of nature as opposed to nurture alone.

Familial Anxiety Spectrum Disorders

Generalized anxiety disorder (GAD), panic disorder, agoraphobia, and obsessive compulsive disorder also cluster in families. As mentioned in Chapter 4, having a close blood relative who suffers from panic disorder or agoraphobia greatly increases your own risk of these illnesses (but generally doesn't increase your risk of other anxiety disorders). GAD is familial but also distinctive from panic disorder; that is, having GAD in your family increases your vulnerability only to GAD.

Likewise, obsessive compulsive disorder (OCD) is more common in identical twins than in fraternal twins. Interestingly, subsequent generations and/or siblings with OCD may have completely different subtypes. One may be a "checker" while another is an obsessional doubter, for example. Compared to panic disorder, generalized anxiety disorder, and major mood disorders, however, OCD is less clearly inherited.

No One Has Perfect Genes

When I tell women about the genetic basis of emotional illnesses, they usually breathe a sigh of relief, basking in a moment in which they feel that the illness is not their fault. For many, the next moment is very uncomfortable: Have I cursed my beloved children? I wish I could make this easier, but I cannot. Yes, your children are at higher risk, your daughters more so than your sons. But, for starters, having an anxiety or depressive disorder does not have to interfere with your own *or* your children's ability to love, laugh, work, and play. These are not such horrible diseases that you should feel morally compelled to prevent them through childlessness. Like every other mother in the world, I understand deeply the wish to protect my children from any harm, however slight, especially one of my own causing. We all bless our children with our good genes but cannot control our bad ones. You do not berate yourself for transmitting a familial risk of high blood pressure, or diabetes, or cancer.

Try to find a way to make peace with yet another example in which we mothers cannot be omnipotent. Many of my patients find comfort knowing that thanks to scientific research, new and better treatments are on the horizon. As one said, "I just have to believe that twenty years from now my daughter will have solutions I can't even imagine."

Also know that there are nongenetic factors that you can address. With the possible exception of bipolar disorder, these same twin studies also show that while the genetic component was great, it was not even close to being the only factor. One way of looking at your tendency to "transmit" emotional illnesses to your children is to recognize that you and they both benefit from your receiving aggressive treatment. Feeling good, feeling less anxious or blue, feeling less out of control will help you to transmit the sense of security and safety that you may have lacked growing up.

DOES THE BRAIN OF A PERSON WITH DEPRESSIVE OR ANXIETY DISORDER LOOK ANY DIFFERENT?

Medical images of the brain include X rays, nuclear brain scans, CT (computed tomography) scans (also called CAT scans), and MRI (magnetic resonance imaging) scans. Each of these ways of looking at the brain provides information about the brain's structure but not its function. It's a little like looking at a photograph taken under the hood of your car: The image doesn't capture how the engine actually works. At this stage of technology, these standard medical images are rarely useful either in making the diagnosis of depression or in illuminating the nature of the problem.*

An electroencephalogram (EEG) tells us about electrical activity of the brain. An EEG draws a rather crude anatomical map of the brain's electrical functioning. Brain cells communicate and function by way of electrochemical activity. Chemicals called neurotransmitters spread electricity between individual brain cells and from one region of the brain to another. Just as the heart's electrical activity can be measured by an electrocardiogram (EKG), the brain's electrical activity can be measured by an EEG, a similarly noninvasive, nonpainful test. Unfortunately, ordinary EEGs give us very little information, unless the emotional symptoms are actually due to a type of epilepsy. Your doctor may be especially likely to recommend an EEG if your symptoms are episodic, suggesting a possible underlying epilepsy, but most women with depression and anxiety do not need an EEG.

In research settings, an expensive and rather elaborate type of EEG called polysomnography has demonstrated a particular biological abnormality seen in clinical depression. Polysomnography studies have repeatedly and consistently documented that the electrical activity during sleep is abnormal in clinically depressed people. Such results were among the early indications that depression has a biological basis, early evidence for the physiologic disturbance in the disease of depression. Clinically, many depressed women have insomnia or escape into excess sleep. At the brain wave level, depres-

---

* Your doctor may order one of these tests to be sure that you do not have a neurologic basis for emotional symptoms. If the results show no abnormality, however, that does not mean that your illness is not real.

sion causes a highly characteristic EEG abnormality called shortened REM (rapid eye movement) latency, which means that dream sleep comes on too quickly in depressed people. While this abnormality is not present in every single case of depression and is sometimes seen in other illnesses (including OCD), it is as close to a diagnostic fingerprint as we have for depression at present. Other sleep abnormalities in depression include increased REM density (more sleep time spent in intense dream states) and decreased non-REM sleep. Practically and financially speaking, it is rarely necessary to sleep in a hospital laboratory with EEG electrodes attached to your head to be diagnosed as having depression, but it is helpful in research and to supply evidence of depression's biological abnormalities.

Some very exciting developments are under way in linking brain imaging with measures of brain functioning, much like moving from a still photograph of the brain to a videotape. The most exciting of these is the PET (positron emission tomography) scan, which is CT scanning modified to include information about blood flow, use of oxygen, and nutritional activity in the brain. (All of these are indirect measures of cellular activity.) PET scans are research tools performed at academic centers and are not now used clinically or covered by insurance.

However, PET scans have given us amazing information about the brain's role in psychiatric illness. How the brain uses oxygen and nutrients can be compared in individuals who are and are not suffering a mental disorder. If individuals with a particular illness show consistent abnormal activity levels in a certain anatomic region of the brain, it would be very difficult to view this as anything but evidence that the brain itself is the problem. PET scans have demonstrated specific brain abnormalities in bipolar affective disorder and obsessive compulsive disorder.

The findings in OCD are quite compelling and give us a fascinating look at how biological and talk therapies can alter brain chemistry. Although the data are preliminary, abnormalities in PET scans of individual suffering from OCD have been localized to specific brain sites (the basal ganglia and the frontal cortex). When the highly specialized psychotherapy called behavioral therapy is successful in relieving the symptoms of OCD, it actually normalizes these PET scan abnormalities, just as serotonin-enhancing medication does.

After successful treatment using talk therapy or medication, the oxygen and glucose abnormalities in these specific sites in the brain can no longer be seen. This is a watershed moment in modern psychiatry: A real brain illness with emotional symptoms has been shown to have a specific abnormality in a specific part of the brain, and this abnormality can be treated successfully using the right words or the right medication.

Like all scientific breakthroughs, this opens a host of intriguing questions. How do words and/or medications fix a brain abnormality? One possible explanation is that, in some highly intricate way, they both modify the chemical messengers of the brain (neurotransmitters) that in turn control the functional activity.

SEROTONIN AND OTHER NEUROTRANSMITTERS AND HOW THEY AFFECT THE BRAIN

Many people have heard of the neurotransmitter serotonin. Other neurotransmitters include norepinephrine (also called noradrenaline), dopamine, and gamma-aminobutyric acid (GABA).

Chemical Messengers

Neurotransmitters are chemical messengers that brain cells use to communicate with one another, to shut off one part of the brain or turn on another. A particular brain cell releases its neurotransmitter into the microscopic space (called a synapse) between itself and other brain cells. That neurotransmitter binds to the adjacent cell(s) at a site called a receptor, leading to electrochemical activity (neuronal discharge) in the receptor cell. To give a simplified model, this is much like sending electricity (the first cell) through the plug in the socket (the neurotransmitter) that turns on the television (the receptor cell).

Re-Uptake of Neurotransmitters

An important part of this process is that the first cell conserves the neurotransmitter by taking it back inside the cell, then recycling and reusing it over and over (called re-uptake, or presynaptic re-uptake).

The receptor cell responds to the reduced amount of neurotransmitter in the synapse by adding receptors, much as you might put a large satellite antenna up in order to pick up more channels.

Gathering information about brain chemistry is inherently difficult; human beings are designed to keep this precious organ as protected as possible. Brain biopsies, spinal fluid taps, and invasive brain chemical measurements obviously are not appropriate for everyday study. The brain's chemical messengers do not pass freely from the brain into the bloodstream, so blood and urine tests can provide only a partial view of what's happening in the brain. However, the amassed indirect evidence shows quite clearly that major mood and anxiety disorders are associated with neurotransmitter dysfunction.

Neurotransmitter Dysfunction and Depression

The first evidence that a deficiency of neurotransmitters could cause depression was seen when the disorder was found to be a direct side effect of an old-fashioned blood pressure medicine called reserpine. Reserpine depletes certain brain neurotransmitters (serotonin and norepinephrine), causing a mood disorder that is clinically identical to ordinary depression.

Scientists then examined the urine, spinal fluid, and blood of people with spontaneous clinical depression to indirectly measure these brain neurotransmitters; they found low levels of the metabolic by-products of the same neurotransmitters. This finding suggests that the same depletion of neurotransmitters causes clinical depression. Almost all antidepressants act to increase the activity of one or both of these neurotransmitters, further "back-door" evidence that these two specific chemicals are malfunctioning in depression.

Serotonin and norepinephrine stimulate activity in receptor cells. It makes intuitive sense that the absence of stimulating neurotransmitters would result in an emotional syndrome characterized by slowing: depression.

Neurotransmitter Dysfunction and Anxiety Disorders

One also might expect that having too little of a neurotransmitter that slows down brain cell activity could result in an emotional syndrome characterized by being overstimulated, racy, wired: anxiety. This is exactly the case. The specific neurotransmitter which is dysfunctional in panic disorder and generalized anxiety disorder is GABA. Unlike other neurotransmitters, which promote nerve cell activity, GABA is an inhibitory neurotransmitter—it quiets electrical activity in the brain. If levels of this calming neurotransmitter are low, the brain receives excessively active distress messages.

There exist other theories about the exact nature of neurotransmitter dysfunction in anxiety disorders. Rather than having too little GABA, one theory states that the receptor cells have faulty reception, like a television with a broken antenna. Decreased sensitivity to GABA would mean that the natural supply of the calming neurotransmitter isn't effective in women with panic disorder.

Some researchers feel that anxiety disorders are caused by dysfunction of norepinephrine at a specific brain site called the locus coeruleus. Chemicals (such as yohimbine) that increase the electrical activity in the locus coeruleus increase anxiety.

HOW MEDICATIONS FOR DEPRESSION AND ANXIETY AFFECT NEUROTRANSMITTERS

All medications for anxiety and depression work by changing the balance of these various neurotransmitters in the brain. They may work by increasing the absolute amount of neurotransmitter present between the cells or, more probably, by making the entire system run more efficiently.

Usually Just One Neurotransmitter Doesn't Cause One Disorder

The fact that two entirely different medications for anxiety (tricyclics and benzodiazepines) act on two entirely different neurotransmitters (norepinephrine and GABA) tells us something interesting: The brain has overlapping, interwoven chemical networks. Because of this, often the entire complex system can be put back in balance simply by affecting one of the components. This principle holds true for depression as well, with serotonin and norepinephrine. Medications that affect either of these two neurotransmitters generally are equally effective antidepressants.

OCD, in contrast, appears to be solely serotonin based. Medications that affect norepinephrine, GABA, or dopamine are ineffective in OCD. Premenstrual depression is in between: Serotonin-enhancing medications are most effective, but medications which affect GABA, norepinephrine, and dopamine may be moderately effective.

More Specifics About Neurotransmitters

Antidepressants inhibit the re-uptake of one or more neurotransmitters, which is the functional equivalent of increasing its activity. Tricyclic antidepressants inhibit the re-uptake of norepinephrine. As their name indicates, the new serotonin re-uptake inhibitors preferentially inhibit the re-uptake of serotonin. To try to visualize why re-uptake inhibition increases the amount of a particular chemical messenger, picture a supply of *T.V. Guides* piling up on the coffee table. You will have as many *T.V. Guides* as the amount coming in minus the amount you "re-uptake." If you get a new one every week but remember to throw the old one away only every two weeks, they pile up.

Delayed vs. Immediate Effects of Antidepressants

When an antidepressant's re-uptake is slowed down, a complex series of chain reactions is set off. The sensitivity and absolute number of the receptors in the second cell is reduced; this finding has led to the notion that rather than a pure deficiency of neurotransmitter, the actual chemical imbalance is supersensitivity in the receptor cell. In other words, because not enough of the chemical messenger has been present in between the two cells, the second cell has tried to restore balance by adding receptors. But this backfires, because, for reasons we don't entirely understand, having more receptors (supersensitivity) compounds the problem. Medications immediately increase the amount of neurotransmitter present between the cells, but they do not reduce the overabundance of receptors in the second cell (a chain reaction called down-regulation) for several weeks. The delay in clinical response to antidepressants mirrors the timing of this chain reaction. Antidepressants act immediately to increase the amount of neurotransmitter, yet no antidepressant combats depression immediately. Instead, it usually takes at least two weeks and up to eight weeks for any antidepressant to take effect. Two to eight weeks is about how long it takes for the secondary down-regulation to occur. The fact that clinical response to antidepressants corresponds very closely to the timing of down-regulation is why researchers believe that down-regulation is the specific way these medications work.

Down-regulation of receptors outside the brain may also explain why early physical side effects almost always get better. When you first take these antidepressants, you may experience side effects from the presence of increased neurotransmitters throughout your body. For example, serotonin is present in the intestinal wall. Immediate increased serotonin from the medication causes the intestines to become more active, which translates clinically into nausea, diarrhea, and cramping. After the receptor cells in the intestine down-regulate, you go back to the original balance you had prior to the medication, and the side effects get better or go away.

At this time there is no absolute consensus about how these drugs work and there are many unanswered questions. Fortunately, while you will have to tolerate the unknowns, the fact that clinical treatment of depression and anxiety is way ahead of full scientific explanations means that often we can fix the problem even if we don't know exactly what we are doing at the cellular level. As one of my former teachers states in a wonderful new textbook of psychiatric medications: "It is now evident that a single neurotransmitter theory does not suffice to explain all known evidence."* Clear as mud?

Are These Changes Permanent?

People usually like to stop taking medication when they feel better. In the case of restoring neurotransmitter balance, however, stopping the medication too quickly will cause the original imbalances to come right back. This is why continuing the medications for a few months to a year is advisable even when you feel like yourself again.

Some chemical imbalances are sure to return without medication. To use the TV comparison, poor reception may be due to a temporary condition (the emotional equivalent of a thunderstorm), or it may be due to an irreversible problem in the TV itself. A single bout of depression or anxiety disorder doesn't indicate that anything is per-

* Philip Janicak, John Davis, Sheldon Preskorn, and Frank Ayd, Jr., *Principles and Practices of Psychopharmacotherapy*, Williams and Wilkins, 1993.

manently "broken," and it would be unnecessary to take corrective measures forever. But bipolar disorder and chronic recurrent depression do indicate an inherent problem that will likely recur if the treatment is removed. Medications for depression and anxiety treat but do not cure the problem.

Neurotransmitters and Anxiety Disorders

Antidepressants reduce activity in the locus coeruleus, and clinically, they reduce anxiety and panic. Benzodiazepines (tranquilizers such as Xanax [alprazolam] and Klonopin [clonazepam]) increase GABA activity, which we assume is how they work to reduce anxiety. Rather than affecting neurotransmitter re-uptake, benzodiazepines attach themselves to the second cell GABA receptor, resulting in immediate slowing down of that cell's electrical firing. As one would expect clinically, tranquilizers have an immediate calming effect, unlike antidepressants, which may take weeks until down-regulation occurs. Many doctors coprescribe tranquilizers for short-term use for a wide spectrum of conditions, including depression and anxiety, until the antidepressant chain reaction kicks in.

WHAT ABOUT HORMONES?

Along with the brain's neurotransmitter deficits, very subtle but real chemical imbalances in the hormones that circulate throughout the body are found in people with depression and anxiety disorders. The neuroendocrine system connects the hormone system of the brain and the body. The neuroendocrine system is a large feedback loop. The brain site (hypothalamus) stimulates the pituitary gland (at the base of the brain) to stimulate the glands scattered throughout the body (including the ovaries, thyroid, and adrenal glands). Levels of circulating hormones feed back to the hypothalamus, which keeps the entire neuroendocrine system running.

Biological regulation via the hormonal neuroendocrine system is clearly dysfunctional in depression; recent studies also indicate that there are subtle abnormalities in the neuroendocrine system in OCD and panic disorder. Unfortunately, these disorders of thyroid or adrenal glands are typically "subclinical"—not so extreme that ordinary blood tests pick up the problem, but presumably bad enough that the brain is affected.

The thyroid feedback loop of the neuroendocrine system is especially likely to be out of kilter in depression and bipolar disorder. Because the thyroid abnormalities are typically subclinical, many psychiatrists add small amounts of thyroid hormone if an antidepressant isn't working. Full-blown low thyroid disease (hypothyroidism) is a well-known cause of secondary depression. Overactivity of the thyroid gland—due to illnesses such as Graves' disease or to overmedication with thyroid hormone—mimics anxiety disorders, causing symptoms of insomnia, a sense of being revved up, and anxiety attacks.

The neuroendocrine system also includes the ovarian reproductive hormones progesterone and estrogen, which are regulated by the pituitary hormones follicle stimulating hormone (FSH) and luteinizing hormone (LH). Estradiol is the naturally occurring estrogen found in the body. Its levels peak twice during the menstrual cycle: just prior to ovulation and about a week before menstruation. Progesterone levels begin to rise at ovulation, peak at the second estradiol peak, and drop back down just prior to menstruation.

Given the unexplained vulnerability of women to mood and anxiety disorders, it is logical to wonder about the influence of ovarian hormones. Both progesterone and estrogen act on neurotransmitter receptors in the brain, but much remains unknown. Reproductive hormones appear to influence actual brain development as well as neurotransmitter-receptor interactions. Further, estrogen inhibits the metabolic breakdown of the neurotransmitter serotonin, which theoretically would cause women to have enhanced moods. There are many, many missing pieces of the puzzle, but, in general, estrogen is probably a mood-enhancing hormone while progesterone may reduce anxiety and/or increase depression. Testosterone (also made by the ovaries in small amounts) is known to affect behavior (aggression) and mood (energy and libido).

It is especially intriguing to look at these hormones at major reproductive transitions. Menarche (the onset of menstruation at puberty) is the time when girls begin to be increasingly vulnerable to depression and anxiety. Until that time, the rates of these disorders in children are roughly equivalent. Once menstruation begins, girls begin to outpace boys in depression and panic disorder, becoming ever more vulnerable by early adulthood. OCD is the opposite: Most children with OCD are boys. Women tend to develop OCD only in early adulthood. The correlation between menarche and increased vulnerability to mood and anxiety disorders is compelling evidence for a biological vulnerability based in reproductive physiology.

Premenstrually, mood changes are the rule. Although only a small percentage of women have true premenstrual depression, most women have mild mood and/or physical symptoms prior to their period. Since all menstruating women have the same hormonal cycles, it may turn out that women have varying degrees of individual sensitivity to the effects of estrogen and progesterone. Many menstruating women do not react neurochemically to reproductive hormone shifts; they do not have premenstrual mood changes. Other women, however, have mild mood reactivity to hormone changes. The third group consists of the small minority of women who are highly sensitive to reproductive hormone fluctuations, which regularly depress mood at major hormone shifts: before menses, during pregnancy, after childbirth, and at or just before menopause.

Reproductive "Kindling"

I believe that hormones affect mood much like ragweed affects allergy sufferers. The hormone shifts are like ragweed in August: present in the environment, but a problem only for vulnerable individuals. This explains why blood tests for hormone imbalances are not useful; the problem is in the brain's response, not how much is in the bloodstream. It also explains why if you have suffered any reproductive-related mood disorder (such as depression due to birth control pills or postpartum depression), you are far more likely to experience a similar mood disturbance during other hormonal transitions. Sensitivity to hormone-induced mood changes has been called kindling. The model of reproductive hormonal kindling proposes that some women's brains are prone to depressed mood during major hormonal shifts (just as allergy sufferers are sensitive to ragweed). Then, having had one bout of hormonal depression renders the individual even more vulnerable to an increasingly mild threshold of hormone changes. It's as if the brain "learns" to become depressed when it is exposed to repeated hormonal fluctuations, much like a fire is rekindled more easily when a few embers remain.

The kindling hypothesis also explains why premenstrual depression appears to become progressively worse over the years and why it is much more common in women over thirty-five and rarely seen in teenagers. Each cycle's repeated hormonal fluctuation rekindles the mood changes, a cumulative problem that increases as one ages. This model can also partly explain why although most women do not have premenopausal mood disorders, a woman with a history of any reproductive mood disorder may suffer greatly during the transition to menopause. And it can account for the much greater vulnerability to depression seen in abrupt menopause (as in women undergoing surgical removal of the ovaries or taking Nolvadex [tamoxifen] for breast cancer or Danazol [danocrine] for endometriosis.): The brain is depleted of hormones so abruptly and dramatically that it has no opportunity to adjust. Finally, the model also can explain why postmenopausal women, even those with past histories of reproductive-related mood problems, generally are less vulnerable to depression once menopause is fully established (once periods stop for a year).

We are just beginning to learn about the relationship between mood and anxiety and reproductive hormones. As we begin to learn more about the role of hormones, we can look at how and when hormones might be an appropriate treatment for mood and anxiety disorders. (See p. 185.)

CONCLUSION

You may be totally confused by all these different explanations for mood and anxiety disorders. If not, go back and reread the text, because the information is indeed conflicting and confusing! While it's natural to search for a single common cause of depression, many illnesses are not so easily explained. Cancer is an example. Certain psychosocial factors affect the risk of dying from cancer, such as the fact that poor women of color are more likely than other women to present with more advanced stages of cervical cancer, since they have less access to early Pap smear screening. Conversely, women affiliated with religious groups that condemn smoking have health benefits based purely on psychosocial factors. Genetics and bad luck often overwhelm the psychosocial factors, and all types of cancers share certain biological abnormalities, regardless of whether you got cancer from exposure to carcinogens at your factory, because of smoking, or, is usually the case, for no known reason except misfortune. Mood and anxiety disorders will undoubtedly turn out to be caused by more than one thing. I expect that we will see more and more evidence of the biological basis of mood and anxiety disorders, but will never come to view psychological or social factors as irrelevant or noncontributory.

But the fact that anxiety and mood disorders are characterized by highly specific neurotransmitter abnormalities in the brain tells us that a chemical imbalance is present. The fact that highly specific medications are effective treatments for highly specific conditions tells us that a chemical imbalance is present. Many women really believe that they have a real illness only when evidence of the success of biological treatment makes it impossible for them to continue blaming themselves.

MEDICATIONS FOR DEPRESSION AND ANXIETY

This section is designed to give specific information about individual medications. After the first page listing the brand and generic names of medications, only the brand name is given.

Please keep in mind that this information is for general informational purposes, to help you communicate better with your doctor, not for self-regulation of medication. Do not make any changes in your medication whatsoever without talking to your doctor, who knows your individual situation. Making changes without doing so could be dangerous to your health and well-being. This general information may not apply to you as an individual and should not be interpreted or used as personal medical advice or treatment.

Your personal physician is the best source of personal medical advice. If your doctor is not open to communication, you should consider changing doctors to one who is receptive to working with you on your terms.

Table B.1 | BRAND AND GENERIC NAMES OF PSYCHOPHARMACOTHERAPEUTIC MEDICATIONS

Brand Name	Generic Name
Adapin	doxepin
Ambien	zolpidem
Anafranil	clomipramine
Ativan	lorazepam
Aventyl	nortriptyline
Buspar	buspirone
Centrax	prazepam
Cibalith, Eskalith, Lithobid, Lithonate, Lithotabs	lithium
Dalmane	flurazepam
Depakote	valproic acid, valproate
Desyrel	trazodone
Doral	quazepam
Effexor	venlafaxine
Elavil	amitriptyline
Endep	amitriptyline
Halcion	triazolam
Klonopin	clonazepam
Librium	chlordiazepoxide
Ludiomil	maprotiline
Luvox	fluvoxamine
Marplan	isocarboxazid
Nardil	phenelzine
Norpramin	desipramine
Pamelor	nortriptyline
Parnate	tranylcypromine
Paxil	paroxetine
Paxipam	halazepam
Prosom	estazolam
Prozac	fluoxetine
Remeron	mirtazapine
Restoril	temazepam
Serax	oxazepam
Serzone	nefazodone
Sinequon	doxepin

Brand Name	Generic Name
Surmontil	trimiprimine
Tegretol	carbamazepine
Tofranil	imipramine
Tranxene	clorazepate
Valium	diazepam
Vivactil	protriptyline
Wellbutrin	buproprion
Xanax	alprazolam
Zoloft	sertraline

Table B.2 | CLASSIFICATION OF PSYCHOTHERAPEUTIC MEDICATIONS

The following classification groups medications as they are generally used in clinical practice. In certain instances, these categories overlap. I've clustered them together the ways I think your doctor may describe them to you.

Medication Type	Clinical Use	Brand Names
Advanced-generation antidepressants: serotonin-enhancing (also called SSRIs)	Depression, panic disorder, OCD, PMD, eating disorders, chronic fatigue syndrome, chronic pain	Anafranil, Desyrel, Effexor, Luvox, Paxil, Prozac, Remeron, Serzone, Zoloft[a]
Advanced-generation antidepressants: atypical	Depression, attention deficit disorder	Wellbutrin
Anxiolytics (benzodiazepines)	Anxiety, agitation, insomnia, agoraphobia, panic disorder	Ativan, Centrax, Klonopin, Librium, Paxipam, Serax, Tranxene, Valium, Xanax
Buspirone	Anxiety, depression, PMD	Buspar
Tricyclic antidepressants (heterocyclics)	Depression, panic disorder, agoraphobia, anxiety, insomnia, OCD,[b] chronic fatigue, chronic pain	Adapin, Anafranil, Aventyl, Elavil, Endep, Ludiomil, Norpramin, Pamelor, Sinequon, Surmontil, Tofranil, Vivactil
Mood stabilizers	Bipolar affective disorder	Depakote, Lithium, Tegretol
Monoamine oxidase inhibitors	Depression, anxiety disorders	Marplan, Nardil, Parnate
Sleeping pills	Insomnia	Ambien, Dalmane, Doral, Halcion, Klonopin, Prosom, Restoril[c]

[a] Effexor and Remeron enhance serotonin and norepinephrine. Also, although Anafranil is a heterocyclic, it is also a powerful serotonin-enhancing antidepressant. Technically, Effexor and Remeron are serotonin and norepinephrine re-uptake inhibitors (SNRIs), and not selective serotonin re-uptake inhibitors (SSRIs). In everyday use, most doctors use the term SSRI interchangeably. This glossary uses the term "SSRIs" to lump together all serotonin-enhancing antide-pressants.
[b] Anafranil is the only heterocyclic that is usually effective against OCD.
[c] In very small doses, Elavil, Desyrel, and Sinequon are often prescribed as sleeping pills. (See Chapter 6.)

ANTIDEPRESSANTS

Table B.3 | A COMPARISON OF ANTIDEPRESSANTS

Classification	Pros	Cons
Serotonin-enhancing antidepressants	Start at therapeutic dose Usually no weight gain Usually not sedating[b] Usually fewest side effects	Sexual side effects common[a] Expensive May worsen sleep May be too stimulating
Tricyclic antidepressants	Often improve sleep Longer track record Blood testing for dose adjustment more reliable than alternatives Not all depressions are serotonin responsive	May cause sedation Constipation, dry mouth, weight gain more common Your system must build up to a therapeutic dose slowly, which can delay clinical response Toxicity in overdose is high
Buproprion	No sexual, weight gain side effects	Two or three-times-daily dosing inconvenient

[a] Remeron and Serzone cause little or no sexual effects
[b] Remeron, Serzone, and Trazodone are frequently sedating

Table B.4 | ANTIDEPRESSANTS THAT INCREASE SEROTONIN

Selective serotonin re-uptake inhibitors (SSRIs) are generally as effective as other antidepressants for depression and panic disorder but more effective than tricyclics and atypical antidepressants for obsessive compulsive disorder and premenstrual depression. Approval status from the Food and Drug Administration indicates that the parent drug company has documented that the medication is effective for a particular disorder. In clinical practice, doctors may prescribe for so-called off-label uses, based on research conducted after the drug company obtains FDA approval. Commonly, SSRIs are prescribed off-label for premenstrual depression, eating disorders (especially bulimia and compulsive overeating), chronic fatigue syndrome, migraines, and panic disorder with or without agoraphobia.

Medication	FDA Approved for Depression	FDA Approved for OCD
Anafranil		✓
Desyrel[a]	✓	
Effexor	✓	
Luvox		✓
Paxil	✓	✓
Prozac	✓	✓
Remeron	✓	
Serzone	✓	
Zoloft	✓	✓

[a] Relatively weak serotonergic, ineffective for OCD

Table B.5 | USUAL DOSE RANGES OF THE SSRIs

As a general rule, the higher-dose ranges are used for major depression and obsessive compulsive disorder, with lower doses often effective for premenstrual disorder and panic disorder. If you have a history of jitteriness from mild stimulants such as caffeine and decongestants, your doctor may recommend an even lower starting dose. Also, psychiatrists often use higher initial doses than other physicians. Dosages typically are halved for women over the age of sixty-five.

Medication	Usual Starting Dose Range	Usual Therapeutic Dose Range	Available Pill Strength	Usual Maximum
Anafranil	25 mg at bedtime	75–200 mg	25, 50, 75 mg	250 mg
Effexor	18.75–37.5 mg twice daily	75–300 mg (split)	25, 37.5, 50, 75, 100 mg	400 mg
Luvox	50 mg at bedtime	150–300 mg	50, 100 mg	300 mg
Paxil	10–20 mg, usually in the morning	10–40 mg	10, 20 mg	50 mg
Prozac	5–20 mg, usually in the morning	10–80 mg	10, 20 mg and as a liquid	80 mg
Remeron	15 mg at bedtime	15–30 mg	15, 30 mg	45 mg
Serzone	100 mg twice daily	150–200 mg twice daily	100, 150, 200, 250 mg	300 mg twice daily
Zoloft	25–50 mg, usually in the morning	50–200 mg	50, 100 mg	200–250 mg

Table B.6 | UNIQUE PROPERTIES OF PROZAC

Since most Americans have now heard of Prozac, many women wonder why a doctor might recommend another selective serotonin re-uptake inhibitor (SSRI) rather than Prozac, or vice versa. The main difference between Prozac and other SSRIs is that Prozac has a much longer half-life. Prozac and its metabolites (by-products) remain in your system for weeks (or months in older women) after you last take the medication. Other SSRIs are usually gone from your system within days.

Potential Advantages of a Long Half-Life	Potential Disadvantages of a Long Half-Life
No withdrawal when stopped. Since Prozac is the only SSRI that can be stopped abruptly without causing discomfort, some doctors prefer it over other SSRIs when they expect to stop the medication eventually.	Longer washout needed when changing to another antidepressant (especially an monoamine oxidase inhibitor). Least acceptable SSRI for nursing because it may remain in the baby's system too long.
Allows for flexible dosing strategies (such as taking a single weekly dose of 60 mg for maintenance therapy or taking it during the premenstrual period alone) and for tiny dose administration. (See Table B.8.)	Prozac remains in your system longer than other SSRIs, so if you become pregnant accidentally and want to stop the medication, it is still in your blood. (So far, however, Prozac is the only SSRI for which there is human data showing no increased risk of major physical birth defects.)
Only antidepressant that can be taken every other day, either on purpose or because you often forget your medication.	The "drug holiday" strategy of skipping a few days' worth of medication for temporary relief of SSRI-induced sexual dysfunction is not effective.

Table B.7 | ADVANTAGES AND DISADVANTAGES OF SHORT-ACTING SEROTONIN-ENHANCING ANTIDEPRESSANTS

Medication	Advantages	Disadvantages
Anafranil	Least likely to cause insomnia or agitation	More side effects than other SSRIs (dry mouth, constipation, weight gain)
Effexor	Fewest interactions with other medications	Must be taken twice daily and discontinued very gradually
	At higher doses, it has a wider and more powerful effect on multiple neurotransmitters	Requires monitoring of blood pressure (may elevate blood pressure in some women)
Luvox	Mildly sedating, low incidence of agitation, introduced in U.S. after wide use in Europe	Greater tendency to cause sleepiness than most other SSRIs
Paxil	Like Luvox, mildly sedating (preferred by many doctors for anxiety disorders)	More likely to cause constipation (which also means less likely to cause diarrhea)
Remeron	No sexual dysfunction	Very sedating
Serzone	No sexual dysfunction	Must be taken twice daily and tends to be sedating
Zoloft	Middle-of-the-road side effects make it the most common antidepressant prescribed by psychiatrists (e.g., is less sedating than Paxil, less stimulating than Prozac)	Absorption varies with full or empty stomach (more absorption after eating a meal)

Table B.8 | HOW TO ADJUST THE PROZAC DOSE DOWNWARD

Some women need to take less than the smallest capsule dosage of Prozac. Women with panic disorder, women with premenstrual depression, and older women may be too sensitive to the stimulation and/or insomnia side effects to tolerate the 10 mg capsule. Under medical supervision, a patient can take smaller amounts of Prozac by one of two methods:

LIQUID PROZAC: A liquid form of Prozac contains 20 mg per teaspoon. A syringe or measuring spoon will allow for doses less than 10 mg per day. While this is the most convenient way to take low doses of Prozac, it is also the most expensive one.

DISSOLVING THE PROZAC: Some doctors instruct their patients to empty a 10 mg capsule into 8 ounces of juice (specifically, lemon-lime Gatorade, cranberry juice, or orange or apple juice), stir very well to dissolve it, and drink two to four ounces depending on the prescribed dose. (The solution stays good for two weeks when refrigerated.) Store the solution safely; make sure that no one confuses it with regular juice.

Table B.9 | COMMON SIDE EFFECTS OF SSRIs

Side Effects	Possible Remedies/Comments
Stomach upset, nausea, and/or diarrhea	Usually resolves. Ginger may help. Over-the-counter stomach preparations usually safe for short-term use
Insomnia or decreased need for sleep	May resolve spontaneously within weeks but may persist. See p. 129
Feeling "revved" (anxiety, and/or like a caffeine overdose), jittery, "wired" or agitated sensations	Drop the dosage and increase more gradually. Consider change to Paxil, Luvox, or Serzone. Use liquid Prozac for tiny dose adjustments. Add mild tranquilizer
Headache (although SSRIs may relieve migraines)	Ask your doctor about taking over-the-counter pain relievers until this resolves

Side Effects	Possible Remedies/Comments
Loss of sex drive and/or inability to have an orgasm	See Chapter 7
Vivid dreams and/or nightmares	May resolve spontaneously but may require comedication. Case reports of successful comedication with Catapres (clonidine) and sleeping pills
Decreased appetite or transient weight loss	Usually most worrisome in the elderly. May be reversed with Periactin (cyproheptadine) or dietary supplements
Sedation/foggy or drowsy feelings	Try to clarify whether the drowsiness is a direct side effect or indirect, due to poor-quality sleep. The former cause may necessitate a different medication if it doesn't wear off, but the latter cause usually gets better with a sleeping pill

Worrisome Side Effects[a]	Comments
Rash, hives, generalized itching	Notify your doctor immediately
Breathing difficulties	Notify your doctor immediately
Joint pains, swelling	Notify your doctor immediately
Racing speech, thoughts, impulsivity, spending sprees, bursts of energy, giddiness or euphoria	Notify your doctor immediately
Heavy menstrual flow with easy bruising or nose bleeds	Notify your doctor immediately

[a] Never hesitate to check with your doctor or nurse about any other significant or worrisome physical or emotional changes that may be medication side effects.

Table B.10 | USUAL DOSE RANGES OF HETEROCYCLIC/TRICYCLIC ANTIDEPRESSANTS

As a general rule, the higher dose ranges are used for major depression and obsessive compulsive disorder (Anafranil only), with lower doses often but not always effective for panic disorder, panic disorder with agoraphobia, and generalized anxiety disorder. Low doses of sedating antidepressants also are used in place of sleeping pills and for a variety of pain syndromes including migraines, chronic pain, fibromyalgia, and when combined with a selective serotonin re-uptake inhibitor or atypical antidepressant for treatment-resistant depression. If you have a history of jitteriness with mild stimulants such as caffeine and decongestants, your doctor may recommend an especially low starting dose for Tofranil, Norpramin, and Vivactil. It is almost always necessary to adjust the dose upward gradually because the therapeutic dose (especially for depressive disorders) usually is too powerful for your system to handle all at once. Psychiatrists often use higher initial doses than other physicians, and they are more likely to increase the dose more quickly (such as every three days). Dosages typically are halved for women over the age of sixty-five. Except for Norpramin and Vivactil, most tricyclics can be taken all at once at bedtime, although spreading the dosage out during the day may help minimize side effects.

Medication	Usual Starting Dose Range	Usual Daily Therapeutic Dose Range[a]	Available Pill Strength	Usual Maximum[b]
Adapin, Sinequon	10–25 mg at bedtime	75–200 mg	10, 25, 50, 75, 100, 150 mg	250 mg
Anafranil	25 mg at bedtime	75–200 mg	25, 50, 75 mg	250 mg
Aventyl, Pamelor	25–50 mg at bedtime	50–150 mg	10, 25, 50, 75 mg	200 mg
Elavil, Endep	25 mg at bedtime	100–250 mg	10, 25, 50, 75, 100 mg	300 mg
Ludiomil	25 mg at bedtime	75–150 mg	25, 50, 75 mg	225 mg
Norpramin	10–25 mg one to three times per day	100–200 mg	10, 25, 50, 75, 100, 150 mg	250 mg

Medication	Usual Starting Dose Range	Usual Daily Therapeutic Dose Range[a]	Available Pill Strength	Usual Maximum[b]
Surmontil	25 mg	75–150 mg	25, 50, 100 mg	200 mg
Tofranil	10–50 mg at bedtime	100–200 mg	10, 25, 50, 75, 100, 125, 150 mg	250 mg
Vivactil	5–10 mg	15–40 mg	5, 10 mg	60 mg

[a] Usual doses for depression and sometimes for anxiety disorders. Doses for many women with anxiety disorders will be much lower.
[b] At higher doses, I recommend a blood test to check the medication level.

Table B.11 | COMMON SIDE EFFECTS OF TRICYCLICS

Pamelor (nortriptyline) and Norpramin (desipramine) are the tricyclics most commonly prescribed by psychiatrists because they tend to cause the fewest side effects in typical doses. Since Pamelor and Norpramin are less likely than other tricyclics to cause these side effects, your doctor may recommend changing from another tricyclic if you are bothered by constipation, sedation or the like. If you cannot tolerate these side effects even on desipramine or nortriptyline, your doctor may recommend either reducing the dose or switching to a selective serotonin re-uptake inhibitor or an atypical antidepressant.

Side Effect	Possible Remedies/Comments
Constipation	Increase fluid and fiber intake Reduce iron supplementation if appropriate Add prunes/prune juice to your diet Avoid regular dependence on laxatives (Perdiem, Citrucel, Metamucil are fine)
Dryness: • mouth • eyes • vagina	Comedicate with Urecholine (bethanecol) only if artificial tears and vaginal lubricants are ineffective See p. 175
Excessive sedation (especially morning sleepiness)	Usually resolves or improves within weeks but may persist. A lower dose, less sedating medication, or more gradual upward dose adjustment may be helpful
Feeling "revved" (anxiety and/or like a caffeine overdose), jittery, or shaky	Drop the dosage and increase more gradually Consider change to Elavil, Sinequon, Pamelor, or Tofranil. Comedication with a benzodiazepine should be a last resort
Dizziness, lightheadedness on standing, or low blood pressure	Increase salt/sodium intake Stand up slowly Switch to nortriptyline, SSRI, or Wellbutrin Comedicate with Florinef Avoid in women at risk for hip fracture

Side Effect	Possible Remedies/Comments
Weight gain, increased appetite	See Chapter 8 Norpramin may be the least likely to cause weight gain
Urinary tract infections, difficulty completely emptying your bladder	10–50 mg bethanechol three to four times daily

Worrisome Side Effects[a]	Comments
Rash, hives, generalized itching	Notify your doctor immediately
Breathing difficulties	Notify your doctor immediately
Joint pains, swelling	Notify your doctor immediately
Racing speech, thoughts, impulsivity, spending sprees, bursts of energy, giddiness or euphoria	Notify your doctor immediately
Suicidal thoughts, impulse to overdose	Notify your doctor immediately
Palpitations, chest pain, fainting	Notify your doctor immediately

[a] Never hesitate to check with your doctor or nurse about any other significant or worrisome physical or emotional changes that may be medication side effects.

Table B.12 | COMPARISON OF TRICYCLIC ANTIDEPRESSANTS

Norpramin vs. Pamelor

In general, either of these two tricyclic antidepressants should be prescribed as the antidepressant of choice if a heterocyclic is recommended, with some exceptions. They differ from one another in the following ways:

Pamelor	May relieve insomnia immediately
Pamelor	Less likely to lower blood pressure
Norpramin	Less sedating (more likely to cause jitteriness and insomnia than Pamelor)
Norpramin	Causes less constipation, dry mouth
Norpramin	The most effective tricyclic for attention deficit disorder

Advantages of Other Heterocyclics

Relative to Norpramin and Pamelor, the following four medications are more likely to cause dry mouth, constipation, and sedation. Nonetheless, they may be preferable to Norpramin or Pamelor for the reasons described.

Elavil	May be especially useful for migraine, chronic pain syndromes, severe insomnia
Anafranil	Only tricyclic effective for OCD.
Sinequon	Antihistamine activity helpful for women with allergies or skin rashes
Tofranil	Preferred by some doctors for panic disorder

Disadvantages of Other Heterocyclics

Ludiomil	Increases susceptibility to seizures

Outdated Antidepressants with No Advantage

Asendin (amoxapine)	May cause irreversible neurologic side effect called tardive dyskinesia
Etrafon, Etrafon Forte, Etrafon 2-10	Contains a medication that may cause tardive dyskinesia
Limbitrol, Limbitrol-DS	Contains a potentially addictive medication
Triavil	Contains a medication that may cause tardive dyskinesia

Table B.13 | UNIQUE ASPECTS OF WELLBUTRIN COMPARED TO SSRIs AND TRICYCLIC ANTIDEPRESSANTS

Advantages:

Safest in bipolar depression
No sexual side effects
No weight gain
No sedation
Few medication interactions
May also be effective in attention deficit disorder

Disadvantages:

Ineffective against anxiety disorders (may precipitate panic)
Less effective for premenstrual depression than SSRIs
Must be taken two or three times per day
May cause insomnia, headaches, stomach upset, tremor
Small increased risk of seizure (therefore, unsafe for women with active eating disorders, alcoholism, or those taking other medications that lower the seizure threshold, such as asthma medications)

Table B.14 | ALTERNATIVES FOR TREATMENT-RESISTANT DEPRESSION

Most women respond to the first or second antidepressant prescribed for them, assuming that side effects don't keep them from reaching a therapeutic dose. However, as many as one in five women have treatment-resistant depression (also called refractory depression). Treatment-resistant depression should be treated by a psychiatrist, preferably one who specializes in the use of medication. Some of the options for treatment-resistant medication include:

Alternative	Comments
Maximize dose	A reasonable first step
Add psychotherapy	A must for those who do not respond quickly to medication. Especially consider cognitive or interpersonal psychotherapy
Switch to Effexor	Commonly done in practice, usually necessary to reach doses of 75 mg twice daily or higher
Switch to a tricyclic	In the Prozac era, these highly effective medications may be overlooked

Augmentation (add another medication to a partially effective antidepressant in order to "squeeze" more benefit from the first one)	Common comedications:
	    Lithium
	    Thyroid hormone
	    10–25 mg tricyclic + SSRI
	    25–100 mg Deseryl
	    Visken (pindolol)
	    stimulants (Ritalin, etc.)[a]
	    Add estrogen[b]
	    Add Buspar
	    Add light therapy
	    Reduce tricyclic dose and add an SSRI
	    Add Tegretol

[a] Stimulants may increase depression in postmenopausal women.
[b] Usually only for perimenopausal women; intermittent progesterone supplementation for endometrial shedding usually advisable.

Alternative	Comments
Switch to monoamine oxidase inhibitor (MAOI) (may be especially effective for atypical depression)	Should be done only under the supervision of an experienced psychiatrist after a careful washout period
	Requires careful dietary changes Requires strict attention to the risks of drug-drug interactions
Electroshock therapy (also called electroconvulsive therapy, ECT, EST). May be especially appropriate for psychotic depression, for severely suicidal depression, in pregnancy and lactation, for medically ill/elderly, and for women with Parkinson's disease, postpartum psychosis, rapid-cycling psychosis, rapid-cycling bipolar disorder	Now performed under general anesthesia with muscle relaxation, ECT is more effective than any medication. Transient memory loss most common side effect Usually contraindicated for individuals with benign or malignant brain tumor or other other mass, recent stroke, arteriovenous malformation, retinal detachment

MOOD STABILIZERS

Table B.15 | MOOD STABILIZERS

Three major medications are used commonly for bipolar disorder (manic-depressive illness): lithium, Tegretol, and Depakote. Lithium is the most commonly prescribed mood stabilizer, but the latter two anticonvulsants are increasingly popular. All three are effective for acute mania and for preventing future episodes of depression or mania. However, they are less effective for acute depression, when a mood stabilizer and an antidepressant is usually best. All three mood stabilizers require regular blood tests for drug levels and to monitor for possible organ damage. All three medications raise the risk of birth defects when taken during the first trimester of pregnancy.

Medication	Usual Starting Dose	Comments
Depakote	250–500 mg twice daily	Common side effects include stomach upset, diarrhea, sedation, tremor. Long-term side effects may include liver damage, weight gain, hair loss, menstrual cycle irregularities
Lithium	300 mg two or three times daily	Common side effects include tremor, nausea, or diarrhea, increased thirst or urination. Long-term side effects may include low thyroid disease, rash/acne, kidney problems, mental slowing, weight gain, hair loss. May worsen cardiac problems
Tegretol	100–200 mg twice daily	Common side effects are stomach upset, sedation, dizziness, clumsiness. Long-term side effects may include liver damage, low blood counts, rash

Table B.16 | AVAILABLE PREPARATIONS OF MOOD STABILIZERS

Lithium, Valproic acid, and carbamazepine are all available in short-acting forms and in sustained-release form. Although the sustained-release forms are more expensive, many women find that the more gradual peaks and valleys of a sustained-release form lead to fewer side effects and are more convenient. The short-acting forms are all available as generics.

Medication	Available Pill Strength	Dosage Frequency
Lithium carbonate (Eskalith, Lithonate, Lithotabs)	300 mg tablets, capsules	Usually three times
Lithium citrate (Cibalith-S)	liquid	Usually three times
Lithobid	300 mg tablets	Two times (sustained-release form)[a]
Eskalith-CR	450 mg tablets	Two times (sustained-release form)[a]
Valproic acid[b]	250 mg capsules or syrup	Three times
Divalproex (Depakote)	125, 150, 500 mg	Two times (sustained-release form)
Tegretol	200 mg capsules or liquid	Three or four times daily
Tegretol-XR	100 mg, 200 mg, 400 mg tablets	Two times

[a] Sometimes taken all at bedtime
[b] A little used substitute for Depakote

Table B.17 | ALTERNATIVES TO MOOD STABILIZERS

In addition to lithium, Depakote, and Tegretol, a wide variety of other medications are used for bipolar disorder illness. In general, these medications should be prescribed by an expert in psychiatric medications.

Medication	Comments
Antipsychotic medications: Examples: Haldol, Loxitane, Navane, Stelazine, Trilafon	Short-term use preferred when possible due to potential for neurological damage
Ativan, Klonopin	Sedative action may be helpful during mania and may curb need for antipsychotic
Atypical antipsychotic medications: Clozaril (clozapine)	Potentially life-threatening side effects make this appropriate only when ordinary medications fail
Risperdal (risperidone), Zyprexa (olanzapine)	Fewer side effects than other antipsychotic medication, including less risk of long-term neurological damage
Calan (verapamil)	Looks promising for treatment of mania
Electroconvulsive therapy (ECT)	Effective for mania or depression
Neurontin (gabapentin)	Promising new anticonvulsant
Nimotop (nimodepine)	Promising for rapid cycling, very expensive
Thyroid hormone	May be helpful to reach high-normal thyroid level on blood testing

ANTIANXIETY MEDICATIONS

Table B.18	A COMPARISON OF PREVENTIVE TREATMENTS FOR PANIC DISORDER WITH OR WITHOUT AGORAPHOBIA		
	Tricyclic Antidepressants	Serotonin Re-uptake Inhibitors (SSRIs)	Benzodiazepines (tranquilizers)
Common side effects	Dry mouth, constipation	Nausea, diarrhea, insomnia	Marked sedation, mental or motor slowing
Major hurdle	Initial jitteriness	Overstimulation "buzzing"	Tolerance Discontinuation may be brutal
Cost	Usually least expensive (many available as generic)	Usually most expensive (none available as generic)	Usually midrange
Potential hazards	Unsafe in many heart conditions, poison risk if taken by children accidentally	Multiple drug interactions	Addictive potential May cause seizures if stopped without doctor's care Unsafe with alcohol
Effect on sleep	Usually improves (Norpramin may cause insomnia)	May cause insomnia, dream changes, increase nighttime wakening	Improves sleep; paradoxically may worsen sleep after discontinuation

Table B.19 | ANTIANXIETY MEDICATIONS: COMPARISON OF BUSPAR (BUSPIRONE) AND TRANQUILIZERS (BENZODIAZEPINES)

Buspar	Benzodiazepines
Not sedating	Sedating
Not addictive	Potential drugs of abuse
Not effective immediately	Provide immediate relief
Must be taken two or three times per day, every day	May be taken regularly or intermittently (prn)
Not effective for panic disorder, agoraphobia	Effective for panic disorder, agoraphobia
Effective for GAD	Effective for GAD
May act as antidepressant	Not effective for depression, may worsen depression
May help premenstrual depression	May help premenstrual irritability
May cause stomach upset	May decrease alertness, memory

Table B.20 | COMPARISON OF BENZODIAZEPINES

Medication	Usual Starting Dose	Comments
Ativan	0.5 mg twice daily	May be preferred for women taking estrogen or Tagamet, and for those with liver disease May be taken under the tongue for rapid onset
Klonopin	0.5 mg at bedtime or 0.25 mg twice daily	Initial daytime/morning sedation common at first, may resolve Easier tapering than Xanax Some women may respond to single bedtime dosing
Restoril	15–30 mg at bedtime	May be preferred for breast-feeding
Serax	10 mg three times daily	May be preferred for breast-feeding, for women taking estrogen or Tagamet, for the elderly, or for those with liver disease
Valium	2–5 mg per day	Disadvantages usually make Valium inferior to alternative agents especially in pregnancy, breast-feeding, and the elderly
Xanax	0.25 mg three times daily	Short-acting, so must be taken throughout the day May have breakthrough symptoms between doses taper off very slowly Rapid onset useful for prn use (especially if taken under the tongue)

GENERAL INFORMATION

Table B.21 | COMMON MEDICATION INTERACTIONS

Medication interactions are a special concern for women, who are more likely to take over-the-counter and other prescribed medications. Always check with your doctor and/or your pharmacist about the safety of combining medications. Certain medicines must never be mixed together, but others just need a dose adjustment and/or blood monitoring for safety. By far, the most common drugs that interact with psychiatric medications are other psychiatric medications. However, many common medications potentially interact with medications for depression and anxiety, as listed. Do not assume that a medication not on this list can be taken safely in combination—check first with your personal physician.

Common Interactions with SSRIs

(Note: Effexor has fewer drug-drug interactions than similar serotonin-enhancing antidepressants; the others vary somewhat.)

Benzodiazepines (such as Xanax and Valium)
Certain heart rhythm prescriptions
Dextromethorphan (many cough syrups)
Diet pills including Redux
Digitoxin
Hismanil (astemizole)
Lithium
MAOIs
Nizoral (ketoconazole)
Propulsid (cisapride)
Other SSRIs or trazodone
Seldane (terfenadine)
Tagamet (cimetadine)
Theophylline
Tricyclic antidepressants
Tryptophan
Warfarin (Coumadin)

Common Interactions with Tricyclic Antidepressants

Alcohol
Benzodiazepines
Blood pressure medications (some)
Certain heart rhythm prescriptions
Depakote (valproic acid)
Diabetes pills (no interaction with insulin)
Estrogen, oral contraceptives, and hormone replacement therapy
MAOIs
Methadone
Smoking
SSRIs
Tegretol (carbemazepine)

Common Interactions with Benzodiazepines

Alcohol
Any sedating comedication has greater sedative potential (tricyclics, antihistamines, etc.)
Barbiturates
Birth control pills
Digitalis, digoxin
Smoking
SSRIs
Tagamet (cimetidine)
Tegretol (carbamazepine)

Common Interactions with Lithium

Alcohol
Ampicillin, possibly tetracycline
Angiotensin-converting enzyme inhibitors (such as captopril, enalopril)
Calcium channel blockers (Diltiazem, Nifedipine, Verapamil)
Diuretics
Nonsteroidal anti-inflammatory agents (such as Advil, Feldene, Indocin, used for arthritis and
          menstrual cramps)
Theophylline, aminophylline

Common Interactions with Tegretol

All major psychiatric medications may interact with Tegretol:
Antidepressants, antipsychotics, anticonvulsants including valproic acid, benzodiazepines, lithium
Antitubercular medications
Birth control pills
Calan (verapamil)
Certain antibiotics (erythromycin, tetracycline)
Clozaril (clozapine)
Coumadin (warfarin)
Danocrine (danazol)
Digitalis, digoxin
Prednisone and other corticosteroids
Tagamet (cimetidine)

Common Interactions with Valproic Acid

Alcohol and other sedatives
Aspirin
Coumadin (warfarin)
Erythromycin
Klonopin or other benzodiazepines
Other anticonvulsants: ethosuximide, felbamate, phenobarbital, phenytoin, primidone

Table B.22 | COST-SAVING MEASURES FOR MEDICATIONS FOR DEPRESSION AND ANXIETY

Since most recently introduced medications for depression and anxiety are not available as generics, they can be incredibly expensive. Sometimes there is no way to cut costs. However, usually the per-pill cost is the same, that is, 50 mg of Zoloft costs roughly the same as 100 mg. If you are at the lower end of the dose range, often you can save money by cutting a larger pill in half rather than taking the equally costly smaller dose. It's a bit less convenient but can save you $40 or $50 per month. Some heterocyclics do not come as generics either, and you can save money by taking a single pill (e.g., 75 mg of Pamelor at bedtime is much cheaper than taking 25 mg in the morning and 50 mg at night).

The following is a table of substitutions that will save you real money on your prescriptions. You will probably need to ask your doctor to write the prescription in this new way.

If Your Dose Is	That's the Same as the Less Expensive
Ambien, 5 mg at bedtime	Half a ten mg tablet[a]
Effexor, 37.5 mg twice daily	Half a 75 mg tablet twice daily
Effexor, 50 mg twice daily	Half a 100 mg tablet twice daily
Klonopin, 1 mg at bedtime	Half a 2 mg tablet
Norpramin, 50 mg three times per day	150 mg once daily
Pamelor, 25 mg three times per day	75 mg at bedtime
Paxil, 10 mg per day	Half a 20 mg tablet per day
Prozac, 10 mg per day	20 mg every other day, or half a capsule diluted
Xanax, 0.25 mg four times daily	Half a 0.5 mg tablet four times daily
Zoloft, 50 mg per day	Half a 100 mg tablet daily

[a] If you have arthritis or some other difficulty splitting the pill, buy a pill cutter (about $4 at a drugstore).

Table B.23 | PREGNANCY RATINGS

The following ratings are guidelines submitted to the Food and Drug Administration by the manufacturer of the medication or assigned by the authors of *Drugs in Pregnancy and Lactation*. As discussed in Chapter 11, these guidelines are not universally agreed upon, and new scientific data rarely lead to changes in a drug's categorization. Since the tricyclics were labeled during a less rigorous scientific period, they tend to be rated as more dangerous than newer drugs, without justification. For example, most experts would agree that Pamelor is a far better choice in pregnancy than Wellbutrin, which is much less well studied in pregnancy. A psychiatrist or obstetrician with expertise in the field can provide you with more useful information.

CATEGORY A: Controlled human studies show no risk to the fetus; risk of harm seems "remote."

CATEGORY B: Animal studies have not shown fetal risk, but controlled studies in women have not been conducted.

CATEGORY C: Animal studies show risk, or there is no human or animal data. "Drugs should be given only if the potential benefit justifies the risk to the fetus."

CATEGORY D: There is evidence of risk in humans but "the benefits from use in pregnant women may be acceptable despite the risk."

CATEGORY X: Known source of birth defects; the medication is contraindicated in pregnancy.

Brand Name	Generic Name	Category
Ambien	zolpidem	B
Anafranil	clomipramine	C
Ativan	lorazepam	D
Buspar	buspirone	B
Cibalith, Eskalith, Lithobid, Lithonate, Lithotabs	lithium	D
Depakote	valproic acid, valproate	D
Desyrel	trazodone	C
Effexor	venlafaxine	C
Elavil	amitriptyline	D
Halcion	triazolam	X
Klonopin	clonazepam	C
Luvox	fluvoxamine	C
Norpramin	desipramine	C

Brand Name	Generic Name	Category
Pamelor	nortriptyline	D
Paxil	paroxetine	C
Prozac	fluoxetine	B
Remeron	mirtazapine	C
Restoril	temazepam	X
Serzone	nefazodone	C
Sinequon	doxepin	C
Tegretol	carbamazepine	C
Tofranil	imipramine	D
Valium	diazepam	D
Wellbutrin	buproprion	B
Xanax	alprazolam	D
Zoloft	sertraline	B

Table B.24 | THE AMERICAN ACADEMY OF PEDIATRICS CLASSIFICATION OF MEDICATIONS BY BREAST-FEEDING WOMEN[a]

Maternal Medication Usually Compatible with Nursing

Chloral hydrate
Depakote
Estradiol
Tegretol

Maternal Medication Contraindicated During Nursing (should not be taken)

Lithium

"Drugs Whose Effect on Nursing Infants Is Unknown but May Be of Concern"

Adapin, Sinequon
Ascendin
Ativan
Centrax
Desyrel
Doral
Elavil
Luvox
Norpramin
Pamelor
Prozac
Restoril
Tofranil
Valium

[a] These classifications represent the consensus of a committee of experts. As discussed in Chapter 12, the issues are highly complex and determined in part by nonscientific factors. Not all experts agree about these classifications. A major drawback is that virtually all new antidepressants and the anti-anxiety medications Klonopin and Xanax have not been classified yet. Presumably, most will end up in the category that contains similar medications that "may be of concern."

Resources

ORGANIZATIONS

The following organizations may be able to refer you to support groups and/or mental health professionals in your area. Many of these organizations provide newsletters and other written information with up-to-the-minute research and clinical trends.

American Psychiatric Association
1400 K Street, N.W.
Washington, D.C. 20005
(202) 682-6000 (Public affairs)

The Anxiety Disorders Association of America
6000 Executive Boulevard, Suite 200
Rockville, MD 20852-3081
(301) 231-9350

Beck Institute (cognitive therapy)
GSB Building, Suite 700
City Line and Belmont Avenues
Bala Cynwyd, PA 19004-1610
(610) 664-3020

Depression After Delivery
P.O. Box 1282
Morrisville, PA 19067
(215) 295-3994
(800) 944-4773

The National Alliance for the Mentally Ill
2101 Wilson Boulevard
Suite 302
Arlington, VA 22201
(800) 950-6264

National Anxiety Foundation
3135 Custer Drive
Lexington, KY 40517-4001
(800) 755-1576

National Depressive and Manic Depressive Association
730 N. Franklin, Suite 501
Chicago, IL 60610
(800) 82-NDMDA

The National Foundation for Depressive Illness
P.O. BOX 2257
New York, NY 10116
(800) 245-4344

National Institute of Mental Health: Depression Awareness, Recognition and
Treatment (DART)
5600 Fishers Lane
Rockville, MD 20857
(800) 421-4211

National Mental Health Association
1021 Prince Street
Alexandria, VA 22314-2971
(800) 969-6642

Obsessive Compulsive Foundation
P.O. Box 70
Milford, CT 06460
(203) 878-5669

The Obsessive Compulsive Information Center (also the Lithium Information
Center)
Dean Foundation
8000 Excelsior Drive, Suite 302
Madison, WI 53717
(608) 836-8070

Postpartum Support, International
927 North Kellogg Avenue
Santa Barbara, CA 93111
(805) 967-7636

For Further Reading

Rita Baron-Faust, *Mental Wellness for Women*, William Morrow, 1997.

Harold Bloomfield and Peter McWilliams, *How to Heal Depression*. Prelude Press, 1994.

K. Edmund Bourne, *The Anxiety and Phobia Workbook*. New Harbinger Press, 1995.

David Burns, *Feeling Good Handbook*. Plume, 1990.

Martha Davis, Elizabeth Eshelman, and Matthew McKay, *The Relaxation and Stress Reduction Workbook*, 4th ed. New Harbinger Press, 1995.

Colette Dowling, *You Mean I Don't Have to Feel Like This?* Bantam Books, 1993.

Rae Dumont, *The Sky Is Falling: Understanding and Coping with Phobias, Panic, and Obsessive-Compulsive Disorders*. W.W. Norton, 1996.

Edna B. Foa, Ph.D., and Reid Wilson, Ph.D., *Stop Obsessing! How to Overcome Your Obsessions and Compulsions*. Bantam Books, 1991.

Mark S. Gold, M.D., *The Good News About Depression: Breakthrough Treatments That Can Work for You*, Bantam Books, 1995.

Elizabeth Hilts, *Getting in Touch with Your Inner Bitch*. Hysteria Publications, 1994.

Kay Redfield Jamison, *An Unquiet Mind—A Memoir of Moods and Madness*. Knopf Books, 1995.

Karen Kleiman and Valerie D. Raskin, *This Isn't What I Expected: Overcoming Postpartum Depression*. Bantam Books, 1994.

Peter Kramer, *Listening to Prozac*. Penguin USA, 1994.

Harriet Lerner, *The Dance of Anger*. HarperCollins, 1989.

Martha Manning, *Under Currents: A Therapist Reckoning with Her Own Depression*. HarperCollins, 1995.

Michael Norden, *Beyond Prozac*, HarperCollins, 1995.

James Perl, *Sleep Right in Five Nights: A Clear and Effective Guide for Overcoming Insomnia*. William Morrow and Company, 1994.

Judith L. Rapoport, M.D., *The Boy Who Couldn't Stop Washing*. Plume Books, 1991.

Domeena Renshaw, *Seven Weeks to Better Sex*. Random House, 1995.

Jerilyn Ross and Rosalyn Carter, *Triumph Over Fear: A Book of Help and Hope for People with Anxiety, Panic Attacks and Phobias*. Bantam Books, 1995.

Ellen Sue Stern, *Running on Empty: Meditations for Indispensible Women*. Bantam Books, 1992.
Susan Swedo and Henrietta Leonard, *It's Not All in Your Head*. HarperCollins, 1996.

INTERNET RESOURCES

World Wide Web
All of the following Web addresses include links to related Web sites.

Anxiety Disorders Association of America

http://www.cyberpsych.org/adaa/index.html

Sponsored by this national self-help group, the site lists nationwide support groups, reports breaking research in anxiety disorders, and offers a comprehensive online bookstore of related books. Also has free Medline searching so that you can locate specific medical references on topics of interest.

Dr. Ivan's Depression Central

http://www.psycom.net/depression.central.html

Another wonderful site, a major Internet clearinghouse with links to dozens of other sites. This site will be of interest to anyone with unipolar depression, bipolar disorder, or dysthymia. Includes specific information on postpartum depression, premenstrual depression, and women's vulnerability to depressive disorder. You also can find links to Internet resources for anxiety disorders here.

Mental Health Infosource

http://www.mhsource.com

This is sponsored by a group that provides ongoing education to psychiatrists and the publisher of *Psychiatric Times*. You can join a weekly mailing list on topics of interest ("listserver"), submit questions for the weekly "Ask the Expert" feature, join chat groups for consumers or professionals, and link to a wide variety of resources. Covers a wide variety of emotional illnesses.

Obsessive Compulsive Foundation

http://pages.prodigy.com/alwillen/ocf/html

The organization's monthly newsletter is reprinted at this site, which also includes book reviews of interest to consumers. Provides a nationwide listing of support and self-help groups.

Psychopharmacology Tips ("Dr. Bob's Virtual En-psych-lopedia")

http://uhs.bsd.uchicago.edu/~bhsiung/tips/tips.html

This is a fantastic Internet site used by both doctors and consumers/patients. It's a compilation of tips passed from one doctor to another, culled from a psychopharmacotherapy bulletin board restricted to mental health professionals. Keep in mind that the postings are not subject to scientific review. Many subheadings cover important women's issues.

OTHER INTERNET RESOURCES

The major online services (America OnLine, CompuServe, Microsoft Network, Prodigy) have information or support available to individuals with psychiatric illnesses. Information ranges from medical references to consumer postings on electronic bulletin boards.

PROFESSIONAL TEXTBOOKS

American Psychiatric Association, *Diagnostic and Statistical Manual of Mental Disorders: DSM-IV*, 4th ed. American Psychiatric Association, 1994.
Kalyna Bezchlibnyk-Butler, J. Joel Jeffries, and Barry Martin, *Clinical Handbooks of Psychotropic Drugs*, 4th ed. Hogrefe & Huber, 1994.
Gerald Briggs, Roger Freeman, and Sumner Yaffe, *Drugs in Pregnancy and Lactation*, 4th ed. Williams and Wilkins, 1994.
Dominic Ciraulo, Richard Shader, David Greenblatt, and Wayne Creelman, *Drug Interactions in Psychiatry*. Williams and Wilkins, 1995.
Robert Hales, Stuart Yudofsky, and John Talbott, *Textbook of Psychiatry*, 2nd ed., American Psychiatric Press, 1994.
Jean Hamilton, Margaret Jensvold, Esther Rothblum, and Ellen Cole: *Psychopharmacology from a Feminist Perspective*. Harrington Park Press, 1995.
Philip Janicak, John Davis, Sheldon Preskorn, and Frank Ayd, Jr., *Principles and Practice of Psychopharmacotherapy*. Williams and Wilkins, 1993.
Jerrold Maxmen and Nicholas Ward, *Psychotropic Drugs: Fast Facts*, 2nd ed., W. W. Norton and Company, 1995.
Laura Miller (ed.), *Postpartum Mood Disorders*. American Psychiatric Press, 1997.
Donna Stewart and Nada Stotland, *Psychological Aspects of Women's Health Care: The Interface Between Psychiatry and Obstetrics and Gynecology*. American Psychiatric Press, 1993.
Depression in Primary Care, Volume 2: Treatment of Major Depression. Order free at (800) 358-9295.
Also available: A *Patient's Guide, Quick Reference Guide for Clinicians, Clinical Practice Guidelines*.

PROFESSIONAL ARTICLES

General Topics

J. L. Abelson and G. C. Curtis, "Hypothalamic-Pituitary-Adrenal Axis Activity in Panic Disorder," *Archives of General Psychiatry*, 53 (1996), 323–331.

American College of Obstetrics and Gynecology, "Depression in Women," Technical Bulletin #182, *International Journal of Obstetrics and Gynecology*, 43 (1993), 203–211.

J. T. Apter and S. F. Kushner, "A Guide to Selection of Antidepressants," *Primary Psychiatry*, 7 (1996), 14–17.

D. J. Castle, A. Deale, et al., "Gender Differences in Obsessive Compulsive Disorder," *Australian and New Zealand Journal of Psychiatry*, 29 (1995), 114–117

D. A. Ciraulo, O. Sarid-Segal, et al., "Liability to Alprazolam Abuse in Daughters of Alcoholics," *American Journal of Psychiatry*, 153 (1996), 956–58.

M. A. Dew, C. F. Reynolds, et al., "Electroencephalographic Sleep Profiles During Depression," *Archives of General Psychiatry*, 53 (1996), 148–156.

L. Ereshefsky, "Drug Interactions of Antidepressants," *Psychiatric Annals*, 26 (1996), 342–348.

J. A. Gazmararian, S. A. James, et al., "Depression in Black and White Women: The Role of Marriage and Socioeconomic Status," *Annals of Epidemiology*, 5 (1995), 455–463.

R. M. Goisman, M. G. Warshaw, et al., "DSM-IV and the Disappearance of Agoraphobia without a History of Panic Disorder: New Data on a Controversial Diagnosis," *American Journal of Psychiatry*, 152 (1995), 1438–1443.

J. M. Gorman, "Recent Developments in Understanding Panic Disorder Leading to Improved Treatment Strategies," *Primary Psychiatry*, 3 (1996), 31–38.

J. A. Horton (ed.), "Mental Health, The Women's Health Data Book," *Jacobs Institute of Women's Health*, 1994, 82–100.

J. W. Jefferson, "Lithium: The Present and the Future," *Journal of Clinical Psychiatry*, 56 (1995), 41–49.

K. S. Kendler, M. C. Neale, et al., "A Longitudinal Twin Study of 1-Year Prevalence of Major Depression in Women," *Archives of General Psychiatry*, 50 (1993), 843–852.

B. L. Kennedy, "Women's Issues in Medicine: An Overview," *Primary Psychiatry*, 3 (1996), 33–34.

J. H. Kocsis, R. A. Friedman, et al., "Maintenance Therapy for Chronic Depression," 53 (1996), 769–774.

I. Lucki, "Serotonin Receptor Specificity in Anxiety Disorders," *Journal of Clinical Psychiatry*, 57 (1996) (supplement 6), 5–10.

R. D. Marshall and D. F. Klein, "Pharmacotherapy in the Treatment of Posttraumatic Stress Disorder," *Psychiatric Annals*, 25 (1995), 588–597.

S. L. McElroy, P. E. Keck, et al., *Practical Management of Antidepressant Side Effects, Practical Clinical Strategies in Treating Depression and Anxiety Disorders in a Managed Care Environment.* American Psychiatric Association, 1996.

D. G. M. Murphy, C. DeCarli, et al., "Sex Differences in Human Brain Morphometry and Metabolism," *Archives of General Psychiatry*, 53 (1996), 585–594.

"New Developments in the Treatment of Obsessive Compulsive Disorder," *Journal of Clinical Psychiatry*, 55, (October 1994) (Supplement). This special issue includes nine articles by the leading scholars in the field, spanning diagnosis and brain imaging to medical and behavioral therapy for OCD.

J. B. Persons, M. E. Thase, et al., "The Role of Psychotherapy in the Treatment of Depression," *Archives of General Psychiatry*, 53 (1996), 283–290.

J. L. Rapoport, "The Neurobiology of Obsessive-Compulsive Disorder," *Journal of the American Medical Association*, 260 (1988), 2888–2890.

K. Rickels, R. Downing, et al., "Antidepressants for the Treatment of Generalized Anxiety Disorder," *Archives of General Psychiatry*, 50 (1993), 884–895.

E. Sacchetti, "Are SSRI Antidepressants a Clinically Homogeneous Class of Compounds?" *Lancet*, 344 (1994), 126–127.

E. Schweizer and K. Rickels, "The Long-term Management of Generalized Anxiety Disorder: Issues and Dilemmas," *Journal of Clinical Psychiatry*, 57 (supplement 7), (1996), 9–12.

J. K. Walsh and C. L. Engelhardt, "Trends in Pharmacological Treatment of Insomnia," *Journal of Clinical Psychiatry*, 53 (1992), 10–17.

M. M. Weissman and M. Olfson, "Depression in Women: Implications for Health Care Research," *Science*, 269 (1995), 799–801.

Pregnancy

L. L. Altshuler, L. Cohen, et al., "Pharmacologic Management of Psychiatric Illness During Pregnancy: Dilemmas and Guidelines," *American Journal of Psychiatry*, 153 (1996), 592–606.

U. Bergman, F. W. Rosa, et al., "Effects of Exposure to Benzodiazepine During Fetal Life," *Lancet*, 340 (1992), 694–696.

C. D. Chambers, K. A. Johnson, et al., "Birth Outcomes in Pregnant Women Taking Fluoxetine," *New England Journal of Medicine*, 335 (1996), 1010–1015.

L. S. Cohen, J. M. Friedman, et al., "A Reevaluation of Risk of In Utero Exposure to Lithium," *Journal of the American Medical Association*, 271 (1994), 146–150.

I. Iancu, E. Lepkifker, et al., "Obsessive-Compulsive Disorder Limited to Pregnancy," *Psychotherapy and Psychosomatics*, 64 (1995), 109–112.

G. Koren and A. Pastuszak, "Prevention of Unnecessary Pregnancy Terminations by Counselling Women on Drug, Chemical and Radiation Exposure During the First Trimester," *Teratology*, 41 (1990), 657–661.

L. J. Miller, "Psychiatric Medications During Pregnancy: Understanding and Minimizing Risks," *Psychiatric Annals*, 24 (1994), 69–75.

A. Pastuszak, B. Schick-Boschetto, et al., "Pregnancy Outcome Following First-Trimester Exposure to Fluoxetine (Prozac)," *Journal of the American Medical Association*, 269 (1993), 2246–2248.

V. D. Raskin, J. R. Richman, et al., "Patterns of Depressive Symptoms in Expectant and New Parents," *American Journal of Psychiatry,* 147 (1990), 658–660.

E. Robert, "Treating Depression in Pregnancy," *New England Journal of Medicine,* 335 (1996), 1056–1058.

M. B. Scolnik, I. Nulman, et al., "Neurodevelopment of Children Exposed in Utero to Phenytoin and Carbamazepine Monotherapy," *Journal of the American Medical Association,* 271 (1994), 767–770.

K. L. Wisner, "Antidepressant Therapy During Pregnancy," *Primary Psychiatry,* 3 (1996), 40–42.

Breast-Feeding and Postpartum Issues

Committee on Drugs, American Academy of Pediatrics, "The Transfer of Drugs and Other Chemicals into Human Milk," *Pediatrics,* 93 (1994), 137–150.

A. J. P. Gregoire, R. Kumar, et al., "Transdermal Oestrogen for Treatment of Severe Postnatal Depression," *Lancet,* 347 (1996), 930–933.

S. Ito, A. Blajchman, et al., "Prospective Follow-up of Adverse Reactions in Breast-fed Infants Exposed to Maternal Medication," *American Journal of Obstetrics and Gynecology,* 168 (1993), 1393–1399.

V. J. M. Pope, H. De Rooy, et al., "Postpartum Thyroid Dysfunction and Depression in an Unselected Population," *New England Journal of Medicine,* 324 (1991), 1815–1816.

V. Raskin, "Pharmacotherapy and ECT for Postpartum Mood Disorders." In L Miller (ed.), *Postpartum Mood Disorders.* American Psychiatric Press, 1997.

D. A. Sichel, L. S. Cohen, et al., "Postpartum Obsessive Compulsive Disorder: A Case Series," *Journal of Clinical Psychiatry,* 54 (1993), 156–159.

Z. N. Stowe and C. B. Nemeroff, "Women at Risk for Postpartum-onset Major Depression," *American Journal of Obstetrics and Gynecology,* 173 (1995), 639–645.

S. Stuart and M. W. O'Hara, "Interpersonal Psychotherapy for Postpartum Depression: A Treatment Program," *Journal of Psychotherapy Practice and Research,* 4 (1995), 18–29.

K. L. Wisner, J. M. Perel, et al., "Antidepressant Treatment During Breast-feeding," *American Journal of Psychiatry,* 153 (1996), 1132–1137.

Women's Side Effects

R. Balon et al., "Changes in Appetite and Weight During the Pharmacological Treatment of Patients with Panic Disorder," *Canadian Journal of Psychiatry,* 38 (1993), 19–22.

B. Bonin, P. Vandel, et al., "Fluvoxamine and Galactorrhea," *Therapie,* 49 (1994), 149–151.

R. Z. Harris, L. Z. Benet, et al., "Gender Differences in Pharmacokinetics and Pharmacodynamics," *Drugs,* 50 (1995), 222–239.

J. Isojarvi et al., "Polycystic Ovaries and Hyperandrogenism in Women Taking Valproate for Epilepsy," *New England Journal of Medicine,* 4 (1993), 1383–1388.

L. J. McKenzie and S. C. Risch, "Fibrocystic Breast Disease Following Treatment with Selective Serotonin Reuptake Inhibitors," *American Journal of Psychiatry*, 152 (1995), 471.

B. L. Szarek and D. M. Brandt, "A Comparison of Weight Changes with Fluoxetine, Desipramine, and Amitriptyline," *Journal of Nervous and Mental Disorders*, 181 (1993), 702–704.

K. A. Yonkers, J. C. Kando, et al., "Gender Differences in Pharmacokinetics and Pharmacodynamics of Psychotropic Medication," *American Journal of Psychiatry*, 149 (1992), 587–595.

Premenstrual Depression

E. Freeman, K. Rickels, et al., "Ineffectiveness of Progesterone Suppository Treatment for Premenstrual Syndrome," *Journal of the American Medical Association*, 264 (1990), 349–353.

T. Pearlstein, "Nonpharmacologic Treatment of Premenstrual Syndrome," *Psychiatric Annals*, 26 (1996), 590–594.

S. K. Severino and M. L. Moline, "Premenstrual Syndrome, Identification and Management," *Drugs*, 49 (1995), 71–82.

M. Steiner and A. Wilkins, "Diagnosis and Assessment of Premenstrual Dysphoria," *Psychiatric Annals*, 26 (1996), 571–575.

K. A. Yonkers and W. A. Brown, "Pharmacologic Treatments for Premenstrual Dysphoric Disorder," *Psychiatric Annals*, 26 (1996), 586–589.

Hormones

P. A. Deci, R. B. Lydiard, et al., "Oral Contraceptives and Panic Disorder," *Journal of Clinical Psychiatry*, 53 (1992), 163–165.

M. Demert, "Estrogen-induced Panic Disorder," *American Journal of Psychiatry*, 151 (1994), 1246.

A. J. Gelenberg, "Symptoms, Drugs, and the Menstrual Cycle," *Biological Therapies in Psychiatry Newsletter*, 16 (1993), 17–20.

L. H. Gise, "What You Can Do About Depression at Menopause," *Menopausal Medicine*, 4 (1996), 1–5.

M. J. Gitlin and R. O. Pasnau, "Psychiatric Syndromes Linked to Reproductive Function in Women," *American Journal of Psychiatry*, 146 (1989), 1413–1422.

J. Jefferson, "Tamoxifen-associated Reduction in Tricyclic Antidepressant Levels in Blood," *Journal of Clinical Psychopharmacology*, 15 (1995), 223–224.

E. L. Klaiber, D. M. Broverman, et al., "Estrogen Therapy for Severe Persistent Depression in Women," *Archives of General Psychiatry*, 36 (1979), 742–744.

B. S. McEwen, "The Brain as a Target Organ of Endocrine Hormones." In D. T. Kreoger and J. S. Hughes (eds.), *Neuroendocrinology*. Sinauer Associates, 1980.

K. F. Mortel and J. S. Neyer, "Lack of Postmenopausal Estrogen Replacement Therapy and the Risk of Dementia," *Journal of Neuropsychiatry Clinical Neurosciences*, 7 (1995), 334–337.

B. B. Sherwin, "Hormones, Mood, and Cognitive Functioning in Postmenopausal Women," *Obstetrics and Gynecology*, 87 (1996), 20S–26S.
B. B. Sherwin, "The Impact of Different Doses of Estrogen and Progestin on
Mood and Sexual Behavior in Postmenopausal Women," *Journal of Clinical Metabolism*, 72 (1991), 336–343.
K. D. Wagner, "Major Depression and Anxiety Disorders Associated with Norplant," *Journal of Clinical Psychiatry*, 57 (1996), 152–157.

Sexuality

R. Balon, "The Effects of Antidepressants on Human Sexuality: Diagnosis and
Management," *Primary Psychiatry*, 2 (1995), 46–51.
A. H. Clayton, J. E. Owens, et al., "Assessment of Paroxetine-Induced Sexual
Dysfunction Using the Changes in Sexual Functioning Questionnaire,"
Psychopharmacology Bulletin, 31 (1995), 397–406.
L. L. Post, "Sexual Side Effects of Psychiatric Medications in Women," *Primary
Psychiatry*, 3 (1996), 47–51.
A. Rothschild, "Selective Serotonin Reuptake Inhibitor-induced Sexual Dys-
function: Efficacy of a Drug Holiday," *American Journal of Psychiatry*, 10
(1995), 1514–1516.

Glossary

affective disorders A synonym for mood disorders, including depressive and bipolar illnesses.

agoraphobia Avoidance of situations in which you fear help would be unavailable or escape impossible or embarrassing, usually secondary to fear of having a panic attack. Typically, this leads to restricted activities, such as avoidance of public transportation, bridges, traffic, grocery shopping and/or driving alone, or fear of leaving the safety of your home.

alopecia Hair loss.

anorgasmia Inability to climax (during intercourse or through masturbation).

antidepressants Medications introduced and/or classified for the treatment of depression. Most "antidepressants" are effective for anxiety disorders.

anxiety A symptom in which you feel worried and fearful about a danger that may be very specific (such as having a heart attack) or quite vague (such as an ill-defined sense of doom). Anxiety is usually both emotional and physical. Physical symptoms may include palpitations, stomach upset, breathing changes, choking sensations, insomnia, and muscle tension. Emotional symptoms may include tension, poor concentration, worry, panic, and apprehension.

bipolar disorder A synonym for manic-depressive illness.

certification Unlike governmental licensure, certification usually is conducted by the practitioner's professional organization or a board of examiners. Psychologists, social workers, and psychiatrists all have professional organizations that may grant certification to the members of their profession.

cognitive therapy A type of psychotherapy that focuses on replacing automatic negative thoughts with more realistic self-appraisal. Cognitive behavioral therapy enhances coping skills and promotes emotionally productive behaviors.

comedication A second medication given to reverse side effects.

comorbidity The presence of more than one emotional disorder.

compulsion Repetitive behaviors designed to minimize anxiety. Examples include compulsive checking, cleaning, or counting.

depersonalization A perception during a panic attack that you are not actively and personally present in the room, as if you are watching yourself, or in a dream.

depression May refer to a temporary mood state or to a cluster of mood disorders, including dysthymic disorder, major depressive episode, postpartum depression, seasonal depression, and bipolar depression.

derealization A perception during a panic attack that things are not real, seem strange, or look "funny."

down-regulation The secondary chemical reaction of a receptor brain cell in response to antidepressant medication. This process takes several weeks and correlates with when antidepressants begin to work.

drug holiday Missing medication for several days in a row, usually used to restore sexual functioning.

DSM-IV ("DSM-four"): An abbreviation for the American Psychiatric Association guide to diagnosis, *Diagnostic and Statistical Manual of Mental Disorders*, fourth edition.

hypersomnia Excessive sleeping.

hypomania Mild to moderate manic mood swing, without psychosis.

insomnia Problems falling or staying asleep.

interpersonal therapy A type of therapy which seeks to improve and enrich a specific important relationship.

libido Sex drive.

license States regulate who can practice, usually based on educational requirements, by granting a license.

mood stabilizer Medications including lithium, Depakote (valproic acid), and Tegretol (carbamazepine) used to stabilize the mood swings of bipolar disorder.

neurotransmitter The chemical messengers of the brain. They include acetylcholine, dopamine, GABA, norepinephrine/noradrenaline, and serotonin.

obsession A repetitive irrational thought, image, or mental impulse that causes anxiety. Examples include obsessive doubting, thoughts of unknowingly harming someone, or excessive worry about germs.

panic May refer to a specific set of symptoms (a panic attack), an illness (panic disorder), or a state of extreme anxiety. A panic attack is caused most often by panic disorder, but it also may be seen in clinical depression or other anxiety disorders.

phobia Excessive fear in response to a specific imagined or real stimulus, such as fear of snakes, flying, or having your blood drawn. Social phobia refers to anxiety about being the object of others' attention.

pharmacotherapy Treatment using medication.

psychiatric nurse In some states, nurses may practice independently as therapists, usually only if they have a master's degree and have met certain licensure requirements.

psychiatrist A medical doctor who has completed four years of additional training and supervised clinical work in the treatment of mental disorders. All states regulate licenses for psychiatrists. While all psychiatrists are able to prescribe medication, a few do not because their training or orientation is toward talk therapy. Increasingly, some psychiatrists do not conduct talk therapy. Many do both.

psychodynamic psychotherapy A type of psychotherapy derived from classical Freudian psychoanalysis. Psychodynamic psychotherapy explores the unconscious recreation of childhood relationships in the therapeutic relationship.

psychologist ("clinical" or "licensed") A psychotherapist, usually with a doctoral degree (Ph.D.) in psychology. Psychologists are not medical doctors and cannot prescribe medication. Traditionally, doctors of psychology have a rigorous academic background that includes a period of supervised clinical therapy. All states license psychologists. Some states permit master's-trained therapists to call themselves psychologists.

psychopharmacotherapy Treatment of psychiatric disorders using medication.

psychotherapy Treatment of psychiatric disorders using talk therapy, stress management, or behavioral and lifestyle changes.

SSRI Selective serotonin re-uptake inhibitor.

SNRI Serotonin and norepinephrine re-uptake inhibitor.

social worker ("clinical" or "psychiatric") A psychotherapist, usually with a master's degree, who conducts talk therapy. Traditionally, social workers have a background that emphasizes the importance of family and community.

TCA Tricyclic antidepressant.

tolerance Reduced sensitivity to the effects of a tranquilizer or benzodiazepine-type sleeping pill when taken over extended time periods. Manifests as increased dose requirements.

unipolar depression The most common form of depression in women, characterized by being episodic but not association with manic episodes.

Index

Abortion, 195, 196–99, 201–203
Adapin (doxepin), 97, 102, 264, 266
   breast-feeding and, 294
   dosage range of, 274
Addiction, 135
   fear of, 100, 124, 132
Advil (ibuprofen), 59, 184
Agoraphobia, 85–87
   cognitive misinterpretation leading
      to, 89–90
   psychotherapeutic medications for,
      95, 285 (table)
Aleve (sodium naproxen), 59, 184
Alternative remedies. See
      Natural/alternative remedies
Ambien (zolpidem), 122, 133, 151,
      239, 264, 266, 291
   breast-feeding and, 239
   pregnancy and, 292
Anafranil (clomipramine), 72, 117,
      118, 151, 239, 241, 243, 264, 266,
      268
   advantages/disadvantages of, 271,
      278
   dosage ranges, 269, 274
   pregnancy and, 292
Anger vs. premenstrual depression,
      60–61
Antianxiety medications, 285–87
      (tables)
   breast-feeding and, 238–39
   comparison of benzodiazepines, 287
      (table)
   comparison of Buspar and
      benzodiazepines, 286 (table)
   for panic disorder, 285 (table)
   in pregnancy, 218

for premenstrual depression, 71–72
Antidepressants, xv, 12, 47–52, 201,
      255–58, 267–81 (tables)
   for anxiety and panic, 93
   atypical, 266 (table)
   for clinical depression, 45–52
   delayed vs. immediate effects of,
      256–57
   length of treatment with, 49
   for obsessive-compulsive disorder,
      117–20
   outdated, 278 (table)
   for postpartum depression, 234–35
   pregnancy and use of, 214, 215–17
   for premenstrual depression, 72–73
   pros and cons of, 267 (table)
   serotonin-enhancing, 268 (table)
      (see also Selective serotonin re-
      uptake inhibitors [SSRIs])
   sexuality and, 149–53
   sleep changes induced by, 129, 134
   tricyclic (see Tricyclic
      antidepressants)
   types of, 50–51
   weight gain caused by, 167–70
Antihistamines, 133
Antipsychotic medications, 284 (table)
Anxiety disorders, xvii, 8n., 11–12,
      79–103 (see also Obsessive-
      compulsive disorder)
   case studies on, 5–6, 79–80, 85–86,
      91, 95–96, 97, 98–99
   causes of, 87–90
   diagnosis of panic disorder as, 82–85
   frequency of, 81
   genetic component of, 87–88,
      248–50

kinds of, 85–87
neurotransmitters and, 254–55, 258
obstacles to care for, 81–82
pregnancy and, 218
psychotherapeutic medications for,
   93–102 (*see* Antianxiety
   medications)
sexual disfunction and, 148–49
sleep disorders and, 127–28, 136
treatments for, 11–12, 90–102
Anxiolytics (benzodiazepines), 266
   (table), 285 (table), 286 (table),
   287 (table)
Asendin (amoxapine), 278
   breast-feeding and, 294
Ativan (lorazepam), 94, 151, 188, 264,
   266, 284
   breast-feeding and, 238, 241, 294
   dosage and comments on, 287
   pregnancy and, 218, 292
Aventyl (nortriptyline), 264, 266
   dosage range, 274

Barbiturates, 135
Baskin, Jill, 175
Beck, Aaron, 42
Behavioral therapy for obsessive-
   compulsive disorder, 113–15
Benzodiazepines, 157, 158, 183, 201,
   238, 266 (table)
   for anxiety and panic, 93, 94–95,
      100–102, 285 (table)
   Buspar vs., 286 (table)
   common medication interactions
      with, 289 (table)
   comparison of, 287 (table)
   for insomnia, 133–34
   pregnancy and, 218
   side effects of, 100–101, 190
   warning on abrupt discontinuation
      of, 102
Bereavement, depression and, 32–33
Biological basis of psychiatric
   disorders, 9–11, 247–62
   anxiety, 87–88
   brain activity and, 251–53
   depression, 38, 40–41
   genetic component, 39–40, 248–50
   hormones and, 258–61
   neurotransmitters and, 39, 40–41,
      253–55
   obsessive-compulsive disorder,
      111–12

psychotherapeutic medications and,
   255–58
in women, 9–11
Biological clocks, mood disorders and,
   65
Bipolar disorder, 25–27, 39
   alternative medications for, 284
      (table)
   medications for, 49, 282 (table), 283
      (table), 284 (table)
   menstrual cycle and, 75–76
   pregnancy, postpartum period and,
      209, 211, 216–17, 229
   sexuality and, 148
   sleep disorders and, 127n., 129
Birth control pills, 187–88
   for premenstrual problems, 69–71
Body. *See* Physical appearance and
   function, psychotherapeutic
   medications affecting
Brain structure and activity
   in anxiety and depression, 88,
      251–53
   in obsessive-compulsive disorder,
      111–12, 252–53
Breast-feeding, 227
   classification of medications used
      while, 294 (table)
   use of psychotherapeutic
      medications while, 50–51,
      230–31, 238–44
Buproprion. *See* Wellbutrin
   (buproprion)
Burns, David, 42
Buspar (buspirone), 71, 72, 101, 119,
   151, 160, 183, 188, 264, 266
      (table)
   benzodiazepines vs., 101, 286 (table)
   pregnancy and, 292
Buspirone. *See* Buspar (buspirone)

Calan (verapamil), 284
Calcium channel blockers, 217
Calcium supplements, 68
Cancer
   depression and, 33–34
   effect of antidepressants on, 191n.
   reproductive hormones and, 191
Catapres (clonidine), 175
Centrax (prazepam), 264, 266
   breast-feeding and, 294
Chemotherapy, effect of, on
   reproductive hormones, 191

Chloral hydrate, breast-feeding and, 239, 294
Cibalith (lithium), 264, 283
 pregnancy and, 292
Clayton, Anita, 159
Clinical depression, xvii, 20–53
 case studies of, 20–21, 37–38, 43–47
 causes of, 36–42
 diagnosis and categories of, 23–29
 frequency of, 21
 genetic component of, 248–50
 medications for, 45–46, 47–52
  (see also Antidepressants)
 neurotransmitters and, 39, 40–41, 254
 premenstrual magnification of, 61–63, 75
 sexuality and, 147–48
 sleep disorders and, 126–27, 135–36
 symptoms of, 22, 24, 28, 45
 treatments for, 11–12, 42–47
 types of, 29–36
 undertreatment of, 21–23
Clonidine, 134
Clozaril (clozapine), 284
Cognitive-behavioral model
 of anxiety, 89
 of depression, 42
Cognitive therapy, 43, 44, 92–93, 235
 for obsessive-compulsive disorder, 113, 115–16
Comorbidity (coexistent illness), 42, 82–83, 110, 128
Compulsion, defined, 109. See also Obsessive-compulsive disorder (OCD)
Constipation, 237
Contraceptive hormones, warning on long-acting, 189
Culture of thinness and body image, 163–64

Dalmane (flurazepam), 134, 135, 188, 264, 266
Danocrine (danazol), 71
Dental caries, 175–76
Depakote (valproic acid, divalproex), 49, 151, 185, 188, 264, 266, 283.
 See also Valproic acid
 breast-feeding and, 243, 294
 dosage and side effects of, 282

pregnancy and, 216–17, 292
Depo-Provera, 189
Depression, xvii, 8n. 11–12. See also Clinical depression; Postpartum depression (PPD); Premenstrual depression (PMD)
 alternatives for treatment-resistant, 51–52, 280–81(table)
 cognitive-behavioral model of, 42
 genetic component of, 248–50
 kindling hypothesis on, 39, 64, 260–61
 panic attacks linked to, 82–83
 psychotherapeutic medications for (see Antidepressants)
 sleep disorders and, 123, 127, 128
Desensitization therapy, 115
Desyrel (trazodone), 119, 133, 134, 151, 264, 266, 268
 breast-feeding and, 241, 294
Diet, premenstrual depression and, 68–69
Divalproex. See Depakote
Doctor-patient communication, xviii, 13–14
 on effect of medications on physical appearance, 164–66
 sexual side-effects of medications and, 145–47
Domestic violence, depression and, 35–36
Doral (quazepam), 264, 266
 breast-feeding and, 294
Doxepin. See Adapin, Sinequon
Dresner, Nehama, 31
DSM-IV (Diagnostic and Statistical Manual of Mental Disorders, Fourth Edition,) 17, 23, 25, 29, 30, 34, 57, 58
Dumont, Rae, 92
Dynamic therapy, 44
Dysmenorrhea, 59
Dysthymic disorder, 25, 28–29
 premenstrual, 57

Eating disorders, 170n.
Effexor (venlafaxine), 13, 72, 99, 129, 151, 157, 174, 264, 266, 268, 291
 advantages/disadvantages of, 271
 dosage ranges, 269
 pregnancy and, 292

Elavil (amitriptyline), 50, 96, 97, 133, 151, 158, 169, 172, 236, 239, 264, 266
    advantages of, 278
    breast-feeding and, 241, 294
    dosage range, 274
    pregnancy and, 292
Electroconvulsive therapy (ECT), 49, 284
Emotional causes of anxiety, 89
Encephalitis, 111
Endep (amitriptyline), 264
    dosage range, 274
Endometriosis, 59
Eskalith (lithium), 264, 283
    pregnancy and, 292
Estradiol, breast-feeding and, 294
Etrafon, 278
Estrogen, 186, 189, 244–45, 259
    medication interactions with, 188
    premenstrual depression and, 71
Evening primrose oil, 68
Evolutionary basis
    of anxiety, 88–89
    of obsessive-compulsive disorder, 112–13
Exercise, 68
    reduced capacity for, 176–77

Familial anxiety spectrum disorders, 249–50
Fastin (phentermine), 170
Fosamax (alendronate sodium), 191

Generalized anxiety disorder (GAD), 87, 101. See also Anxiety disorders
Genetic component
    of anxiety, 87–88
    of clinical depression, 39–40
    of premenstrual depression, 65
Gise, Leslie Hartley, 241
Grief, depression and, 32–33

Hair loss, medication-induced, 173
Halcion (triazolam), 134, 135, 188, 264, 266
    pregnancy and, 292
Haldol, 185, 217, 284
Halo response, 67
Heart attack, panic disorder and fear of, 84–85

Heredity. See Genetic component
Heterocyclics. See Tricyclic antidepressants
Hormone replacement therapy, 69, 186
    warning about, 189–91
Hormones, reproductive
    depression and, 35–37, 64–66
    during pregnancy, 207–8
    psychiatric disorders and effects of, 36–37, 258–61
    treating postpartum depression with, 244–45
    treating premenstrual depression with, 69–71
Hormones, reproductive, interaction of psychotherapeutic medications with, 179–92
    birth control pills, 187–88
    case studies, 179–80, 185, 186–87
    chemotherapy and, 191
    contraceptive hormones, 189
    hormone replacement therapy, 189–91
    hormones as treatment, 185–87
    menstruation and, 181–85
    obstacles to care, 181
Hyperandrogenism, 185
Hypersomnia, 127, 132
Hypoglycemia, 84
Hypomania, 25–27, 129
Hytrin (terazosin), 175

Inderal, 176
Insight-oriented therapy, 92
Insomnia, 124–29
    anxiety and, 127–28, 136
    depression and, 126–27, 135–36
    as effect of antidepressants, 129, 134
    frequency of, 122
    obstacles to care for, 123–24
    postpartum depression and, 232
    posttraumatic stress and, 128
    primary, 125–26
    stress-induced, 125
    treatments for, 130–36
Interpersonal therapy (IPT), 43, 44, 212
Irritability, premenstrual depression and, 56–57

Jamison, Kay Redfield, 209

Karr, Mary, 39
Kindling of depression, hormones and, 39, 64, 260–61
Klonopin (clonazepam), 96, 100, 119, 134, 151, 158, 188, 201, 264, 266, 284, 291
    dosage and comments on, 287
    pregnancy and, 196–97, 218, 292

Lerner, Harriet, 61
Librium (chlordiazepoxide), 264, 266
Life circumstances
    depression and, 37–38, 41–42
    gender-linked, 9–11, 31–35
Lifestyle changes, premenstrual problems and, 68–69
Light therapy, 30–31
Limbitrol, 278
Lithium, 49, 119, 151, 182, 188, 264, 266
    breast-feeding and, 241, 294
    common medication interactions with, 289 (table)
    dosage and side effects of, 282
    pregnancy and, 209, 216–17, 221, 292
    preparations of, 283
Lithobid (lithium), 264, 283
    pregnancy and, 292
Lithonate (lithium), 264, 283
    pregnancy and, 292
Lithotabs (lithium), 264, 283
    pregnancy and, 292
Loxitane, 284
Ludiomil (maprotiline), 237, 264, 266
    disadvantages of, 278
    dosage range, 274
Lupron (leuprolide), 71
Luvox (fluvoxamine), 13, 50, 72, 117, 129, 151, 157, 264, 266, 268
    advantages/disadvantages of, 271
    breast-feeding and, 241, 294
    dosage ranges, 269
    pregnancy and, 292

Magnesium, 68
Maintenance medication, 49
Major depressive episode, 25, 27–28
Manic-depressive illness, 25–27, 129.
    See Bipolar disorder

Marplan (isocarboxazid), 264, 266
Medications
    interactions between, 97, 197, 288–90 (table)
    for premenstrual problems, 67–68
    psychotherapeutic (see Psychotherapeutic medications)
    for restoration of orgasm, 160
Melatonin, 136
Menopause, 33
    hormone treatment for abrupt, 186–87
    medical, 71
    premenstrual depression and, 64, 65, 74–75
Menstruation
    depression and (see Premenstrual depression [PMD])
    effects of, on psychotherapeutic medications, 181–83
    effects of psychotherapeutic medications on, 183–84
    missed, and medications, 184–85
    painful, 59
Mental illness, cultural perspectives on, 4
Migraine headaches, 59
Miller, Laura, 215
Miltown (meprobamate), 135
Mitral valve prolapse, 84
Monoamine oxidase inhibitors (MAOI), 51, 151, 197, 266 (table)
Mood stabilizers, 27, 49, 266 (table), 282 (table)
    alternatives to, 284 (table)
    available preparations of, 283 (table)
    breast-feeding and, 243
    pregnancy and, 216–17
Mouth, excessively dry, 175–76

Nardil (phenelzine), 151, 264, 266
Natural/alternative remedies
    during pregnancy, 212–13
    for premenstrual problems, 66–69
    for sexual dysfunction, 153–56
    for sleep disorders, 130–32
Navane, 185, 284
Neurotransmitters, 10–11, 253–55
    anxiety and, 93, 254–55
    depression and, 39, 40–41, 254
    effect of psychotherapeutic medications on, 255–58
Neurontin (gabapentin), 284

Nightmares, 134
Nimotop (nimodepine), 284
Norplant, 189
Norpramin (desipramine), 50, 97, 129,
    134, 151, 158, 236, 239, 264, 266,
    291
  breast-feeding and, 241, 242, 294
  dosage range, 274
  Pamelor vs., 278
  pregnancy and, 292

Obsession, defined, 109
Obsessive-compulsive disorder (OCD),
    104–20
  case studies, 104–7, 114–15, 117
  causes of, 111–13
  diagnosis and kinds of, 108–10
  frequency of, 107–8
  obstacles to care for, 108
  postpartum, 104–8, 112–13, 225,
    232
  SSRIs approved for, 268 (table)
  treatments for, 113–20
Orgasm, restoration of, 153–60
Orudis (ketoprofen), 59, 184
Over-the-counter medication for
    menstrual problems, 67–68, 184

Pamelor (nortriptyline), 50, 136, 151,
    158, 167, 172, 188, 236, 264, 266,
    291
  breast-feeding and, 239, 242–43
  dosage range, 274
  Norpramin vs., 278
  pregnancy and, 293
Panic disorder, 82–85
  fear of heart attack associated with,
    84–85
  obsessive-compulsive disorder and,
    110
  postpartum, 88–89, 225, 232
  postpartum panic, 210
  psychotherapeutic medications for,
    93–102, 169, 285 (table)
  symptoms of, 83
Parnate (tranylcypromine), 151, 264,
    266
Patient control, 15–18
  getting good help, 15–16
  information in this book to facilitate,
    16–18
  self-care and, 18–19

Paxil (paroxetine), 50, 72, 99, 129,
    151, 157, 172, 174, 201, 264, 266,
    268, 291
  advantages/disadvantages of, 271
  dosage ranges, 269
  pregnancy and, 216, 224, 293
Paxipam (halazepam), 264, 266
Periactin (cyproheptadine), 160, 171
Personality traits, anxiety vs., 81
Perspiration, medication and excessive,
    175
Physical ailments, anxiety disorders as
    mimics of, 81–82, 84–85
Physical appearance and function,
    psychotherapeutic medications
    affecting
  case studies, 162–63, 165
  dry mouth or dental cavities, 175–76
  excessive perspiration, 175
  hair loss, 173
  obstacles to care for, 163–67
  reduced exercise capacity, 176–77
  skin changes, 174
  tremor, 172, 176
  weight gain, 167–70
  weight loss, 170–72
Physicians Desk Reference (PDR),
    144–45, 214
Pondimin (fenfluramine), 170
Postpartum depression (PPD), 30,
    223–46
  case study, 223–24, 242–43
  breast-feeding and
    psychotherapeutic medication for,
    230–31, 238–44
  diagnosis of, 231–33
  frequency of, 225
  hormone treatment and, 244–45
  length of treatment with medication
    for, 245–46
  obstacles to care for, 225–28
  risk factors for, 229–31
  side effects of medications for,
    235–37
  treatment for anxiety and, 234–35
Postpartum obsessive-compulsive
    disorder, 104–8, 112–13, 225,
    232
Postpartum panic disorder, 88–89, 225,
    232
Postpartum psychosis, 232–33
Posttraumatic stress disorder, 35
  sleep disorders and, 128
Pregnancy, accidental, 184, 193–203

case study, 194, 196–97, 198–99
choosing to continue, 199–201
choosing to end, 196–99
doctor's role and, 196
frequency of, 195–96
psychotheraputic medications and, 197–98, 199–203
Pregnancy, use of psychotherapeutic medication in, 50–51, 199–203, 204–22
best alternatives for, 213–18
case study, 205
effects on fetus, 199–201, 208–10, 214–18
frequency of, 206–8
medications ratings for, 292–93 (table)
nonmedical alternatives to, 212–13
obstacles to care and, 208–10
other concerns regarding, 220–21
stopping medication, 218–20
weighing risks of mental illness vs., 206–7, 210–12
Premarin, 71 (see also Hormone replacement therapy, Hormones, reproductive)
Premenstrual depression (PMD), 54–78
alternative diagnosis to, 63–64
case studies, 4–5, 7, 55–56, 61–62, 73–74
causes of, 64–66
charting, 77–78
controversy about, 58
diagnosis of, 56–58
disorders other than, 58–61
premenstrual magnification (see Premenstrual magnification [PMM])
premenstrual syndrome (PMS) vs., 54–55, 63–64
treatment for, 66–74
treatment length for, 74–75
Premenstrual magnification (PMM), 61–63
treatments for, 75–76
Premenstrual syndrome (PMS), 54–56, 63–64, 179, 182
Primary insomnia, 122, 125–26
PRN basis, medications given on, 93–95
Progesterone, 64, 71, 180, 244, 259
warning about, 186 (see also Depo-Provera)

Prosom (estazolam), 134, 264, 266
Prozac (fluoxetine), 12–14, 46, 50, 72, 72, 99, 117, 129, 141, 151, 155, 156–57, 174, 184, 236, 264, 266, 268
adjusting dosage of, downward, 272
breast-feeding and, 241–42, 294
cost-saving measures for, 291
debate about, xv–xvi
dosage ranges, 269
pregnancy and, 201, 202–3, 205, 215, 293
unique properties of, 270
Psychosis, 232–33
Psychotherapeutic medications, xv–xviii. See also Side effects of psychotherapeutic medications
allergic reaction to, 174
antidepressants, 267–81 (tables) (see also Antidepressants)
for anxiety, 93–102, 285–88 (tables) (see also Antianxiety medications)
brand and generic names of, 264–65 (table)
breast-feeding and (see Breast-feeding)
classification of, 266 (table)
common medication interactions, 197, 288–90 (table)
cost-saving measures for, 291 (table)
cultural attitudes on, 7–9
for depression, 45–52
effect of, on neurotransmitters, 255–58
mood stabilizers, 282–84 (tables)
for obsessive-compulsive disorder, 116–20
in pregnancy (see Pregnancy, use of psychotherapeutic medication in)
pregnancy ratings for, 292–93 (table)
for premenstrual depression, 69, 71–75
for sleep disorders, 132–36
Psychotherapeutic medications, decision to take, 3–19
case studies, 3–9
depression, anxiety, and, 11–12
biochemical basis of emotional illness in women and, 9–11
patient control and, 15–19
Prozac revolution and, 12–14
Psychotherapy. See Talk therapy

Rape, 34–35
Redux (dexfenfluramine), 170
Remeron (mirtazapine), 50, 264, 266, 268
   advantages/disadvantages of, 271
   dosage ranges, 269
   pregnancy and, 293
Renshaw, Domeena, 154
Response prevention, 115
Restoril (temazepam), 134, 238, 264, 266
   breast-feeding and, 241, 294
   dosage and comments on, 287
   pregnancy and, 293
Risperdal (risperidone), 185, 284

St. John's wort, 68
Seasonal affective disorder, 30–31
Seconal (secobarbital), 135
Secondary insomnia, 126–27, 136
Selective serotonin re-uptake inhibitors
   (SSRIs), 50, 72–73, 182, 266
   (table)
   advantages/disadvantages of short-
      acting, 271 (table)
   for anxiety and panic, 98–99, 285
      (table)
   common medication interactions
      with, 288 (table)
   dosage ranges for, 269 (table)
   FDA-approved, for depression and
      OCD, 268 (table)
   for obsessive-compulsive disorder,
      116, 117–20
   for postpartum disorders, 234–35
   pros/cons of, 267 (table)
   Prozac as (see Prozac [fluoxetine])
   side-effects of, 98, 99, 119, 122,
      129, 144, 152, 170–72, 272–73
      (table)
   weight loss and, 170–72
Serax (oxazepam), 95, 188, 264, 266
   dosage and comments on, 287
      (table)
Serotonin, 66
   antidepressants that increase, 268
      (table)
   effect of, on brain, 253–55
   obsessive-compulsive disorder and,
      113, 117–18
   sexual responsiveness and, 152
Serotonin syndrome, 119, 170

Serzone (nefazodone), 13, 50, 72,
   73–74, 99, 117–18, 150, 151, 152,
   158, 174, 264, 266, 268
   advantages/disadvantages of, 271
   dosage ranges, 269
   pregnancy and, 293
Sexual assault, depression and, 34–35
Sexual dysfunction, 147–49
Sexual side effects of
      psychotherapeutic medications,
      119, 141–61
   case studies, 141–42, 144, 156
   comparison of, 150–52
   diagnosis of, 147–50
   frequency of, 143–45
   medical interventions for, 156–60
   obstacles to care for, 145–47
   postpartum, 237
   reasons for, 152–53
   reducing, 153–56
Side effects of psychotherapeutic
      medications affecting body
      appearance and function, 162–78
   of benzodiazepines, 100–101
   jitteriness, 97–98
   postpartum depression and, 235–37
   during pregnancy (see Pregnancy,
      use of psychotherapeutic
      medication in)
   reproductive hormones,
      menstruation, and, 179–92
   serotonin syndrome, 119
   sexual, 141–61
   of SSRIs, 99, 129, 272–73
   of tricyclics, 97, 276–77
Sinequon (doxepin), 133, 151, 158,
   165, 236, 241, 264, 266
   advantages of, 278
   dosage range, 274
   pregnancy and, 293
Skin, medication-induced changes in,
   174
Sleep, habits for good, 130–31
Sleep apnea, 124
Sleep deprivation and fatigue, 36
   obsessive-compulsive disorder and,
      113
   panic disorder and, 88–89
   postpartum, 234–36
Sleep disturbances, 121–37
   case studies, 121–22, 125, 126, 136
   diagnosis and types of, 124–29
   frequency of, 122
   obstacles to care for, 123–24

postpartum, 232
  treatments for, 130–36
Sleeping pills, 266 (table)
Spinelli, Margaret, 212–13
SSRI. *See* Selective serotonin re-
  uptake inhibitors (SSRIs)
Stelazine, 284
Stress
  depression due to, 37–38
  insomnia due to, 123, 125
Surmontil (trimipramine), 265,
  266
  dosage range, 275
Sydenham's chorea, 111–12
Symmetrel (amantadine), 159,
  160

Talk therapy, xiv, 12
  for anxiety, 90–93
  for depression, 42–45
  for obsessive-compulsive disorder,
    113–116
  in pregnancy, 212–13
  providers of, 15–16
Tegretol (carbamazepine), 49, 151,
  190, 265, 266
  breast-feeding and, 243, 294
  common medication interactions
    with, 188, 290 (table)
  dosage and side effects of, 282
  pregnancy and, 216–17, 293
Thyroid gland/hormone, 124, 206,
  284
  postpartum depression and, 245
  underactive, 19, 23–24, 59, 84, 167
Tofranil (imipramine), 50, 97, 151,
  158, 167, 188, 239, 265, 266
  advantages of, 278
  breast-feeding and, 294
  dosage range, 275
  pregnancy and, 293
Tourette's syndrome, 111–12
Tranquilizers. *See* Benzodiazepines,
  Anxiolytics
Tranxene (clorazepate), 95, 265,
  266
Treatment-resistant depression,
  51–52
Tremor, medication-induced, 172,
  176
Triavil, 278
Tricyclic antidepressants, 13, 50, 158,
  182, 220, 234, 266 (table)
  for anxiety and panic, 96–98, 285
    (table)
  common medication interactions
    with, 289 (table)
  comparison of, 278 (table)
  dosage ranges of, 274–75 (table)
  pros and cons of, 267 (table)
  side effects of, 97, 129, 150, 153,
    172, 190, 276–77 (table)
  weight gain caused by, 167–69
Trilafon, 284

Unipolar depression, 25, 27–28
Urecholine (bethanechol), 160

Valium (diazepam), 94, 95, 188, 265,
  266
  breast-feeding and, 241, 294
  dosage and comments on, 287
    (table)
  pregnancy and, 293
Valproic acid, 49, 243, 283. *See also*
  Depakote
  common medication interactions
    with, 290 (table)
Vitamins, 67, 68
Vivactil (protriptyline), 129, 265,
  266
  dosage range, 275

Weight gain caused by
  psychotherapeutic medication,
  167–70, 236–37
Weight loss caused by
  psychotherapeutic medication,
  170–72
Wellbutrin (buproprion), 13, 49, 96,
  129, 134, 150, 151, 152, 158,
  159, 160, 170, 172, 237, 265,
  266
  advantages/disadvantages of, 279
    (table)
  pregnancy and, 293
  pros and cons of, 267 (table)
Wisner, Katherine, 220, 231, 239
Women and emotional illness, xiv
  biochemical and social component
    of, 9–11
  depression, 36–42
  gender-linked life circumstances
    affecting, 31–35

Xanax (alprazolam), 72, 91, 94, 95, 96,
   100, 151, 158, 188, 201, 239, 265,
   266, 291
   dosage and comments on, 287
      (table)
   pregnancy and, 218, 224, 293

Yocon (yohimbine), 159, 160

Zoloft (sertraline), 13, 19, 50, 52,
   72, 98, 129, 151, 157, 172,
   174, 180, 236, 265, 266, 268,
   291
   advantages/disadvantages of,
      271
   dosage ranges, 269
   pregnancy and, 201–2, 216,
      293